B2 Business Vantage Trainer

Six Practice Tests with answers

1

WITH RESOURCES
DOWNLOAD

Cambridge University Press
www.cambridge.org/elt

Cambridge Assessment English
www.cambridgeenglish.org

Information on this title: www.cambridge.org/9781108716505

© Cambridge University Press and Cambridge Assessment 2020

This publication is in copyright. Subject to statutory exception
and to the provisions of relevant collective licensing agreements,
no reproduction of any part may take place without the written
permission of Cambridge University Press.

First published 2020

20 19 18 17 16 15 14 13 12 11 10 9 8 7 6 5 4 3 2 1

Printed in Dubai by Oriental Press

A catalogue record for this publication is available from the British Library

ISBN 978-1-108-71650-5 Student's Book with answers with Resources Download

The publishers have no responsibility for the persistence or accuracy
of URLs for external or third-party internet websites referred to in this publication,
and do not guarantee that any content on such websites is, or will remain,
accurate or appropriate. Information regarding prices, travel timetables, and other
factual information given in this work is correct at the time of first printing but
The publishers do not guarantee the accuracy of such information thereafter.

It is normally necessary for written permission for copying to be obtained *in advance*
from a publisher. The answer sheets at the back of this book are designed to be copied
and distributed in class.

The normal requirements are waived here and it is not necessary to write to
the publishers for permission for an individual teacher to make copies
for use within his or her own classroom. Only those pages that carry the wording
'REPRODUCED WITH PERMISSION (C) CAMBRIDGE ASSESSMENT 2020 Photocopiable '
may be copied.

Contents

Introduction		5
Training and Exam Practice		
Test 1	Reading	10
	Writing	28
	Listening	34
	Speaking	45
Test 2	Reading	54
	Writing	68
	Listening	72
	Speaking	81
Practice tests		
Test 3	Reading	87
	Writing	96
	Listening	98
	Speaking	103
Test 4	Reading	106
	Writing	115
	Listening	117
	Speaking	122
Test 5	Reading	125
	Writing	134
	Listening	136
	Speaking	141
Test 6	Reading	144
	Writing	153
	Listening	155
	Speaking	160
Speaking task cards		163
Audioscripts		169
Keys		190
Sample answer sheets		218

Introduction

Who is *B2 Business Vantage Trainer* for?

This book is suitable for anyone who is preparing to take *Cambridge English: B2 Business Vantage*, also known as Cambridge Business English Certificates (BEC) Vantage. You can use *B2 Business Vantage Trainer* in class with your teacher or on your own at home.

What is *B2 Business Vantage Trainer*?

B2 Business Vantage Trainer contains six practice tests for *Cambridge English: B2 Business Vantage*, each covering the Reading, Writing, Listening and Speaking papers. The first two tests are 'guided tests', which means that they contain extra training and support to help you with each of the tasks in the exam. Tests 3–6 are purely practice tests. All six tests are at *Cambridge English: B2 Business Vantage* level and match the exam in format and standard.

Test 1 consists of a Training section and an Exam practice section for each part of each paper. The Training sections give information about each part of the exam and provide advice and practice to help you prepare for it. They focus on grammar, vocabulary and functional language directly relevant to particular task types. This is supported by work based on correcting common grammar and vocabulary mistakes made in the exam by *Cambridge English: B2 Business Vantage* candidates, as shown by the **Cambridge Learner Corpus**. (For more information on the Cambridge Learner Corpus, see page 6.) The Exam practice sections consist of the test itself accompanied by an Action plan, giving step-by-step guidance for each task, with tips on general strategy and advice linked to the specific questions.

Test 2 also consists of a Training section and an Exam practice section for each part of the exam. The Training sections are shorter than those in Test 1. They review the information provided in Test 1 and also include further practice for that part of the test. The Exam practice sections provide additional tips and advice.

Tests 3–6 are complete practice tests without advice or training. They give you the opportunity to practise the skills you have acquired while working through Tests 1 and 2.

There are explanatory Keys (see below) for all tests.

Features of *B2 Business Vantage Trainer*

- **Material** for the Speaking paper in all six tests.
- **Explanatory Keys**, not only giving information about which answers are right, but also, where appropriate, explaining why certain answers are correct and other options are not.
- **Notes** in the **Keys** for all Writing tasks to explain what is required and **model answers** for each task type.
- **Downloadable resources** consisting of audio recordings for the six Listening tests, as well as keys and audioscripts. These resources can be downloaded from http://esource.cambridge.org.
- **Audioscripts** for all recordings.
- **Photocopiable answer sheets** for the Reading and Use of English and Listening papers. Before you take the exam, you should study these so that you know how to mark or write your answer correctly. In the Writing exam, the question paper will have plenty of lined paper for you to use for your answers.

How to use *B2 Business Vantage Trainer*

Test 1 Training

- For each part of each paper, you should begin by studying the **Task information**, which tells you the facts you need to know, such as what the task type tests and the kinds of question it uses.
- Throughout Test 1, you will see information marked **TIP**. These tips give you practical advice on how to tackle each task type.
- In all papers, training exercises help you develop the skills you need (e.g. working out meaning from context) by working through example items.
- Answers to all the training exercises are in the **Keys**.
- Throughout Test 1, there are **Useful language** sections, which present and practise grammatical structures, vocabulary or functional expressions that are often tested by particular task types.

- Many exercises involve focusing on and correcting common language mistakes made by actual *Cambridge English: B2 Business Vantage* candidates, as shown by the **Cambridge Learner Corpus** (see below).
- In **Listening**, you are prompted to use the downloadable audio, with the track number clearly identified:

   You will also need a watch or clock to make sure that you keep to the time allowed for each part of the test.

- In **Writing**, the Keys contain **model answers** for the tasks. Although there are many different ways of answering each question, it is worth studying these and thinking about the structure and language of each of the answers provided.
- In **Speaking**, you are sometimes prompted to use the audio recordings and do tasks as you listen. You can practise speaking on your own, with a partner or in a group of three, using what you have learnt in **Useful language** and in **Tips**.

Test 1 Exam practice

- Look first at the **Action plan**, which gives you clear step-by-step guidance on how to approach each task type.
- Read any further **Tips** for that part of the exam.
- Work through an exam-style task, following the **Action plan** and making use of the **Advice** boxes, which suggest ways of dealing with specific items.
- Answers to all items are in the **Keys**, which also explain why the correct answers are right and others are wrong. For **Listening**, the parts of the **Audioscripts** which identify the correct answers are underlined.

Test 2 Training

- Look at the **Tips** and work through the exercises, which focus on other useful exam techniques and language to help with this part of the exam.
- There is further work based on mistakes frequently made by *Cambridge English: B2 Business Vantage* candidates, as shown by the Cambridge Learner Corpus.

Test 2 Exam practice

- Think about the **Action plan** in Test 1 for each part of the exam. Use the cross-reference if you need to.
- Use any **Tips** on strategy and **Advice** relating to specific questions to help you work through the exam task.
- Do the task under exam conditions if possible, i.e. not using a dictionary and spending an appropriate amount of time on the task.
- Check your answers in the explanatory **Keys**.

Tests 3–6 Exam practice

- In Tests 3, 4, 5 and 6, you should apply the skills, techniques and language you have learnt in Tests 1 and 2.
- You can do these tests and the four papers within them in any order, but you should always try to keep to the time recommended for each paper.
- It will be easier to keep to the exam instructions if you can find somewhere quiet to work and ensure there are no interruptions.
- For the Speaking paper, it is best if you can work with a partner or in a group of three, but if that is not possible, you can follow the instructions and do all four parts on your own.
- You can check all answers and explanations for them, and also study the Listening audioscripts, after you have completed the tasks.

Audio

For the Listening papers, you will always hear the recordings played a second time with full instructions and appropriate pauses, as in the exam.

The Cambridge Learner Corpus (CLC)

The CLC is a large collection of exam scripts written by candidates taking Cambridge English exams around the world. It currently contains over 55 million words and is growing all the time. The CLC is error coded to show the mistakes students tend to make and also what they tend to do well. It forms part of the Cambridge English Corpus (CEC) and it has been built up by Cambridge University Press and Cambridge Assessment English. The CLC currently contains scripts from:

- over 220,000 students
- 173 different first languages
- over 200 different countries.

Level of *Cambridge English: B2 Business Vantage*

- *Cambridge English: B2 Business Vantage* is at Level B2 in the Common European Framework of Reference for Languages (CEFR). Achieving this level means that your English is good enough for you to study or work in most situations where English is the main language used.
- A pass mark at *Cambridge English: B2 Business Vantage* is given a grade: A, B or C.
- Achieving a grade A means that your English is considered to be at Level C1 on the CEFR.
- If you do not get enough marks for a grade C in the examination, you may get a certificate stating that your English is at Level B1, provided you have demonstrated that is the case.

Grading

- The overall Cambridge English Scale score that you receive for the exam is the average of the separate scale scores you receive for each of the four skills and Use of English.
- The overall score determines your grade and CEFR level.
- There is no minimum score for each paper, so you don't have to pass all four papers to pass the exam.
- Whatever your grade, you will receive a Statement of Results. This includes your overall scale score, your scale score in each of the four skills and Use of English, your CEFR level and your grade.
- For more information on grading and results, go to the Cambridge Assessment English website (see *Further information* on page 9).

Content of *Cambridge English: B2 Business Vantage*

Cambridge English: B2 Business Vantage has four papers, each with several parts in it. For details on each part, see the page reference under the *Task information* heading in the tables on the following pages.

Reading (1 hour)

There are five parts to this paper and they are always in the same order. Parts 1–3 contain a range of texts and accompanying reading-comprehension tasks. Parts 4–5 contain texts with accompanying grammar and vocabulary tasks.

The texts used are from newspapers, magazines, journals, books, leaflets, brochures, etc.

Part	Task type	No. of questions	Format	Task information
1	Matching	7	Four short texts on a related theme, or one continuous text divided into four sections, with seven statements or phrases related to the texts. This mainly tests the identification of specific information and detail, although some questions may focus on gist.	page 10
2	Matching	5	A text that has six sentences removed from it, and a set of seven sentences labelled A–G. This mainly tests understanding of text structure as well as meaning.	page 14
3	Multiple-choice	6	A text accompanied by six 4-option multiple-choice questions. This mainly tests reading for gist and specific information.	page 18
4	Multiple-choice cloze	15	A text with 15 gaps, most of which test lexical items and may focus on correct word choice, lexical collocations and fixed phrases. This mainly tests understanding of vocabulary and structure.	page 22
5	Proofreading	12	A text into which words have been introduced in error. This mainly tests understanding of sentence structure and ability to identify errors.	page 26

Introduction

Writing (45 minutes)

There are two parts to this paper, each containing one compulsory task. Part 1 carries one-third of the total marks available and Part 2 carries two-thirds of the total marks available. In each task, you are told what kind of text you must write, who you are writing to, and why you are writing.

Part	Task type	No. of words	Format	Task information
1	Message, memo or email	40–50	You have to write an internal company communication, using a written prompt. You may be required to give instructions, explain a development, ask for comments, request information or agree to requests.	page 28
2	Business correspondence, short report or proposal	120–140	You are given a rubric and a short text, which may contain visual or graphic information and have 'handwritten' notes on them. Features of this task may include explaining, apologising, reassuring, complaining, describing, summarising, recommending or persuading.	page 31

Listening (approximately 40 minutes)

You will both hear and see the instructions for each task, and you will hear each of the three parts twice. You will hear pauses announced and you can use this time to read the questions. There is one mark for each question in this paper. At the end of the test, you will have five minutes to copy your answers onto the answer sheet.

Part	Task type	No. of questions	Format	Task information
1	Note completion	12	You hear three telephone conversations or messages with a gapped text to go with each. This part of the test mainly focuses on your ability to retrieve factual information.	page 34
2	Matching	10	There are two sections with five short monologues in each, with eight options in each section. This part tests your ability to identify topic, context, function, etc.	page 38
3	Multiple-choice	8	You hear a longer monologue, discussion or interview and have to answer eight multiple-choice questions, each with three options: A, B, and C. This part tests your ability to follow the main points of a text and retrieve specific information.	page 41

Speaking (14 minutes)

You will most likely do the Speaking test with one other candidate, although sometimes it is necessary to form groups of three. There will be two examiners, but one of them does not take part in the conversation. The examiner will indicate who you should talk to in each part of the test.

Part	Task type	Format	Task information
1	Short conversations between one of the examiners and each candidate (3 minutes)	The examiner asks you both some questions about yourself, your interests and experiences, and encourages you to express personal opinions. This part tests your ability to respond to questions and expand on responses.	page 45
2	Individual 'long turn' with brief response from partner (6 minutes)	You are each given prompts; the examiner will ask you to give a 'mini-presentation' about these for about a minute. You are asked to give a short response after your partner has finished their 'long turn'.	page 48
3	Collaborative task (5 minutes)	You are given a topic to discuss with your partner, and you have to talk for three minutes. The examiner then asks further questions related to the theme of the discussion. This part tests your ability to communicate, negotiate, initiate and respond in an appropriate way.	page 50

Further information

The information about *Cambridge English: B2 Business Vantage* contained in *B2 Business Vantage Trainer* is designed to be an overview of the exam. For a full description, including information about task types, testing focus and preparation for the exam, please use the *Cambridge English: Business Certificates* Handbook, which can be obtained from Cambridge English Language Assessment at the address below or from the website at www.cambridgeenglish.org.

Cambridge Assessment English
The Triangle Building
Shaftesbury Road
Cambridge
CB2 8EA

Training Test 1 — Reading Part 1

Task information

- In Part 1, there may be four short texts on a related theme or a single text divided into four sections.
- There are seven statements and you match each of these with the relevant short text or section. There is an example given.
- Part 1 mostly tests your ability to find specific information and detail in a text.
- You could also be tested on your understanding of topic, the target reader and the purpose for writing.
- The information you are looking for may not be in the same order as the statements.

READING FOR GIST

1 Quickly read the text *Launching a new product*. Ignore the underlined phrases. Decide whether the purpose of the text is to
   a provide ideas about successfully introducing a product to the market.
   b outline typical mistakes and things to avoid when promoting a product.

IDENTIFYING KEY WORDS AND PHRASES IN THE STATEMENTS

2 Read statements 1 – 7 below without looking at the text on page 11. Underline two of the words or phrases in bold that show you where to look in the text. The locating words in the example have already been underlined.

  TIP Don't try and match words in the statements with the same words in the text. Instead, think about how language in the options might be paraphrased.

Example:

0 A product may quickly <u>be forgotten</u> by people when **other products** receive their <u>attention</u>.

1 An **endorsement** from the wrong person could **lead** to **falling** product sales.
2 Take into account any **negative feedback** to **help** you **improve** your product.
3 **Customers** must be **persuaded** that a product will **make a difference to their lives**.
4 **In order to** create **interest**, begin to promote your product **well ahead of** the launch date.
5 Accept that the **traditional way** of launching a **product** is **not effective**.
6 **Be clear** about the **group of people** who might be interested in **buying** your product.
7 Even when a **launch** has been successful, it is still **necessary** to **draw attention to** the product.

Advice

1 It is usually famous people that endorse products. Look for examples of people who might be considered famous.

7 Look for ways that a company could continue to promote its product after a launch.

 TIP If you can't find the information for a particular statement, move on to the next one. At the end, once you have matched all the statements you can, you should have a better idea of where to look for the last piece of information.

3 Read the text again, more carefully. Which section of the text (**A, B, C** or **D**) does each statement (**1 – 7**) in Exercise 2 refer to? Use the underlined phrases in the text to help you.

Launching a new product

A Long-established companies may recall a time when launching a new product <u>simply involved arranging interviews with reporters</u>. <u>Reviews would then be published</u> around the launch date, guaranteeing publicity. However, <u>unless companies are willing to recognise that this approach no longer holds consumer attention, the product is likely to fail</u>. Today, even though a newspaper may post a stunning review online, it will quickly be replaced with other content. *<u>There is always a 'newer' new product to read about</u>, and <u>consumers' memories can be short</u>. Alternative strategies are therefore required.

B Before considering a possible launch date, <u>ensure you know your target market</u>, so you can avoid wasting time making announcements to the wrong audience. <u>Once you have identified your core audience</u>, offer them a free trial or demonstration. <u>Don't be defensive if they find flaws</u>; their comments will allow you to <u>strengthen your product</u> before it goes to market. Taking the time to evaluate similar products put out by competitors can also be beneficial.

Advice

* **0** Use the example to help you. Look in the text for the answer to clarify what you need to do. Here, the answer for the example is in section A of the text.

C When you are confident you have the best possible version of your product, <u>start making announcements at least eight weeks before it goes on sale</u>. A pre-launch video campaign, for example, <u>will awaken customers' curiosity</u>. Many companies also make products available to influencers first; that is, social media celebrities or popular bloggers. <u>A good review from an influencer</u> can mean thousands of fans taking notice and spreading the word about your product. Having said that, choose your influencer carefully. <u>If they somehow damage their reputation</u>, you will quickly see your <u>profit margins decline</u>.

D If sales take off after the official launch date, you can congratulate yourself on a job well done. However, you <u>must now</u> intensify your efforts to <u>keep your product in the spotlight</u>. Posting a customer satisfaction survey or a short article about customers' experiences are strategies many companies adopt. Another idea is to publish an infographic <u>convincing people of the need for</u> your product; explain <u>what problem your product was created to solve or how it will help them do something better</u>.

4 For Part 1 in general, which of the following are more likely to be locator words?
1. a word contained in the title of the text
2. nouns / noun phrases that can be paraphrased in the text
3. a word which also occurs frequently in a text, e.g. *customer*
4. a linking phrase, e.g. *as a result of* / *lead to*
5. main verbs such as *persuade* or *improve*
6. words like *necessary* and *essential* that can be replaced by modals, e.g. *need to, must*

Exam Practice Test 1 — Reading Part 1

ACTION PLAN

1 Read the instructions and title, and note any headings to find out what kind of text it is and the topic.
2 Read the statements and underline the key words and ideas.
3 Match the information in the text with the questions.
4 Read the questions again and check the evidence in the text.
5 Read the first section. Check which questions are answered in this section.
6 Repeat for the other sections.

Follow the exam instructions, using the advice to help you.

Questions 1 – 7

- Look at the statements below and the views given on the opposite page on innovation in business.
- Which statement (**A, B, C** or **D**) does each view **1 – 7** refer to?
- For each statement **1 – 7**, mark one letter (**A, B, C** or **D**) on your Answer Sheet.
- You will need to use some of these letters more than once.

TIP Make sure you understand the complete meaning of each statement.

Example:

0 Having new ideas is more important than the processes by which they are judged.

TIP Look for the information in the questions which you need to match with a clause or sentence, or with a longer section of text.

1 Using our past experiences in innovation projects helps keep new ones on target.
2 Experiencing a well-known product in a new situation has enabled employees to be more innovative.
3 You should consider changing your marketing strategy if initial customer feedback is disappointing.
4 Take into account the fact that benefits of innovations take time to become apparent.
5 You need to accept that not all innovations will be successful and act quickly and decisively.
6 Conducting extensive research into an idea can have a negative impact on the original concept.
7 Innovation has had the most effect in areas of the business that might not seem the most obvious.

Advice

1 Find evidence of a company's past experience.
2 Look for the idea that employees personally experience an activity.
3 Find a reference to negative customer feedback.
4 Look for the point about how long it takes to be successful.
5 Find some advice about why it's important to make quick decisions.
6 Identify an explanation of a possible problem with trialling.
7 Find the idea of surprise in the texts.

Experts' views on business innovation

A   **Tom Willington:** A common pitfall when launching a new product or service is not reacting flexibly to the unforeseen frustrations that it might cause your consumers in the first few weeks after launch. There might be greater advantages in repackaging the existing product or service, rather than always rushing to change or replace it. Another error that perhaps goes against logic is spending too long testing every single aspect of an idea to the point where you lose sight of your original concept. You could end up with a product that looks good 'on paper', but has actually lost its sparkle – the thing that attracted you to the idea in the first place.

B   **Agnieszka Kowalski:** Innovation is resource-heavy, whether that's in terms of money, people or research and development – and for this reason, it's important to demonstrate its positive impact on the overall business strategy. We do this by setting benchmarks up front, both from a short- and long-term perspective – not forgetting that most innovation will require a period of time to pass before its impact can be felt or observed. We have a long history of innovation across all sectors of our business, which enables us to look at our back catalogue to set these benchmarks effectively.

C   **Arjun Sharma:** We often think innovation is all about new technology, but that doesn't consider how companies can innovate the services they already offer. In fact, some of the most impactful innovations have occurred in unexpected areas of the value chain, like delivery services taking the place of physical supermarkets, or customers accessing positive or negative reviews on a holiday company's website to help them make decisions. By challenging our own ideas about what we think our business should be providing, thinking outside our comfort zone, we can affect consumer expectations.

D   **Sara Halton:** Some of our most successful innovations have come from trying to stay clear of our own cultural expectations. As a company, we found ourselves returning to well-tried concepts, so for the release of our latest car, designers went abroad and stayed with families with similar vehicles to understand how they use a car today. Of course, every business is different. But you must be open to change, and be willing and brave enough to quickly kill an idea where necessary. The mechanisms for capturing ideas and measuring success are secondary.

Training Test 1 — Reading Part 2

Task information

- In Part 2, there is a text with six gaps. Each gap represents a missing sentence. These sentences are in a list (**A – G**), but will be in a jumbled order. You have to put the sentences into the right gaps.
- The first gap is done for you as an example, using one of the sentences **A – G**.
- For the other five gaps, you should use each of the remaining sentences once only. There is one extra sentence you do not need.
- Part 2 tests your understanding of the overall structure of the text, and the development of an argument, ideas or opinions.

READING FOR MAIN IDEAS

It is important to be able to identify the main ideas in each paragraph, and do this quickly. This will help you follow the writer's argument, and rule out some of the unlikely options.

1 **Quickly read the text *How colour affects consumer behaviour.* (Ignore the gaps and the underlined words.) Choose a summary sentence from a – e below to match with each paragraph 1 – 5.**

   a   Companies often make generalisations about the colours customers prefer. ....
   b   Colours should be appropriate for the situation they are used in. ....
   c   Colour is important to companies in many areas of design. ....*1*.......
   d   People giving advice about colour psychology do not always understand it. ....
   e   Companies must make it easy for customers to notice a colour. ....

> **TIP** Underline key vocabulary in sentences A – G, in particular main verbs and nouns. Then look for synonyms or paraphrasing in the text *before* and *after* a gap.

RECOGNISING THE FUNCTION OF LINKING PHRASES

For Part 2, it is a good idea to highlight linking phrases in sentences A – G. These phrases may help you work out whether a sentence fits into a gap or not.

2 **Look at the words and phrases 1 – 7 taken from the missing sentences A – G on page 15. Match the phrases with explanations a – g.**

   1   In this way
   2   For example
   3   however
   4   In contrast with
   5   It's more the case
   6   Similarly
   7   Indeed

   a   for adding a comment which is surprising or which differs from what has just been said.
   b   when mentioning a fact or situation that is related to the one we just mentioned.
   c   to provide evidence that something we already said is true
   d   when comparing two things which are very different
   e   to introduce a further comment or statement which strengthens the point we have already made
   f   to refer to the likely consequence of an action/situation we just mentioned
   g   to show disagreement with a previous view or statement, and introduce a view or statement we support

3 **Read the text again and choose the best sentence A – G to fill each of the gaps (1 – 5).**

> **TIP** Cross out the example from the list, and then each time you choose one of the other sentences, cross that out too. In this way, you won't have to keep reading through the whole list.

How colour affects consumer behaviour

1. We do not need psychologists to tell us that specific colours may evoke a particular emotion or create a particular mood. We may be less conscious, however, of the extent to which companies rely on colour psychology to build brand awareness and encourage us to spend. **(0)** ......*G*...... . This is a widespread practice, especially amongst larger corporations.

2. In fact, colour psychology *can* be useful to companies, but they must question claims made in the numerous online articles on this subject. **(1)** .... These suggestions do not reflect the complex way that colour psychology works, however. In truth, while writers of business websites may have expertise in many aspects of running a successful venture, they are unlikely to have spent time studying the human mind. It becomes necessary, therefore, for them to simply repeat information from other poorly researched articles about colour psychology. **(2)** .... Predictably, many of them are related to gender preference.

3. Companies often rely on marketing databases to reveal whether customers are mostly male or female, and select colours for products accordingly. But just because some manufacturers continue to create pink products for women, this doesn't mean it's the colour all women prefer or that there is genuine demand for it. **(3)** .... Likewise for men, not all are instinctively drawn to dark colours. Therefore, to expand their customer base, design and marketing departments must take into account people's personal preferences.

4. Instead of choosing colours on the basis of an emotion they might represent, companies should, instead, predict what colours might be a good fit for a product. It is traditional, for instance, to produce kitchen appliances in 'hygienic' white. **(4)** .... Sales suggest this has been a positive move. But would customers accept these products in, say, brown? While brown may be perfectly acceptable for chocolate and coffee adverts, implying warmth and luxury, it may suggest dirt in a kitchen context. Orange might not be the colour many consumers want for motorbikes, but could make an energy drink look tempting.

5. Companies that really understand colour psychology will also know that a colour must demand attention. For instance, some banks opt for red to represent their brand, unlike the majority that use blue. By choosing red, they can easily distinguish themselves. **(5)** .... Customers are far more likely to remember a brand or take action when directed if a colour stands out.

A **In this way**, the same, oversimplified messages about the way customers respond to colour continue to spread.

B **For example**, it is often stated that health products or services are best promoted in green, while fast food outlets should stick to red.

C There has recently been a shift in thinking, **however**, and now they are also available in blue and yellow.

D **In contrast with** the Western view, it can also represent sickness, courage, and envy, depending on the cultural background of the customer.

E **It's more the case** that this group of consumers may be forced to buy an item in this colour, since there is no alternative.

F **Similarly**, buttons such as 'Buy Now' or 'Get Started' will contrast sharply with the other text or images on a webpage.

G **Indeed**, everything from the colour of the logo to the colour of the store lighting is chosen in the belief that it will affect consumer behaviour.

Advice

1. The sentence after the gap begins with **these suggestions**. Look for examples of suggestions or recommendations in sentences A – G.

2. The sentence before the gap talks about the need to **repeat information**. Look for an example of paraphrasing in A – G.

3. The topic before the gap is discussing company beliefs about women's colour preferences. Look for language in A – G that might refer to the main subject, e.g. women.

USEFUL LANGUAGE: LINKING PHRASES

4 The text contains some underlined phrases which are similar in meaning to the phrases in Exercise 2. Match each underlined phrase with a phrase from Exercise 2, e.g. *Indeed = In fact* (paragraph 2).

Exam Practice Test 1 — Reading Part 2

ACTION PLAN

1 Read the instructions, title and subtitle (if there is one), so you can see what kind of text it is and what the topic is.
2 Quickly read through the main text to get an overall idea of what the text is about.
3 Then read the seven sentences, A – G, to see if you think any obviously fit into any of the gaps.
4 For each gap, look closely at the ideas and words that come before and after it.
5 Look for related ideas in the sentences and the texts.
6 In both the main text and the sentences A – G, underline any vocabulary links, reference words such as *this*, *these* and linking expressions like *also*, *so* and *additionally*.

Follow the exam instructions, using the advice to help you.

 TIP Don't spend too much time on words you don't know.

Questions 8 – 12

- Read the article on page 17 about negotiating a pay rise.
- Choose the best sentence below to fill each of the gaps.
- For each gap **8 – 12**, mark one letter (**A – G**) on your Answer Sheet.
- Do not use any letter more than once.
- There is an example at the beginning (**0**).

 TIP Look carefully at pronouns to make sure they match the nouns before/after the gap.

Example:

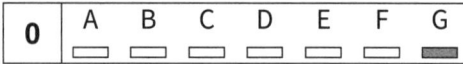

A Being able to supply records of specific achievements and events is essential.

B Your line manager will certainly be involved, even if they don't have the power to make the final decision.

C Perhaps there are elements of your current role that could be expanded, or exchanged for new challenges and more responsibility.

D Doing so helps you stay in control and avoid the possibility of making a decision you might regret.

E Recruitment companies are also useful sources of information.

F Additionally, you must be aware of the organisation's process for making pay awards.

G This is usually done as part of the performance management process.

How to negotiate a pay rise

The art of salary negotiation is a key career skill that will help you throughout your working life. Asking for a rise can, however, be unwelcome to employers, so it's essential you get your timing right. If not, you might get a reputation for being difficult at the very time you want senior decision-makers to be thinking about your value. It may well be possible to submit your request in line with a general company pay review. **(0)** ....G.......... . If your company, however, does not have a regular time for this – or you've just missed it – raising the subject of salary during a performance development review is a good option.

Negotiating a pay rise is about understanding your value. One way of getting a realistic figure is by speaking to people in similar roles within your company or sector, particularly people you know well. **(8)** .... Then, when you start negotiating, you can have the goal you've set yourself at the front of your mind. Be clear about why this is so important to you and your rationale behind it. Why does negotiating a pay rise have to be done now? Where does your salary fit in your overall career objectives? **(9)** .... Find out how it works, and who has influence regarding any offer.

You will be expected to present a watertight business case, and evidence of your skills. **(10)** .... You should include details of your work and any completed projects, and how you work with different teams and key people. Most importantly, you'll need to demonstrate the ability to work on tasks that are above and beyond what might be expected of someone in your current position.

Expect frank discussions about your pay. As with any negotiation process, you must have a clear understanding of what is acceptable to you, and you need to consider how much scope for flexibility you are willing to allow. You always have the opportunity to go back with a compromise and other suggestions, so think about a solution that could fit in with your overall pay package strategy. **(11)** .... You'll clearly know what these options are if you have identified them in advance. Naturally, when you're under contract, your employer is likely to try and hold you at the lowest possible rate. That doesn't mean you can't create a package that works well for you, so just be clear about why you deserve what you want.

Finally, don't be tempted into accepting an early offer. An appropriate initial response might be, 'Thanks for that, I'm going to get back to you on it.' Each situation is different and you may need more or less time to consider any offer. Even if you think that the offer is perfect, give yourself at least a night to think it through. **(12)** .... The people you are negotiating with should respect your need to consider an offer carefully before committing to it.

Advice

8 The topic here is places to get advice, and the phrase **One way** suggests that another is to follow, so look for a linking word that does this.

9 Look for a sentence with a word that connects to the idea of an **offer** after the gap, and that has a correct pronoun reference.

10 Look for a sentence that has examples of the topic of the sentence before the gap, and fits with the idea of including information in the following sentence.

11 The word **these** in the following sentence gives you a clue that you are looking for more than one idea here.

12 Look for the linker in the sentences that connects to the ideas before the gap.

Training Test 1 — Reading Part 3

Task information

- In Part 3, you read a text followed by six questions with four options: **A, B, C** or **D**.
- Questions often test your ability to understand opinion and attitude. You may also need to understand main ideas such as cause and effect, problems and solutions, or why a particular example has been used.
- You may need to infer meaning. This means using clues in the text to understand things that aren't directly stated.
- There may sometimes be a question that tests your understanding of a word or phrase. You should be able to use the context to work out its meaning.
- Questions always follow the order of information in the text.

PREDICTING TEXT CONTENT

1. Read the title and the subheading in italics. What do you think the text will be about?
2. Quickly read the two paragraphs. How accurate was your prediction?

RECOGNISING AND RULING OUT DISTRACTION

Only one of the four options **A – D** is the correct answer. However, there might be something in each paragraph to make you think one of the other options is the correct answer. This is called *distraction*.

3. Read the paragraphs more carefully. Then look at multiple-choice questions 1 and 2 and decide which is the correct answer, A, B, C or D.
4. Now think about the three options that are incorrect for questions 1 and 2. There is something in the paragraphs that might make you *think* these are the correct answers. For each of the incorrect options, underline this distraction.

TIP Sometimes the stem (the question or statement that comes before the options) will tell you which paragraph to look at. Use only information in this paragraph to choose the correct option.

TIP Sometimes the stem will contain words that are the same or similar to words in the text, e.g. people's names or dates, or business-related nouns like *modern technology, new strategy, training courses, workplace survey*. Use these words to locate the relevant part of the text.

Make meetings count

It's the quality of meetings, not the quantity, that helps companies fulfil goals

It goes without saying that collaboration is vital to the success of any business. Yet the responses to recent workplace surveys may surprise some CEOs. It seems that no matter the industry, there is growing frustration amongst staff regarding the meetings they feel obliged to attend. Respondents report having to spend up to 25% of their working day sitting around tables with colleagues, often listening in to discussions about projects that do not directly concern them. Every minute spent at a meeting is time they could otherwise have spent on getting through tasks actually assigned to them. But, despite this widespread sense of resentment, they admit that every time a meeting invitation pops up on their calendars, they accept without question.

However, by modifying their own behaviour, an employee may be able to encourage others in the office to change theirs. When replying to a colleague's invitation, a respectful 'The project sounds interesting,' should appear in the opening line. Following that, the employee can enquire what their colleague specifically hopes to achieve by having the meeting and how they can help their colleague achieve it. If no clear objective is provided, and the employee's expected contribution remains vague, the employee can politely decline the invitation, but offer to send data electronically in advance of the meeting. In some cases, the sender may decide a sit-down meeting is unnecessary after all.

---

1   According to the writer, workplace surveys reveal that employees

   A   are unwilling to express their real opinions during meetings.
   B   set up meetings so they can avoid criticism from senior management.
   C   worry that meetings impact on their own productivity.
   D   fail to realise how meetings offer opportunities for teamwork.

2   In the second paragraph, the writer recommends that an employee

   A   seek information about the purpose of individual meetings.
   B   suggest fewer meetings being scheduled with their department.
   C   offer assistance to co-workers with organising meetings.
   D   be tactful with people in the office who may be over-sensitive.

Exam Practice Test 1 — Reading Part 3

ACTION PLAN

1. Read the instructions, title and subtitle (if there is one). These will tell you important information about the text, its subject and the writer.
2. Quickly read the text to get a clear idea of what the complete text is about.
3. Read the first question and underline the key words or points.
4. Find the relevant part of the text. Most questions relate to one paragraph.
5. Read the four options **A – D** and choose the option you think is correct.
6. If you really aren't sure, cross out the ones you think are wrong and make a guess.

Follow the exam instructions, using the advice to help you.

 TIP Pay attention to the general theme of each paragraph.

Questions 13 – 18

- Read the article below about a fashion retailer called FrontRow, and the questions on the opposite page.
- For each question **13 – 18**, mark one letter (**A, B, C** or **D**) on your Answer Sheet for the answer you choose.

 TIP Remember that the options in the question may mean something similar to the text, but not have the same meaning.

FrontRow: a fashion success story

The fashion retail sector is well known for being highly competitive. With its high-value clothes, online retailer FrontRow is giving large retailers like New Style a run for their money as it targets fashion-hungry 16 – 24-year-olds.

FrontRow has an impressive track record, from a standing start ten years ago to profits of nearly £12m from sales of £110m in the last year. The board of the newly listed company has just agreed measures to maximise capacity in the company's UK warehouses, which will eventually be able to handle sales of £1bn. This will include products being shipped to the ever-increasing numbers of overseas customers, which account for 40% of all items transported from the central depots to distribution points abroad. This is a direct result of a global shift in the fast-fashion market to online shopping, with more international customers discovering the brand every day.

Inevitable comparisons have been drawn between the development of FrontRow and online giant Atmos, the fashion website which, until recently, was a stock market favourite. And indeed, in the run up to flotation, this parallel proved useful for FrontRow, with the launch securing £230m for the owners and the board. However, earlier this month Atmos blamed both supply chain problems, which left customer orders unfulfilled, and also heavy discounting for a massive profit warning. This wiped as much as 35% off its share price and FrontRow found itself pulled down with it, despite its business not being affected by the same issues.

Many retailers stock a range of third-party products, which results in a wide product range – up to around 75,000 in the case of Atmos. FrontRow focuses on a range of around 8,000 own-brand lines, using its designers and manufacturers with whom it has built strong working relationships. Chief Executive Ana Langley explains how being able to set its own charging structure is fundamental to the company plan. It also avoids the challenges that businesses doing international trade face with regard to foreign exchange rates. FrontRow manages stock levels in a different way to many other retailers. Ms Langley explains that because in this industry products have to be constantly new and exciting, it generally only stocks between 700 and 1,000 pieces at a time, but over a much larger range than competitors, around 25 styles, where others might focus on three or four. In this way, the overall volume requirement is covered, but only the best sellers get repeat orders.

Jonathan Denton, FrontRow's Chief Financial Officer, said that the company's success with its mostly 'millennial' customers had been driven by its focus on encouraging popular celebrity bloggers and social media influencers to post about the clothes on various social media platforms, thereby instantly reaching a huge market. He declined to say how much people are paid for brand promotion, but added that some are genuinely interested in fashion, and post online in return for seeing the latest designs before the general public, or receiving free samples.

FrontRow has had recent success in the US, where sales grew by 140% compared with 33% in the UK. Analysts at stockbrokers Dawson Partners upgraded their pre-tax profit forecast to £40m, explaining that strong trading momentum from autumn/winter is likely to have provided a good start to the new season, trading updates are unlikely to disappoint and the medium-term outlook remains encouraging.

---

13 FrontRow's current business development plans include

  A developing the numbers of overseas distribution hubs.
  B creating a more targeted online presence.
  C increasing its storage capabilities.
  D reorganising the management structure.

14 What point is made about a comparison with the online retailer Atmos?

  A Atmos's previous track record helped make FrontRow attractive to investors.
  B FrontRow was forced to slash prices in order to remain competitive.
  C Atmos's pricing structure encouraged FrontRow to alter its business plan.
  D FrontRow's similar business model meant it could fill a gap in the market.

15 How does FrontRow benefit from selling own-brand merchandise?

  A Manufacturing costs are controlled as there is no outsourcing.
  B There is no outside influence determining prices.
  C In-house designers understand FrontRow customers better.
  D The supply chain of goods is more streamlined.

16 What is FrontRow's policy on stock management?

  A It purchases items in bulk to remain competitive.
  B It focuses on delivering a small product range.
  C It monitors customer spending before reordering larger volumes.
  D It encourages return sales by changing lines.

17 In Jonathan Denton's opinion, what has been the most important part of FrontRow's advertising strategy?

  A making use of people that the target demographic admire
  B keeping costs low by using the power of social media
  C creating a platform that can respond quickly to changes in fashion trends
  D using input from people in the world of fashion to keep the brand relevant

18 In the final paragraph, what do we understand about FrontRow's financial position?

  A Recent sales figures are explained by a downturn in the UK market.
  B Future figures are expected to be in line with current predictions.
  C Growth in the medium term is not predicted to meet current expectations.
  D Seasonal fluctuations are responsible for the recent increase in profits.

Advice

13 *Make sure you choose an option that relates to the **current** plans.*
14 *Sometimes the answer is implied, so you have to read the text carefully to get the answer.*
15 *Make sure that the option you choose fully answers the question, not just part of an idea.*
16 *Read the correct section of the text closely, as the information is quite dense.*
17 *Look for the idea of the 'most important' part of the advertising strategy here.*
18 *Read the details carefully so that you understand the figures and trends and find the right answer.*

Training Test 1 — Reading Part 4

Task information

- In Part 4, you choose from words **A**, **B**, **C** or **D** to fill in 15 gaps in a text.
- Part 4 mainly tests vocabulary, but you may also need to understand grammatical links between words, or the text as a whole.
- Words that often go together, called *collocations*, are often tested and so are words followed by a preposition, e.g. *invested in*. You might also be tested on fixed phrases and phrasal verbs, e.g. *to be in the black*, *to take* (a new employee) *on*.

GETTING AN OVERVIEW OF THE TEXT

1. Quickly read the business report *Halfords goes back to basics* on page 23, then answer the questions. Ignore the **A – D** options.
   a What does Halfords' CEO plan to do? Why?
   b Why are investors concerned about the plans?

> **TIP** Don't choose an option simply because it looks longer or shorter than the other three, or you think it seems to be a harder word than the others. Use your knowledge of collocation, fixed expression, etc. to make your choice.

USING THE CONTEXT TO PREDICT THE MISSING WORD

2. Read the report again and focus on the questions with words highlighted in bold: these test collocation, fixed expression and phrasal verbs. Match each question with the general meaning or function (**a – g**) of the missing words.

   0 ....c....   a It must help form an expression meaning something like *create* or *develop*.
   1 ....   b The missing word in this noun phrase must mean something like *amount*.
   2 ....   c This missing word must mean something like *told people about*.
   5 ....   d It must help form an expression which means something like *to pay for* or *provide the money*.
   6 ....   e The missing noun must mean something like *strategy* or *action*.
   8 ....   f The missing verb must mean something like *stay* or *continue to be*.
   9 ....   g It must help form an expression which means something like *benefit from*.

> **TIP** The options all have a very similar meaning, but only one fits the context, collocation or phrase, so try each word in the gap. Check whether it fits the grammar of the sentence.

FOCUSING ON PREPOSITIONS

For Part 4, a knowledge of dependent prepositions is also helpful.

3. Match the sentence halves below. Use the underlined words and the prepositions in bold to help you.

   1 a The service should be <u>accessible</u>   i   **to** anyone.
      b It should be <u>possible</u>   ii **for** anyone to use the service.

   2 a The company is <u>known</u>   i   **for** its sustainable practices.
      b You will need to be <u>familiar</u>   ii **with** company procedures.

   3 a We need to <u>add</u>   i   **into** retaining younger staff.
      b We need to <u>put</u> more effort   ii **to** our efforts to retain younger staff.

   4 a The brothers have been **in**   i   <u>trade</u>, but are now retraining.
      b Both of the brothers are builders **by**   ii <u>business</u> since 1989.

   5 a Advance orders have put manufacturers **under**   i   considerable <u>pressure</u>.
      b According to manufacturers, the product is in   ii great <u>demand</u>.

---

22 Training Test 1   Reading Part 4

4 Choose the best word or phrase to fill each gap from **A, B, C** or **D**.

HALFORDS GOES BACK TO BASICS

Halfords, the UK's biggest bike retailer, **(0)** ......C...... a back-to-basics **plan** yesterday. Chief executive Graham Stapleton told investors that he wants to **(1)** .... **advantage** of rising sales of electric vehicles, so that Halfords can **(2)** .... **competitive** with much larger, internet-based retail companies. By reducing the sale of products such as camping gear, the company can focus on the categories they are best **(3)** .... for: cycling and motoring.

Interest in electric bikes has surged in recent years, as they are popular with young people but also make cycling **(4)** .... to older people. Prices at Halfords start at £600 for a folding electric bike, while mountain bikes can go up to £3,000.

Stapleton hopes that impressive **sales (5)** .... will convince investors in Halfords that doubling the number of bike shops is **the right (6)** .... **forward**. Halfords also currently has about 800 shops and garages offering testing and repair services to vehicle owners, and Stapleton aims to raise this to 1,000.

Not all investors have welcomed the proposals. The strategy involves **(7)** .... more money into the business – £60m a year rather than £40m. This investment would **(8)** .... **the cost** of opening additional garages and shops, and **(9)** .... **training programmes** for staff. Profits will be flat for the next two years, putting the company under financial **(10)** .... , and news of this has seen shares drop by 9% to 305p.

Stapleton is yet to confirm whether Halfords will be among the bidders for Evans Cycles, its old rival now struggling to stay in **(11)** ....

Example:

| | A stated | B expressed | C announced | D indicated |

0 A ☐ B ☐ C ■ D ☐

1	A	achieve	B	get	C	form	D	take
2	A	remain	B	stand	C	maintain	D	keep
3	A	represented	B	known	C	identified	D	regarded
4	A	possible	B	manageable	C	accessible	D	doable
5	A	percentages	B	records	C	margins	D	figures
6	A	direction	B	way	C	change	D	shift
7	A	putting	B	spending	C	supplying	D	advancing
8	A	supply	B	spread	C	cover	D	provide
9	A	setting up	B	drawing on	C	running over	D	carrying out
10	A	crisis	B	pressure	C	difficulty	D	tension
11	A	venture	B	market	C	commerce	D	business

Exam Practice Test 1 — Reading Part 4

ACTION PLAN

1. Read the title, and the first sentence with the example.
2. Without filling in any of the gaps, read the text quickly to get an idea of what it's about.
3. Read the text again more slowly and fill in each gap with one of the four options.
4. Look at the words around each gap, as the missing word might be part of a collocation.
5. Check that the completed sentence makes sense.
6. Check that the missing word fits with any prepositions before or after the gaps.

Follow the exam instructions, using the advice to help you.

Questions 19 – 33

- Read the advice below about customer loyalty.
- Choose the best word (or phrase) to fill each gap from **A, B, C** or **D** on the opposite page.
- For each question **19 – 33**, mark one letter (**A, B, C** or **D**) on your Answer Sheet.
- There is an example at the beginning (**0**).

 TIP Complete the gaps you are sure about first.

 TIP Make sure you follow the meaning of the text as you work through it.

Customer loyalty

Loyal customers are hard won and easily lost. But there are (**0**) ....C.... ways to encourage repeat business. A technique many businesses choose to (**19**) .... is to offer a loyalty card. But how attractive are these nowadays? It's certainly true that customers compare cards carefully to see what the (**20**) .... that are on offer are actually worth. Many card-based schemes (**21**) .... points in proportion to money spent, for customers to (**22**) .... as they wish. Some experts suggest, however, that the future of consumer spending will be characterised by personalisation, with promotions targeted (**23**) .... at individuals, based on their preferences. For this to work, businesses must (**24**) .... consumer trust. If not, it's unlikely that customers will be willing to share data.

Small businesses can have an advantage over big players in terms of service, as they can have a more personal relationship with their customers. This allows them to take (**25**) .... of simple, low-cost ways of making customers feel special. Small acts like adding a handwritten card or free sample to an order can be (**26**) .... enough for customers to talk about their purchases to their friends, increasing public (**27**) .... of your brand.

For any business owner, creating a strong brand is crucial in order to (**28**) .... from everyone else in a crowded marketplace, and have the chance of winning repeat orders. When a customer sees a company logo, there should be immediate, positive (**29**) .... , proving the strength of the brand. For small businesses, the reason for deciding to set up the business is often what customers buy into. Having a story means these businesses can (**30**) .... themselves from big faceless brands, and (**31**) .... with customers on a personal level.

A final piece of advice is to respond to all customer reviews, including the positive ones. It's easy to focus (**32**) .... on negative feedback, but it's important to thank customers who've taken the trouble to (**33**) .... a great experience.

Example:

	A applicable	B possible	C effective	D promising

0 A☐ B☐ C▓ D☐

		A		B		C		D
19	A	agree	B	sponsor	C	value	D	adopt
20	A	bonuses	B	perks	C	additions	D	promises
21	A	award	B	arrange	C	accept	D	allow
22	A	select	B	transfer	C	redeem	D	remove
23	A	exactly	B	specifically	C	absolutely	D	definitely
24	A	expect	B	make	C	give	D	build
25	A	advantage	B	note	C	benefit	D	control
26	A	incentive	B	resolution	C	purpose	D	determination
27	A	notification	B	enjoyment	C	response	D	awareness
28	A	bounce back	B	stand out	C	break through	D	get away
29	A	recognition	B	appreciation	C	commitment	D	obligation
30	A	transform	B	specialise	C	differentiate	D	adapt
31	A	connect	B	motivate	C	join	D	persuade
32	A	consideration	B	time	C	attention	D	concern
33	A	advertise	B	support	C	feature	D	highlight

Advice

19 Choose the word that means **to implement** something – in this case, a marketing decision – and that also collocates with **technique**.
20 Choose the word that describes types of extra benefits customers can receive.
21 Choose the word that means **to give**. In this case, the items being given are **points**, and the answer must collocate correctly with this word.
22 Choose the word that describes the process of exchanging points for a reward.
23 Choose the word that expresses the idea of targeting each customer.
24 Choose the word that collocates with **trust** to express the idea of developing a feeling.
25 Choose the word that collocates correctly with the word **take** in this sentence and fits the context of the sentence.
26 Choose the word that means a reason for someone to do something – in this case, customers to share views with their friends.
27 Choose the word that forms a phrase fitting the context of generating interest in your product.
28 Choose the phrasal verb that has the meaning of **being different from others** – in this case, from others in a crowded marketplace.
29 Choose the word that explains what a business would want in order for its logo to be remembered.
30 Choose the word that goes with **from** later in the sentence and expresses the idea of **uniqueness**.
31 Choose the word that fits with the preposition that follows the gap.
32 Choose the word that collocates with the preceding verb and uses the preposition that follows to form a common phrase.
33 Choose the word that means what a customer might do to **draw attention to something** – in this case, a great experience.

Training Test 1 — Reading Part 5

Task information

- In Part 5, there is a short text, with 14 numbered lines, including two example lines (0 and 00).
- You read through the text to identify any additional or unnecessary words that make a sentence incorrect or do not fit with the meaning of the text. You write these words on the answer sheet.
- Some of the lines may be correct and contain no errors. In this case, write CORRECT on the answer sheet.

IDENTIFYING LANGUAGE WHICH MAY BE TESTED

1 A student has underlined some words she thinks are extra in various Part 5 sentences (1 – 8). Match the extra words with one of the strategies (A – H) for doing Part 5.

TIP Read the text at least twice to understand the gist and the points the writer is trying to make. In this way, it will be easier for you to spot errors.

1 The company has managed to keep <u>on</u> sales steady for the last ten years. As a …
2 Customers dislike hearing that their enquiry <u>was</u> not properly <u>been</u> dealt with. In order …
3 Since 2016, we have managed to <u>increase</u> almost <u>double</u> our staff retention rates and …
4 We have come <u>up with</u> several possible solutions that may help us through this …
5 In <u>most of</u> people's opinion, this kind of gender-based advertising is outdated and no …
6 … while the time spent commuting went down, the time <u>it</u> spent working from home went up.
7 … but designers with many years' experience, <u>unlike to</u> their junior colleagues, will find this …
8 … and so recruiters would <u>rather than you</u> be honest about your qualifications before you …

A Underline pronouns. Work out what subject, if any, they refer to.
B Highlight words which are similar in meaning and are close together in a sentence.
C Highlight words that can be followed by different grammatical structures.
D Check the structure of linking words and phrases.
E Underline pairs of prepositions. Decide if they are *both* necessary for a phrasal verb or not.
F Highlight any quantifiers. Think about the correct structure.
G Highlight pairs of auxiliary verbs. Decide whether they are *both* required or not.
H Underline single prepositions. Decide whether these are required after a main verb or not.

2 Find the sentence in Exercise 1 which is correct.

Advice

34 Read carefully to make sure all the shorter words are needed.
35 Check word formation after any relative pronouns.
36 Think about the accuracy of language used for comparison.
37 Check phrasal verbs for inaccurate or unnecessary words.
38 Think about whether a definite article is necessary.
39 See if there really is an idea of comparison in the sentence.
40 Read carefully to make sure all the shorter words are needed.
41 Check that reference words are linked to another word or phrase.
42 Think about possible structures that would follow the **-ing** verb form.
43 Check any adverbs are used correctly in the context of the sentence.
44 Read carefully to check for accurate use of singular/plural words.
45 Read carefully to make sure all the shorter words are needed.

Exam Practice Test 1 — Reading Part 5

ACTION PLAN

1 Read the instructions carefully.
2 Read the title and the whole text quickly to get the gist of the topic.
3 Look at the first two example sentences and find the incorrect extra word.
4 Read the text carefully line by line.
5 Underline the incorrect words in each line, and remember some lines are correct.
6 Check again, then write the incorrect word, or the word 'CORRECT' on your answer sheet.

Follow the exam instructions, using the advice on page 26 to help you.

TIP Remember the word must be incorrect, not unnecessary.

Questions 34 – 45

- Read the article below about business collaboration.
- In most of the lines **34 – 45** there is one extra word. It is either grammatically incorrect or does not fit in with the meaning of the text. Some lines, however, are correct.
- If a line is correct, write **CORRECT** on your Answer Sheet.
- If there is an extra word in the line, write **the extra word** in CAPITAL LETTERS on your Answer Sheet.
- The exercise begins with two examples (0) and (00).

TIP Read the whole sentence to make sure the word is really incorrect.

Examples:
0	C	O	R	R	E	C	T
00	S	O					

The Benefits of Collaboration between Businesses

0	Successful business models include approaches focusing on maximising productivity
00	while reducing waste. It is, of course, undeniable that these are so key points for
34	any plan. However, in order to meet the increasing demand for various products
35	which resulting from an expanding population, some businesses are now
36	benefitting many more by working together. This can be seen in the example of a
37	group of photocopier manufacturers. By coming up together, they have been
38	successful in increasing overall product efficiency by sharing the expertise and
39	research data. This is as good for consumers in two ways. In addition to being
40	cheaper to run, the machines are less expensive to buy. An issue manufacturers
41	previously experienced was when a company put those financial resources into
42	developing of more efficient machines, the cost was passed on to the consumer.
43	The product was, therefore, not most attractive to consumers, even though the idea
44	of greater efficiency certainly was. Working together allowed each manufacturers
45	to share research and development costs and offer their customers better prices.

Training Test 1 — Writing Part 1

Task information

- The writing task in Part 1 tests your ability to produce an internal company communication, e.g. a message, email or memo of between 40 and 50 words.
- You have to identify the key information you need to communicate. You have to write to another person inside the same business organisation in order to give instructions, explain a development, ask for comments, request information, apologise, or agree to requests.
- You must express the information concisely and accurately.
- You should use an appropriate business style, clearly organising the information.
- You will need to use accurate grammar, spelling and punctuation.

UNDERSTANDING THE TASK

1. Read this Writing Part 1 question. Think about how you would answer it.
   - You are the Head of Client Relations in your company. Some of your clients have recently complained about problems accessing the building your company works in.
   - Write an **email** to John Smith, the site manager of your company:
     - explaining the problem
     - requesting a meeting to discuss solutions
     - providing contact details.
   - **Write 40 – 50 words.**

 TIP You should spend no more than 15 minutes on this question. (It is worth one third of the total marks.)

2. Read these statements about the question in Exercise 1. Mark them T (true) or F (false).
   1. The email is an internal company communication. ....
   2. The email should be neutral to formal in style. ....
   3. You must write up to 60 words. ....

3. Read three answers (A – C) to the question in Exercise 1. Which one is the best? Why?

 TIP Stay on topic and make sure that you include all the content points.

A

```
To: John Smith
From:
Subject: Access problems
```

Mr Smith,

Some of our clients have recently complained about problems accessing the building our company works in. I want a meeting to discuss this problem. My telephone number is 555 4141.

Yours,
Ms G. Ward

B

Hi John,

I'm Georgina from Wing Business up on the 13th floor. We've had a few small problems with people not being able to see us because the security guards will not let them in. One client also reckoned the guards were very rude.

I want a meeting with you on Monday at 9 a.m. in my office.

My phone number is 555 4141.

All the best,
Georgina

C

Dear Mr Smith

My name is Georgina Ward. I am the Head of Client Relations for Wing Business on the 13th floor.

Unfortunately, we have had some complaints from clients saying it was difficult to enter the building. Would it be possible to arrange a meeting so we could discuss this problem?

You can call me on 555 4141.

Yours sincerely,
G Ward

Exam Practice Test 1 — Writing Part 1

ACTION PLAN

1. You have to answer the Part 1 question.
2. Before you write anything, make sure you read the question carefully so that you understand who you are writing to and why. These factors affect the register and function.
3. There are always three points which you must include in your answer. You will need to invent details for one or more of the points.
4. Underline any key words in the question. Use these to help you plan your answer.
5. Plan your answer so that what you write is well organised, but don't spend too long on this. You need to leave enough time for Part 2, which is worth two thirds of the marks for the paper.
6. Make sure that you aim to write between 40 and 50 words.
7. Check your work for mistakes, especially the kind of mistakes that you may have made in other pieces of writing.
8. Make sure that all three points from the question are clear to the reader.

1 **Read the exam task below and answer these questions.**
   1 Who are you writing this email to?
   2 Is there any difference between *saying what*, *explaining* and *telling* in this question?
   3 What kind of language could you use to start and end this email?

- You work as a manager for a retail company. You need to ask staff to attend a special meeting about a new marketing campaign next week.
- Write an **email** to all staff:
   - saying what the meeting will be about
   - explaining the arrangements for the meeting
   - telling staff to contact you if they cannot attend the meeting.
- Write 40 – 50 words.

2 **Do the exam task.**

TIP Think about any meetings you have been to. Could you use the experience in your answer?

TIP In your answer, you need to demonstrate your range of vocabulary and grammar to the examiner, so try not to use exactly the same words or phrases as in the question, e.g. you could write *unable to come to the meeting* instead of *cannot attend the meeting*.

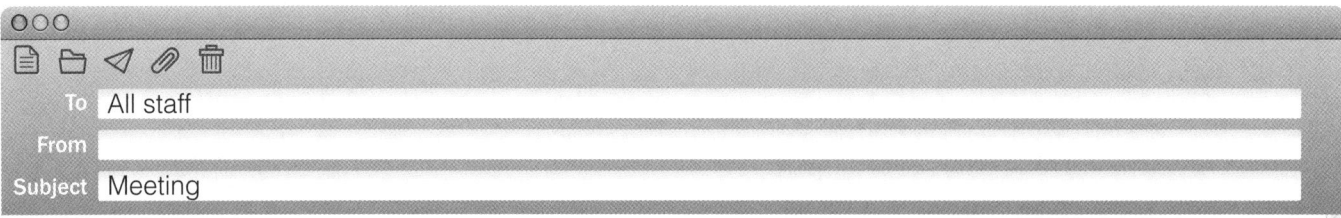

To: All staff
From:
Subject: Meeting

Training Test 1 — Writing Part 2

Task information

- The writing task in Part 2 tests your ability to produce a text relating to a business context, e.g. a report or proposal.
- You have to read and respond to input material, e.g. a letter, advert or graph, which often includes handwritten notes with further information.
- You have to write between 120 and 140 words in 30 minutes.
- You must explain, describe, complain, apologise, summarise, recommend or persuade, depending on the task.
- You should cover all the points in the task.
- You must use your own words, expressing ideas succinctly and clearly.
- You should use an appropriate business style, using the right text structure.
- You will need to use accurate grammar, spelling and punctuation.

UNDERSTANDING THE TASK

1 Read these statements about Part 2 of the Writing Paper. Mark them T (true) or F (false).
   1 You have a choice of tasks in Part 2. ....
   2 You will need to write a text relating to a business context. ....
   3 You should write in quite a formal, business style. ....
   4 You can choose which of the handwritten notes to write about. ....
   5 You should spend about 30 minutes writing your answer. ....

2 Match the descriptions (1 – 3) with the type of text you might be asked to write.

   report   proposal   business correspondence

   1 A letter or an email from one business to another. ....
   2 A document in which you recommend what action to take and explain why. ....
   3 A document in which you describe a problem or a situation. You might make a recommendation, but this is not the main focus of the text. ....

3 Read the example Part 2 task below. What do you have to include in your answer?

- You have recently attended a two-day course to help you improve your presentation skills. You have been asked to write a report for the HR department on your experiences, so that your company can decide if they should send other people on the course.
- Look at the leaflet about the course on which you have already made some handwritten notes.
- Then, using **all** your handwritten notes, write a **report** to the HR manager.
- Write 120 – 140 words.

TIP Carefully read the information and the notes before you start to write. Remember, you must cover all of the handwritten notes that may be provided in your answer.

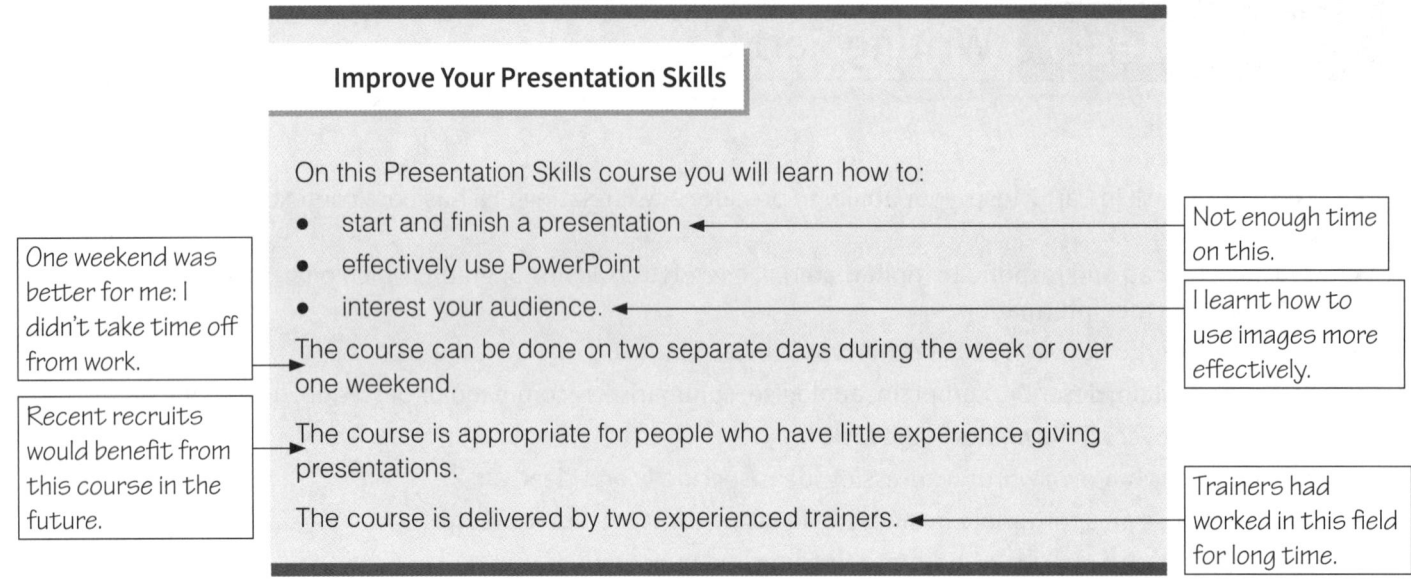

4   Read this answer. Is all of the important information included?

This report will inform management of my experience on the course 'Improve Your Presentation Skills'.

<u>Course Contents</u>
The trainers were excellent and very experienced. The most important part was the ideas for using images to catch people's attention. However, there could have been more time on beginning and ending a presentation.

<u>Course Duration</u>
The course lasts two days. While you can do the course on two separate days, I chose to do it on one weekend. I believe this is better as I did not miss any days at work.

<u>Course Level</u>
The course is for people who do not have much experience. As a result, I believe some of the new employees would find this course very useful.

<u>Conclusion</u>
I learnt a lot and I would recommend it to future employees.

TIP Using headings for a report or recommendation can help you to efficiently organise your answer.

USEFUL LANGUAGE: LINKING WORDS AND PHRASES

5   Using linking words and phrases is an important part of this task. Use these words from the model answer in Exercise 4 to complete the sentences.

while   as   as a result   and

1   .... we appreciated the presentation, we thought the product was too expensive.
2   We would like to place an order for 150 computers .... 75 printers.
3   I decided to look for a new job .... there were very few opportunities for promotion.
4   The company was experiencing financial difficulties. .... they made 100 people redundant.

6   Substitute the words in Exercise 5 for one of the words or phrases below.

as well as   because   although   due to this

Exam Practice Test 1 — Writing Part 2

ACTION PLAN

1. You have to answer the Part 2 question, which can be a proposal, report or business correspondence.
2. There are usually handwritten notes with further information which you must include in your answer.
3. Before you write anything, make sure that you read the question, the text and the handwritten notes.
4. Ensure that you understand what you are writing about and who you are writing to.
5. Consider using headings and subheadings in your report. These are not essential, but may be helpful in your writing and show the examiner that you have written about each of the five points from the question.
6. Try not to include information that the reader will already know. For example, if the report is for someone in the same company, you don't need to tell them which company you work for.
7. Start the report by saying what the aim of the report is.
8. Finish the report with a clear conclusion.
9. Make sure that you write at least 120 words. If you write less, then you might not give enough detail to answer the question properly.

1. **Read the exam task below and answer these questions.**
   1. Who will read this report when it is finished?
   2. What is the aim of the report?
   3. How should the report finish?

> **TIP** For points in the question where you do not have to invent information, like *always good*, it is still a good idea to try to add more details, so the examiner can see examples of your own language.

> **TIP** In this task, you have to decide if the supplier should get another contract. In situations like this where you have to say what you think about something, you should always try to give a reason.

- You work for a manufacturing company. The Purchasing Manager has asked you to write a report on one of your company's suppliers, MCP Ltd.
- Look at the information below, on which you have already made some handwritten notes.
- Then, using **all** your handwritten notes, write your **report**.
- **Write 120 – 140 words.**

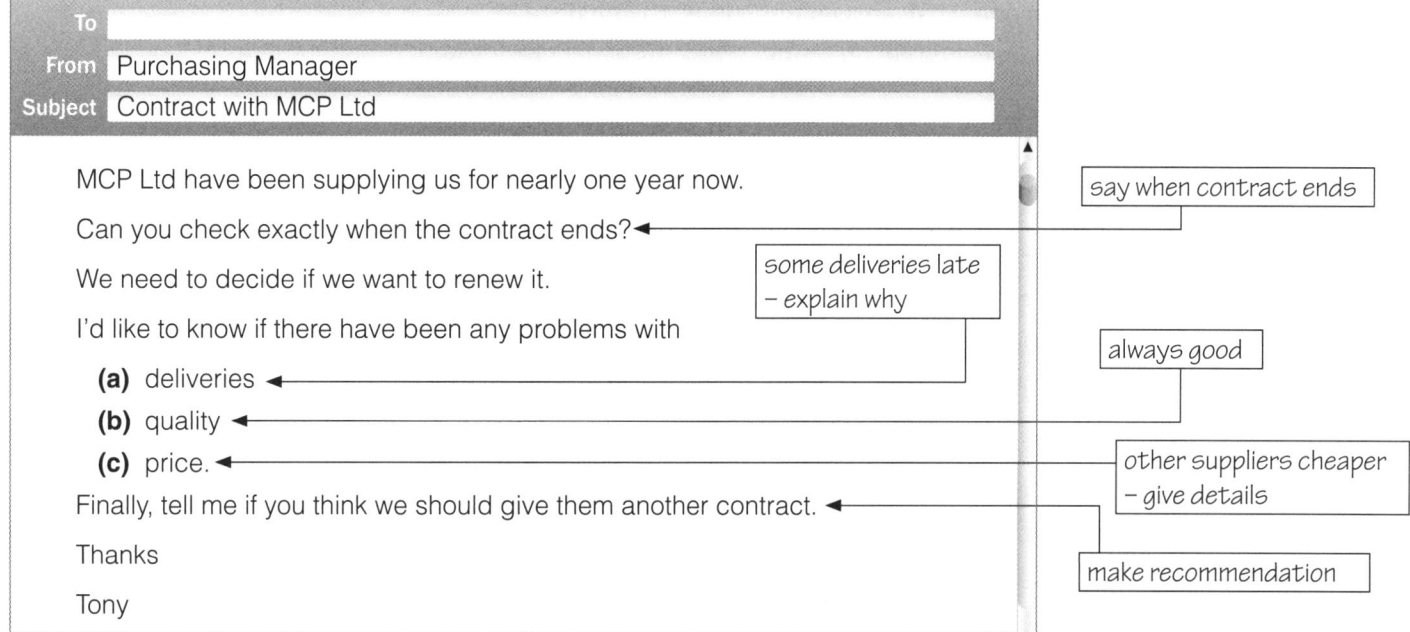

2. **Do the exam task.**

Training Test 1 Listening Part 1

Task information

- In Part 1, you will hear three monologues or dialogues.
- You will hear each extract twice.
- The texts are often telephone conversations or short messages.
- For each recording, you have to listen and fill in four gaps in a short text, such as a form.
- The recording for each question is about 1 minute long.
- There is a sentence that will inform you of the context of the recording, so you will know who is speaking and what they are speaking about.
- The questions will test your ability to listen to and write down specific information.

TIP Look at information before and after the gaps. Each gap needs to be filled by one or two words or a number. Think about the type of word(s) required.

PREPARING TO LISTEN

1 What kind of information is missing from the notes?

> Talk to Mrs (1) .... about moving date
>
> Deposit: (2) £ ....
>
> Location: 34 Willow Street (3) ....

2 You will hear two colleagues talking. Listen and complete the gaps. Were your predictions in Exercise 1 correct?

3 Read the instructions and the notes from three recordings. Note down who will be talking to whom and the situation in each one. Then answer questions a – f on page 35.

   1 You will hear an HR manager discussing some problems with her colleague.

   > ### Issues with Peter McCarthy
   >
   > First client complaint received: (1) .... September
   >
   > Submitted (2) .... late
   >
   > Arrived at work wearing (3) .... on 4th October
   >
   > Has lately been causing some (4) .... on some projects

34 Training Test 1   Listening Part 1

2 You will hear two friends talking about what to wear to a job interview.

Job interview attire tips

Call your friend or (5) .... for advice.

Scan the company's (6) ....

Overdressing can send the message that you cannot understand your (7) ....

Ask questions about people's suits and (8) ....

If in doubt, go with smart business casual.

3 You will hear a coach talking to a team of managers.

Decision fatigue

Our daily (9) .... ability is limited.

Famous study of (10) ....: examined their decisions made in morning and afternoon.

Business owners should eliminate thinking about what to (11) .... or wear.

Alternatively, make these decisions the night before.

Create a (12) ....

- **a** Which recording is likely to be a monologue?
- **b** Which recording is going to contain a list of negative things?
- **c** Which recording is probably quite informal?
- **d** Which recording will contain mostly suggestions?
- **e** Which recording will include tips based on some scientific research?
- **f** In which recording is the tone of the speaker(s) likely be upset or worried?

4 Listen and check if you were right.

Exam Practice Test 1 — Listening Part 1

ACTION PLAN

1. Read the instructions to get an idea of the situation. Who will be talking to whom? What's the situation?
2. Look at the heading and quickly read the notes before you listen. This will help you get a better idea of what the recording is going to be about.
3. Before you listen, decide what kind of information (e.g. a noun, adjective, verb; a name, a number, etc.) you will need to catch for each gap.
4. The first time you listen, write your answer with a question mark. You might decide to change it on the second listening.
5. When the second listening has finished, check that the sentences all make sense and are grammatically correct as well. Don't forget about any words after a gap. The answer has to fit with the words after the gap, as well as those before it.
6. At the end, check that you have followed the word count. Remember, you have to write one or two words.

Follow the exam instructions, using the advice to help you.

Questions 1 – 12

- You will hear three telephone conversations or messages.
- Write **one or two words or a number** in the numbered spaces on the notes or forms below.
- You will hear each recording twice.

TIP If the notes contain lists, try to notice when the speakers start going through the items to catch the one(s) that are missing from these.

Conversation One
(Questions 1 – 4)

- Look at the notes below.
- You will hear a woman telephoning a business school.

Writing Effective Business Content

Course starts in (1) ....

Heavy focus on (2) ....

Other common topics:

– how many (3) .... to hire

– who to choose: (4) .... or content writing ones

---

Conversation Two
(Questions 5 – 8)

- Look at the notes below.
- You will hear an architect telling prospective investors about a construction project.

Urban Cow (fully furnished apartments)

Location: in the centre, near the Cathedral and the **(5)** ....

Average monthly price: **(6)** ....

Included in the price: utilities (including **(7)** ....) and housekeeping

Further unique selling points:
- **(8)** contracts for .... available
- each equipped with washer and dryer

Conversation Three
(Questions 9 – 12)

- Look at the notes below.
- You will hear a woman telephoning a research company.

The Internet of Things (IoT)

Projected number of IoT tools by 2025: **(9)** ....

Number of IoT devices in 2017: **(10)** ....

Popularity of **(11)** .... (e.g. smart watches) projected to grow

Also likely to influence the **(12)** ....

Advice

1. What kind of date (i.e. day? month? year?) would make sense here that goes with the preposition **in**?
2. The man says **The course will deal with that a lot!** What is he referring to?
3. What synonym of the word **topic** can you think of?
4. What word is used instead of **choose** that signals the answer?
5. What two locations in the centre are mentioned? Which one is not listed in the notes?
6. What type of information do you expect to catch after the word **price**?
7. How is the phrase **included in the price** expressed by the woman?
8. How are the place's **unique selling points** introduced?
9. What synonym do you hear used for the word **tool**?
10. When the man says **this is way higher than ...**, what is he referring to?
11. What are **smart watches** and **fitness trackers** examples of, according to the man?
12. What key word is used to mean **influence** in the recording?

Training Test 1 — Listening Part 2

Task information

- In Part 2, you listen to two sections.
- In both sections, you will hear five short monologues.
- The two sections always test different topics or business issues.
- Each monologue will be approximately 30 seconds long.
- In both sections, you have to choose from a list of eight options, depending on which one best matches what you hear. There will be three options that you don't have to use.
- The options A – H don't follow the order of the information in the recording.
- In this part of the exam, the questions test your understanding of gist, detail, attitude, opinion, feeling and purpose, etc.

IDENTIFYING AND PREDICTING CONTENT WORDS

1   You are going to hear five people talking about working with introverts. For each recording, you will have to decide what each speaker is talking about. Read options A – H and underline no more than three key words in each option that will help you choose the right answers.

   A   They manage uncertainty well.
   B   They pay attention.
   C   They can work well alone.
   D   They can be more modest.
   E   They understand more complex problems.
   F   They do not waste time.
   G   They are more cautious.
   H   They handle money well.

2   Before you listen, decide which of these words and phrases might be used by the speakers in options A – D above.

   A   unsure / not sure, unclear / not clear, (no) guarantee, questionable, (to) doubt, poorly
   B   good at listening, pay, distracted
   C   on their own, pay cheque, isolated / in isolation, without, (a) team
   D   arrogant, to tell somebody off, conceited, to boast, humble, humility

   TIP Trying to imagine what words and phrases the speakers might use before you listen can help you catch the correct answers.

3   Now try to predict some words or phrases that the speakers might use in options E – H above.

   E   ....
   F   ....
   G   ....
   H   ....

4   Listen and write one letter (A – H) from Exercise 1 next to the number of the recording. Do not use any letter more than once. You will hear the five recordings twice.

   04
   1   ....
   2   ....
   3   ....
   4   ....
   5   ....

   TIP It's OK to not be sure about the correct answer by the end of the first listening. In these cases, write down the options you are considering for each question and pick your answer after the second listening.

5   Check the audioscript on page 170. Which of the words in Exercise 2 were used by speakers 2 – 5?

Exam Practice Test 1 — Listening Part 2

ACTION PLAN

1. Read the instructions and options A – H in Section One.
2. Read options A – H again and underline any key words in each one.
3. Before you listen, try to predict any words or phrases that the speakers might use to talk about the topic.
4. During the first listening, focus on the general idea of what each speaker is saying.
5. Try to choose an answer to most of the questions during the first listening, but be open to revising these the second time you listen.
6. Confirm your guesses the second time you listen and check that the options you eliminated were really not right.

Follow the exam instructions, using the advice to help you.

Questions 13 – 22

Section One
Questions 13 – 17

TIP Sometimes a speaker's opinion is conveyed using negatives (e.g. *Nothing is worse than*), while the answer may be worded positively, as a suggestion (e.g. *Be a ... / Make sure you ...*, etc.). Focus on the global meaning of the excerpt to notice these parallels.

- You will hear five short recordings. Five people are talking about how they manage their stress when giving a presentation.
- For each recording, decide what strategy each speaker mentions.
- Write one letter (**A – H**) next to the number of the recording.
- Do not use any letter more than once.
- You will hear the five recordings twice.

13 ....
14 ....
15 ....
16 ....
17 ....

A considering your tools
B tailoring it to your audience
C reminding yourself to breathe
D thinking of your own expertise
E smiling and being friendly
F rehearsing it a lot in advance
G moving around
H making sure the material is well organised

Advice

A What **tools** might a presenter need? Try to catch these things being mentioned.

B How can a presentation be **tailored** to an audience?

C Be careful about what the overall message of each speaker is. Which speaker mentions breathing? What is their main idea?

D Listen for words that mean the same as **expert** or **expertise**.

E Although **being kind and welcoming** is mentioned by a speaker and this is similar to **smiling and being friendly**, check what their main message is.

F Listen for words that describe **rehearsing** a presentation before giving it.

G Which speaker mentions **walking around**? Is it used in a positive or a negative meaning?

H What might make a presentation cohesive, **closely linked**?

Section Two
(Questions 18 – 22)

- You will hear another five recordings. Five business leaders are talking about advising their teams of big changes.
- For each recording, decide what strategy each speaker finds useful.
- Write one letter (**A – H**) next to the number of the recording.
- Do not use any letter more than once.
- You will hear the five recordings twice.

18 ....
19 ....
20 ....
21 ....
22 ....

A Monitor for any resistance
B Convince some key employees first
C Provide the right training beforehand
D Follow up later
E Break it down into smaller steps
F Share the reasons
G Get help from Human Resources
H Admit that change is difficult

TIP Try to notice if more concrete examples are used to represent a more abstract or general category (e.g. *room* and *the technology* for *environment*).

Advice

A What might be some signs that employees are **resisting** a change?
B Which employees might be **key** at a company?
C What synonyms can you think of for **training**? Are any mentioned by the speakers?
D Be careful with how the words **follow** and **follow up** are used.
E How is the word **minor** used by one of the speakers? Is he/she talking about introducing change in **smaller steps**?
F Many of the speakers mention communicating about the change with their teams, but only one describes it as their strategy.
G Who uses the words Human Resources? Are they talking about **getting help** from it?
H Listen for synonyms of the key words **admit** and **difficult**.

Training Test 1 — Listening Part 3

Task information

- In Part 3, you will hear one longer conversation or monologue (an interview, discussion, presentation, etc.) and will have to answer eight comprehension questions.
- You have to listen to the recording and choose the right answer (**A**, **B** or **C**) for each question.
- You will be tested on your ability to understand both main idea and detail, including the speakers' attitudes, feelings and opinions, etc.
- The questions follow the order of the recording.
- The instructions will let you know who the speakers are and what they will be talking about.
- The recording will be about four minutes long.
- You will hear the recording twice.

USING KEY WORDS TO MAKE PREDICTIONS

1 You are going to hear an interview with Angela Kemp, a successful business owner and entrepreneur. For each question 1 – 8, you will have to mark one letter (**A**, **B** or **C**) for the correct answer. Underline the most important words in the first lines of the questions.

1. Angela believes that …
2. The first key thing to consider is …
3. The second question is whether you …
4. What does Angela think about freedom?
5. What should an entrepreneur do after a networking event?
6. You can get better at sales by …
7. Angela believes that if you have a family …
8. What does Angela say about charging money?

> **TIP** Sometimes there is a key word in the main line of the question that will help you orientate, and sometimes you will see a sequencer such as *The first point to consider is …* or *The second question is if you …* .

> **TIP** Before you listen, read through the questions and options and try to imagine the context. Who will be talking with whom? What about? How much do you know about the subject from your own life?

2 What might the topic of the interview be, based on the extracts in Exercise 1? Brainstorm some ideas.

3 Read the complete questions. Do you still think the same? Underline any key words.

1. Angela believes that before someone becomes an entrepreneur they should
   - **A** transition into a leadership position first.
   - **B** think about some important questions.
   - **C** not depend on anybody.
2. The first key thing to consider is
   - **A** how to acquire new customers.
   - **B** why you want to leave your day job.
   - **C** your current paid projects.

3 The second question is whether you
   A have enough available clients.
   B are not confusing your clients.
   C accept being disturbed on holiday.

4 What does Angela think about freedom?
   A Entrepreneurs have more autonomy than employees.
   B Entrepreneurs are freer before their company really takes off.
   C Entrepreneurs need to bear others in mind too.

5 What should an entrepreneur do after a networking event, according to Angela?
   A offer further help to new contacts
   B make new friends diligently
   C be willing to be needed

6 You can get better at sales by
   A believing in your value for the customer.
   B thinking through your strategy in advance.
   C going to lots of business networking events.

7 Angela believes that if you have a family, you should
   A postpone becoming an entrepreneur.
   B feel more motivated about the change.
   C have enough money for a few months.

8 What does Angela say about charging money?
   A Having a portfolio can make it easier.
   B Entrepreneurs need to communicate about it early on.
   C Be firm with dishonest clients.

4 **Listen to the interview. For each question 1 – 8 above, mark one letter (A, B or C) for the correct answer. You will hear the recording twice.**

Exam Practice Test 1 — Listening Part 3

ACTION PLAN

1. Read the instructions carefully. What is the situation? What is the subject? Who will be speaking?
2. Before you listen, read the first line of each question and underline the key words in each.
3. Try to read the rest of the questions before the first listening. This will give you an idea of what the recording will be about and what information you should listen for.
4. Listen for expressions with similar or opposite meanings to the key words you underlined.
5. Follow the recording by listening for the answer to each question. As soon as you've chosen the answer to a question, listen for the answer to the next one. Don't get stuck on a question you couldn't answer. Instead, try to 'move along' with the recording.
6. Check all your answers on the second listening. Then transfer them to the answer sheet at the end of the Listening test.

Follow the exam instructions, using the advice to help you.

Questions 23 – 30

- You will hear a radio interview with a woman called Vanessa Campbell, talking about monetising a podcast.
- For each question 23 – 30, mark one letter (**A**, **B** or **C**) for the correct answer.
- You will hear the recording twice.

23 According to Vanessa, podcasts

    A require an audience that is good with technology.
    B can be produced by anybody with a mobile device.
    C are produced in various industries.

 Be careful if you hear the same words that are in an option. For an option to be correct, it is not enough that the same words are used. The whole sentence should fit with what the speakers are generally saying.

24 Vanessa says that podcast producers often release their shows

    A in bulk.
    B for expert audiences in different fields.
    C after they have found a way to monetise it.

 Don't forget to pay special attention to the beginning of the sentence (stem) in a question. The options have to be understood in conjunction with it.

25 Podcast listeners find it surprising that

    A podcasters are experts on their topic.
    B podcasts do not cost money.
    C podcasts can be of top quality.

26 According to Vanessa, affiliate marketing

    A yields a reliable income.
    B has another common name.
    C works best with online retailers that produce educational content.

27 Affiliate marketing is ideal

    A with small start-ups.
    B if the audience is already familiar with the product.
    C if the podcaster also likes the products advertised.

28 In the traditional advertising model, it is important for the podcaster to

    A actively seek out sponsors.
    B have high download rates.
    C calculate the number of purchases accurately.

29 Why do beginner podcasters prefer affiliate marketing?

    A because they do not have a large audience
    B because it engages their audience more
    C because they receive a fixed fee

30 Podcast listeners might receive their discount by

    A downloading their voucher first.
    B using their given names.
    C using a key word while making a purchase.

Advice

23 The key words in the options are **technology**, **mobile device** and **industries**. What does Vanessa say about each?

24 Be careful with how prepositions may modify meaning (e.g. **for**, **by**, **in**, **after**).

25 Always pay attention to who the subject of the sentence is (e.g. here **podcast listeners**) and which of the options is explicitly true about them.

26 If you **only earn money when...**, does that sound like a **reliable income**?

27 The key words in the options are **start-ups**, **familiar** and **likes**. Which of these do you hear? How are they used? Be careful: the correct answer may not use any of these but a synonym instead.

28 How is the word **calculate**(d) used in the recording?

29 Who uses the word **engage** and which monetisation model are they talking about?

30 Whose **given name** is mentioned?

Training Test 1 — Speaking Part 1

Task information

- Speaking Part 1 is a short introductory conversation, lasting about three minutes.
- There are two phases. The first phase is based on personal questions, e.g. where you come from and whether you work or study. The second phase is based on a business topic and usually asks for your opinions.
- Part 1 tests your ability to use language for social purposes, e.g. to make introductions, ask and answer questions, express and give reasons for personal opinions.
- You have to answer each question appropriately – usually in two or three sentences.
- Sometimes you are asked an independent question, sometimes you are asked the same question as your partner.

UNDERSTANDING THE TASK

1 What happens in Part 1 of the Speaking test? Complete the text with words from the box.

> examiners   paper   three   morning   marksheet   anything

You and your partner will sit outside the examination room. Someone, for example a teacher or a receptionist, will give you a piece of **(1)** .... This paper is your **(2)** .... and it should have your name on it.

There will be two **(3)** .... in the room. The first examiner will ask you to sit down and say 'Good **(4)** .... / afternoon / evening.' This examiner will then introduce himself / herself and the other examiner in the room.

The first examiner will ask you your names, take your marksheets and then ask you questions for about **(5)** .... minutes. The second examiner will fill in the marksheets but will not say **(6)** .... during the test.

2 Match each question a – i with a topic in the table. Some questions might fit more than one topic.

Home	Studies	Job

a Where are you from?
b Do you work or are you a student?
c What do you like most about your work or studies?
d What qualifications do you need for a job like yours?
e Could you tell me how important tourism is for your local economy?
f How did you get started in this area of work?
g Do you have opportunities to continue your studies in your work?
h How important for you is the opportunity to work in a different country?
i Could you tell me the effect of international business on work habits in your country?

TIP The questions may ask you to talk about the past, present or future, so listen carefully and use the correct tenses in your responses.

3 Look again at the questions in Exercise 2. For each question, decide if it is likely to be in Phase 1 (general, personal questions), or Phase 2 (questions on a business-related topic).

4 Read the checklist for providing appropriate answers. Then listen to three answers for the first three questions in Exercise 2 and decide which ones are good answers.

To provide good answers for Part 1 you should
- ✓ reply with a full description.
- ✓ avoid short answers.
- ✓ give answers that are relevant to the question.
- ✓ speak clearly.
- ✓ use a variety of appropriate vocabulary.
- ✓ use different grammatical structures correctly.

USEFUL LANGUAGE: TALKING ABOUT YOUR JOB

5 Complete the sentences with words from the box.

| report to | deal with | responsible for | oversee | involves | intern | producing | in charge of |

1 I .... my line manager.
2 In my job, I'm .... making sure all the accounts are prepared correctly and on time.
3 I am .... all decisions made in my department.
4 I have to .... any customer enquiries or complaints.
5 My main duty is .... written feedback reports for HR.
6 I .... a small group of people working in compliance.
7 My work .... coordinating communication between groups in different countries.
8 I study at university in the mornings and in the afternoons I'm an .... in a civil engineering company in my home city.

TIP Practise talking about your duties and responsibilities in your job and studies.

Exam Practice Test 1 Speaking Part 1

ACTION PLAN

1. Try to look and sound friendly and confident when you meet the examiners.
2. Listen carefully to all of the examiner's questions.
3. If you don't understand any of the examiner's questions, just ask him or her to repeat them.
4. Speak clearly so that everybody can easily hear you.
5. Don't just say yes, or no, when the examiner asks a question. This won't tell them anything about your language ability. Always try to give reasons, examples or more detail if possible.
6. When the examiner asks you about yourself and where you are from, keep your answer simple and don't give a prepared answer. This won't sound natural and the examiner can usually tell it is prepared.

Part 1 3 minutes (5 minutes for groups of three)

1. Work in pairs. One of you takes the role of the interlocutor and asks the questions, while the other answers the questions. Then swap roles.

Interlocutor: Good morning / afternoon / evening.
- What's your name?
- And where are you from?
- Do you work or are you a student?
- What do you like most about your work or studies?

Thank you. Now I'm going to ask you some questions about finding a good job.
- Do you think it's getting easier or more difficult to find a good job at the moment? (Why? / Why not?)
- Do you think schools and colleges should teach young people how to find a good job? (Why? / Why not?)
- Do you think that having good qualifications helps people to find a good job? (Why? / Why not?)

Thank you.

TIP If you know your exam partner, try to speak English as much as possible, even outside class. You will soon get used to each other's way of speaking and will sound more relaxed together. If you don't know them, try to have a quick chat in English before you go into the examination room.

TIP Don't worry if you don't know exactly how to answer any of the questions. It is all right to say *It's the first time I've thought about this, but I'd say that ...* to give yourself time to think. It still shows the examiner good use of English.

Training Test 1 — Speaking Part 2

Task information

- In Speaking Part 2, you have to give a short presentation of about one minute, followed by a brief question for your partner, based on what you said.
- Part 2 tests your ability to organise your ideas and speak fluently.
- You have to quickly read three cards and choose one to talk about.
- You have one minute to prepare your short presentation.
- You should talk about the topic for one minute.
- You listen to your partner's presentation and say what the most important point is.

UNDERSTANDING THE TASK

1 What happens in Part 2 of the Speaking test? Complete the paragraph with words from the box.

> make   brief   stop   three   pay

The examiner will give you a piece of paper with (1) .... tasks. You have one minute to decide which task you want to talk about and to (2) .... notes or think about what you want to say. After your preparation, you need to talk about the question for one minute. At the end of the minute the examiner will (3) .... you and invite your partner to ask you a question about what you have just said. You should give a (4) .... answer to your partner's question. When your partner is answering his/her question, you should (5) .... attention to what is being said so you can ask a relevant question at the end.

USEFUL STRATEGIES: MAKING NOTES

2 Look at the card and the notes a candidate has written. What do you think the candidate is going to say? Listen and check your ideas.

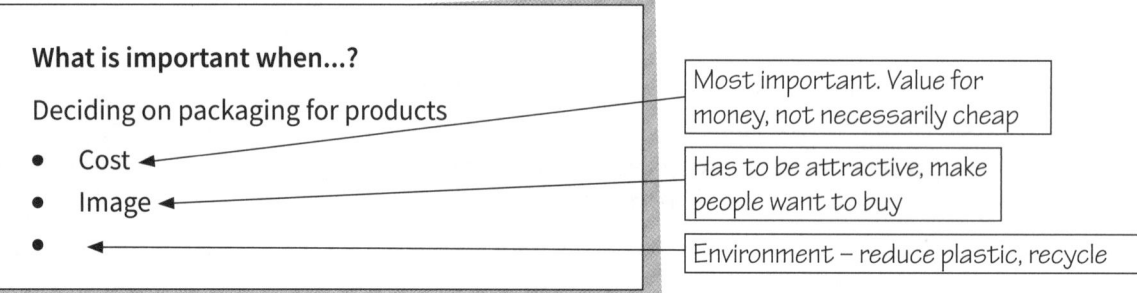

USEFUL LANGUAGE: STRUCTURING YOUR PRESENTATION

3 Listen to the candidate in Exercise 2 again. Which of the following sentences does she use to structure her presentation?

1 I'd like to talk about …
2 First of all …
3 The second factor to consider is …
4 This brings me on to my next point …
5 While cost is important, we should not forget …
6 Another very important thing is …
7 My final point is …
8 In conclusion, I'd say …

TIP Time yourself when practising for this part of the test. It can be a challenge to talk for a minute.

Exam Practice Test 1 — Speaking Part 2

ACTION PLAN

1 Listen carefully to the examiner's instructions.
2 Use the one minute of preparation time to make notes, but write key words or ideas, not sentences – there won't be enough time.
3 Remember to add at least one idea of your own to the two ideas on the task. The examiners will be looking for that.
4 Don't speak too quickly, especially at the beginning, when you might be more nervous. Try to speak at a natural speed.
5 Try to speak for the full minute, but don't worry if the examiner interrupts you after that time.
6 When it is your partner's turn to speak, listen very carefully to their presentation. Make notes to help you think of a question to ask at the end.

Part 2 6 minutes (8 minutes for groups of three)

1 Work in pairs, A and B. One of you should take the role of the examiner and give the instructions below.

  TIP Use presentation language, such as *that brings me to my next point*, to improve the structure of your presentation.

Interlocutor: Now, in this part of the test, I'm going to give each of you a choice of three different topics. I'd like you to select one of the topics and give a short presentation on it for about a minute. You will have a minute to prepare this and you can make notes if you want. After you have finished your talk, your partner will ask you a question.

All right? Here are your topics on page 163 *(A)* and page 165 *(B)*.

[1 minute – A and B should now choose their topic and prepare their presentation]

2 One of you takes the role of the examiner and gives the instructions, while the other follows the instructions. Then swap roles.

  TIP Try to link your question to something your partner said in their presentation. For example, *you mentioned the importance of ... Why do you think that?* or *You said that ... Do you have any experience of that yourself?*

Interlocutor: Now, *(A)*, which topic have you chosen, A, B or C?

Would you like to talk about what you think is important when *[state A's chosen topic]?*

(B), please listen carefully to *(A)*'s talk, and then ask him/her a question about it.

[1 minute – A speaks about the chosen topic]

Interlocutor: Thank you. Now *(B)*, please ask *(A)* a question about his/her talk.

Training Test 1 — Speaking Part 3

Task information

- Speaking Part 3 is a collaborative task, about two-minutes long, between you and your partner, followed by an extended discussion of about three minutes with the examiner.
- Part 3 tests your ability to take part in a conversation related to a business topic.
- You have to read a task the examiner gives you and talk about it with your partner.
- You should try to agree a decision with your partner.
- You must manage the conversation by, for example, asking questions, agreeing and disagreeing, giving opinions, negotiating and exchanging information.

UNDERSTANDING THE TASK

1 **These sentences describe what happens in Speaking Part 3. Which one is false?**
   1 The examiner will give you a task to talk about with your partner for about three minutes.
   2 Stop talking when you have said one or two things about each point.
   3 During your discussion, you should try to make sure that both you and your partner have an opportunity to talk.
   4 You do not have to agree on everything, but you should be polite when disagreeing.

USEFUL LANGUAGE: SUGGESTING, AGREEING AND DISAGREEING

2 **Match the phrases with the correct category.**

What do you think about …?	Are you ready to start?	I agree to a point, but …
I understand what you're saying, but …	Would you like me to start?	Personally, I believe …
In my opinion …	How about if we …?	I'm not sure I agree.
From my experience, I've found …	I couldn't agree more.	I'd say …
That sounds good to me.	Let's start.	Would it be possible to …?
That's right.	OK, but what about …?	Do you think it would be a good idea to …?
Shall we start by talking about …?	Yes, absolutely.	

Starting the discussion	Giving an opinion	Making a suggestion

Agreeing	Disagreeing

TIP Maintain eye contact with your partner and use positive body language. This can help you understand each other and communicate better.

TIP If your partner is quiet, encourage him or her to get involved by asking simple questions.

USEFUL LANGUAGE: GIVING AND JUSTIFYING REASONS

3 Complete the sentences with a word from the box.

   actually   would   believe   seems   view

   1 I .... say it's not necessary for all meetings to be face to face nowadays.
   2 I .... think it's a good idea if all employees are responsible for their own training.
   3 It .... to me that a pay rise is the best solution.
   4 From my point of .... team-building days are a waste of time.
   5 I don't .... it is a good thing for people to work late all the time.

4 Match the opinions from Exercise 3 with reasons a – e.
   a Because people need a good work/life balance.
   b As lots of things can be done on the internet instead of travelling to see people.
   c That way, they will be able to set their own goals and objectives.
   d But then, I have a job where I can't be out of the office for a whole day.
   e I mean, who doesn't want more money?

Exam Practice Test 1 — Speaking Part 3

Part 3 5 minutes (7 minutes for groups of three)
Phase 1

ACTION PLAN

1 Before you start speaking, use the 30 seconds the examiner gives you to read the task carefully and make sure you understand what you have to discuss and decide about.

2 You can ask the examiner to repeat a question, but don't ask them for the meaning of words because they are not allowed to give explanations.

3 The most important thing in this part of the test is to make sure you both have the chance to speak. It is intended to be a discussion, which means you should both put forward and respond to ideas.

4 To keep the discussion moving, always try to bring in your partner. Ask them things like *What do you think (about ...)?* or *Do you agree?*

5 You do not have to agree about every point in the discussion, but always try to give reasons why you disagree with your partner.

6 Try to look interested and involved in what your partner is saying. Positive body language like nodding your head and smiling can help here.

Interlocutor: Now, in this part of the test, you are going to discuss something together. You will have 30 seconds to read this task carefully and then about three minutes to discuss and decide about it together. You should give reasons for your decisions and opinions. You don't need to write anything. Is that clear?

TIP Remember that there are no right or wrong answers in the discussion and you are not being tested on your business knowledge. As long as you try to discuss the situation and try to reach agreement, that's fine.

[30 seconds – Candidates look at the task on page 167]

Interlocutor: I'm just going to listen and then ask you to stop after about three minutes. Please speak so that we can hear you.

TIP The aim in this part is not to speak as much as possible. Try to make sure that each of you takes part in the discussion. Also, don't be afraid to interrupt your partner politely to make a point. These are things the examiner will be looking for.

[3 minutes – Candidates discuss the situation in the task]

Interlocutor: Thank you.

Phase 2

ACTION PLAN

1. Listen carefully to the examiner's questions and ask them to repeat a question if you didn't understand it.
2. The questions in this part are generally more challenging than earlier in the test and you will need to give your opinion, so practise this kind of language beforehand, e.g. *As I see it ...* and *From my point of view ...*
3. Try to give full answers to each question, including reasons for your opinion. If you don't, the examiner will usually ask *Why?* or *Why not?*
4. If you don't know anything about the topic of a question, or you haven't got an opinion, it's fine to admit that. Use expressions like *I've never really considered that before, but I suppose ...* or *I'm not quite sure what to say about that, but maybe ...* You will still get marks for your English.
5. Listen carefully to your partner's answers because the examiner might ask you the same question.
6. If the examiner asks you the same question as your partner, try to link your answer to theirs, or to add something extra, e.g. *I completely agree with [name] because ...* or *I thought what [name] said was interesting, but I think that ...*

Take it in turns to ask these questions.

- Do you think profit is the most important reason for increasing production? Why? / Why not?
- Do you think managers and staff should receive a bonus if production increases? Why? / Why not?
- Why do you think that some companies choose to outsource extra production?
- Why do you think some companies decide to produce less than they could?
- Do you think the staff should be told about a company's business plans? Why? / Why not?

 Involve your partner in the discussion by asking them what they think when you have finished answering the question.

 Try to vary your language when giving opinions, don't just say *I think ...* each time.

Training Test 2 — Reading Part 1

REVIEW

1 How many questions do you answer for Part 1?
2 Are the questions in the same or a different order to the text?
3 Are you tested mainly on specific information and detail, or attitude and opinion?
4 Will the key words in the options be exactly the same as words in the text?

PREDICTING WHAT KIND OF INFORMATION IS REQUIRED

The statements in Part 1 are sometimes full sentences, but they can also start like this:
1 *problems associated with employees being promoted to managerial positions*
2 *aspects of staff training which are often overlooked by employers*
3 *cultural differences causing communication problems within some international teams*

TIP Check that *all* parts of an option are relevant to the section you choose. For statement 5, for example, there should be language in the section which paraphrases *aspects of communication*, but also paraphrases or refers to *customers*, *staff* and *problematic*.

1 Read the Part 1 statements below. (There is no accompanying text, but the statements include useful information even when studied in isolation.) Match the statements with a strategy (a – h) that would help you find the relevant part of a text.

Statements

1 <u>reasons why</u> customers may delay making a formal complaint ......*d*........
2 <u>a way of</u> ensuring that a customer's complaint is handled appropriately ....
3 <u>failure</u> to confirm whether customers are satisfied with the outcome of their complaint ....
4 the <u>consequences</u> of relying on technology to deal with complex complaints ....
5 <u>aspects of</u> communication between customers and staff that are often identified as problematic ....
6 the <u>common situation</u> of customers blaming staff for problems they are not responsible for ....
7 the <u>importance</u> of showing appreciation to customers for bringing a problem to the company's attention ....
8 the <u>possibility</u> of staff being unable to resolve a particular complaint ....

Strategies

a Look for paraphrases such as *a familiar experience* or *this behaviour seems to be widespread*.
b Look for modals like *may, might* or *could, if* clauses or adverbs such as *likely, probably*.
c Look for synonyms or paraphrasing, e.g. *don't always succeed in, don't take the necessary steps to*.
d Look for phrases such as *This is because / Another explanation for this is …*
e Look for at least two examples in a section, connected by linkers such as *and, as well as, not only … but*.
f Look for phrases such as *As a result / This is likely to lead to …*
g Look for adjectives like *critical, essential*.
h Look for a description of a process or method, and phrases like *can be used to (do), by + -ing*.

Exam Practice Test 2 — Reading Part 1

Follow the exam instructions, using the advice to help you.

Questions 1 – 7

- Look at the statements below and the information about a Home Improvement retail group called Kingfisher on the next page.
- Which section (**A, B, C** or **D**) does each statement **1 – 7** refer to?
- For each statement, mark one letter (**A, B, C** or **D**) on your Answer Sheet.
- You will need to use some of the letters more than once.

TIP There will be some similar information across the sections, so you need to read them all carefully to find the right answer.

TIP Look for ideas in the sections that are similar to or the same as the ones in the statements. The ideas will be expressed in different language.

Example:

0   an increasing lack of confidence in Kingfisher's plans from some people

1. local conditions adding to Kingfisher's difficulties earlier in the year in one region
2. Kingfisher viewing the profile of its customers differently to other people with knowledge of the business
3. the wide-reaching nature of Kingfisher's plans being the reason for current financial forecasts
4. Kingfisher not looking to change its fundamental management style
5. Kingfisher being unlikely to accept pressure to sell part of the business
6. the chance of opportunities presented to Kingfisher by a competitor's difficulties being reduced due to a discount brand entering the market
7. Kingfisher having various assets that could be a suitable target for investors

Advice

1. Look for another way of describing **local conditions**.
2. Find an example of the company expressing a different opinion.
3. Locate language which explains a situation.
4. Look for a reference to Kingfisher's management style.
5. Find an expression which shows an action is not being taken.
6. Locate the part of the text which expresses this situation in different words.
7. Find examples of items that could be assets.

A	Kingfisher believes its plan will boost profits by £500m over five years, despite growing scepticism among analysts. The DIY / home improvement group is halfway through a programme to cut costs, simplify ranges and increase online sales. The target of £500m in additional profit was announced by chief executive Véronique Laury in January, but analysts forecast an increase of only £300m, with shares currently a fifth below previous level. Ms Laury argues that seeing the benefits of the programme will take time, as changes go deeper than other business restructuring proposals.
B	Most people understand the benefits of unifying buying teams and eliminating duplication, but some industry experts question Kingfisher's wish to standardise product ranges across different countries. Kingfisher replies, however, that research shows customers' needs are more similar than dissimilar. And there have been significant market changes since Kingfisher started formulating the plan. In the UK, traditional rival Homebase has experienced problems, offering Kingfisher a chance to increase its UK business. However, low-cost chain B&M now plans to move into DIY sales, which could limit the size of any extra market.
C	Trading has been volatile, with the first quarter affected by poor weather in the UK. But despite doubts about targets, many analysts are buying Kingfisher stock. It has been noted that shares in US company Home Depot trade at higher valuations even though it operates a very similar business. This company is currently in the middle of a takeover bid for its high-street stores. With £3.5bn of property, no debt, a surplus in its pension scheme and nine separable businesses, the Kingfisher group could also be an attractive proposition.
D	Kingfisher has rejected attempts to impose a more central management structure. Its business model is to maintain a varied portfolio, including Screwfix, which targets the professional building trade from smaller sites on trading estates, and also online. This is a different approach to rivals such as B&Q, who sell to home DIY enthusiasts through out-of-town retail parks. Screwfix is a key part of the Kingfisher group. 'I'd expect they will come under increasing calls to split it off, which they will resist,' says retail analyst Steve Collinge.

Training Test 2 — Reading Part 2

REVIEW

1 How many sentences do you choose for the gapped text?
2 Read this sentence from an article about employees who are perfectionists:

However, it can also result in perfectionists becoming extremely frustrated when others in the team do not live up to their high standards.

Which of these approaches to doing the task do you agree with?

a Look for the word *perfectionists* in the main article.
b Look for a positive outcome or situation in the text before the gap.
c Look for a paraphrase of *result in* in the text before the gap.
d Look for synonyms of *frustrated* in the text after the gap, or examples of people expressing their frustration.
e Look for text after a gap which includes the word *standards or standard*.

USEFUL LANGUAGE: PRONOUNS

1 **Look at the underlined pronouns in these sentences. Decide if they are referring to something *already mentioned* (AM) or introducing something *new* (N).**
   1 Atkinson objects to this suggestion, claiming that it would never work in practice. ....
   2 The report suggests they are no longer concerned about breaking into the European market. ....
   3 It is getting the attention of potential investors that matters most. ....
   4 This is what surprised the team at first, who had expected quite different results. ....
   5 These could be sent out electronically, provided customers have the facilities to download them. ....
   6 Jansson said it would only work if there was commitment from other retailers. ....
   7 It is because they can be installed so easily that customer demand has soared. ....
   8 That decision was taken only after junior staff had sent in their feedback. ....
   9 In such circumstances, there may be no option but to walk away from a merger. ....
   10 What they need is a commitment from suppliers to get goods delivered on time. ....

2 **Which sentence or sentences in Exercise 1 contain(s) a pronoun that**
   a refers to people?
   b refers to objects or things?
   c refers to an idea, activity or situation?
   d is followed by a noun that would have a synonym or be paraphrased before the gap?

Exam Practice Test 2 — Reading Part 2

Questions 8 – 12

- Read the article below about companies choosing a recruitment agency.
- Choose the best sentence from the opposite page to fill each of the gaps.
- For each gap **8 – 12**, mark one letter (**A – G**) on your Answer Sheet.
- Do not use any letter more than once.
- There is an example at the beginning (**0**)

 TIP Keep checking your answers – if you are finding one sentence particularly difficult to place, you may have already used the correct answer in the wrong place.

Essential Questions to Ask

If you decide to use a recruitment agency to find the right candidate for a vacancy, here are a few tips to make sure you get the most out of them.

Outsourcing your recruitment process can be the most effective way of finding new permanent members of staff. However, if you've never worked with an agency before, it can be hard to find the right one. In addition to industry-specific questions, there are some vital questions to ask. **(0)** ....*G*.... Recruitment agencies' fees can vary from 8 – 25% depending on the agency and the salary. They tend to charge in one of two ways: a percentage fee, or a retainer. The percentage fee is based on the starting salary of the candidate and is normally payable once the candidate starts work, and is the most common structure. However, if you don't find a suitable candidate, you don't pay the agency anything.

Alternatively, you could choose a retainer fee. This is split into two parts, with the first being required upfront. **(8)** .... Of course, once the new employee does begin work, there is nothing more disheartening than seeing them leave after you have paid a fee to an agency. Most agencies will offer some form of a rebate of their fee should a candidate leave within a defined period. In many cases this is 12 weeks, generally in line with a probationary period. **(9)** .... Make sure that you negotiate the structure with an agency, and get this in writing.

You need to be confident that the agency understands the role you are looking to fill, and the sort of applications you want. Asking if they have placed candidates in similar roles will help to ensure that you are selecting the right one. **(10)** .... Reading these will help greatly if you are still unsure. The whole point of outsourcing recruitment is to save you time and money. You don't want to be inundated with applications that you have to spend hours sifting through to find relevant candidates. **(11)** .... You need to know if they speak to each applicant, and what information they will be obtaining. Also ask them how many CVs they anticipate providing you with.

Once you have found your successful candidate, references will need to be checked before a new employee can start. **(12)** .... It is a time-consuming process, but a vital one, and knowing that identities will be confirmed and ex-employers spoken to should give you more confidence in the candidates that are supplied.

There is certainly a lot to consider when choosing a potential agency, but it's worth taking time to find the one that you feel comfortable representing your business in the search for new staff.

Example:

A   It is normally based on a sliding scale, and the amount of reimbursement depends on how long the candidate has been employed.

B   Hiring an agency that specialises in a particular business sector is not, therefore, always the most economic option.

C   Making sure this is done might not be part of an agency's agreement, and you need to know whether they handle these on your behalf.

D   Even better, get them to provide examples and, if possible, customer testimonials.

E   The outstanding balance is then due when the successful candidate starts their employment.

F   Ask how an agency manages this crucial initial screening process.

G   Perhaps the most fundamental is how much the service will cost you.

Advice

8 Look for an idea that links to the phrase ... **the first** ... in the sentence before the gap.
9 Find a sentence that continues the theme of money and costs, and check that pronoun references are accurate.
10 Look for a sentence which has the correct pronoun referencing, as well as following the topic logically.
11 Think about the stage of the process that the text is describing here.
12 Find a sentence that follows on smoothly on the same topic, checking that plural and singular referencing is consistent.

Training Test 2 — Reading Part 3

REVIEW

1 How many questions do you have to answer?
2 What information might be contained in the stem to help you locate the right part of the text?
3 Which of these strategies might help you in Part 3?
  a Read the stem, and then read the paragraph. Work out the answer for yourself, and then check your idea against the four options.
  b Underline vocabulary in the options and look for the same words in the text.
  c Use your own knowledge of business to help you choose an option, so that you don't need to waste time reading the text.
  d Underline language in the options and look for how it might be paraphrased in the text.

USEFUL LANGUAGE: PHRASAL VERBS

1 Match the phrasal verbs in sentences 1 – 8 with a more formal word or phrase a – h.

1 Richards is planning to **step down** from his role as CEO later this year.
2 In order to **get on** in the world of advertising, excellent communication skills are vital.
3 We **keep up with** developments in the industry, and that allows us to remain competitive.
4 We do not intend to **lay** any of our factory workers **off**, despite the economic downturn.
5 After taking over, Wu managed to **turn** the struggling company **around** in just six months.
6 Small companies must budget for any unexpected problems that **come up**.
7 By investing in automation, the company hopes they can **speed up** the manufacturing process.
8 Employees should be able to **carry out** their work without constantly seeking assistance.

a perform
b make redundant
c occur or happen
d remain aware of / informed about
e make something faster and more efficient
f resign / retire
g make progress
h make a venture successful after it was once unsuccessful

2 Choose the correct verbs in *italics*.

1 A loan is often required to help young entrepreneurs *run / set / draw* **up** their small business.
2 If there are no opportunities for promotion, *back / pull / turn* **down** the offer but do so politely.
3 The deal seemed promising early on, but the company *ended / broke / added* **up** losing money.
4 A number of staff have *called / allowed / spoken* **for** changes in the way performance reviews are conducted.
5 Any investment the company makes in staff training will *take / pay / put* **off** in the long run.
6 Even after a contract has been *set / made / drawn* **up**, it is still possible to make changes.
7 If they are not fully prepared, it may be necessary to *call / put / cut* **back** your meeting until everyone can contribute.
8 Don't assume customers will automatically see the advantages. You may need to *spell / show / stand* them **out**.

Exam Practice Test 2 — Reading Part 3

Follow the exam instructions, using the advice to help you.

Questions 13 – 18

- Read the article below about a new energy drink, and the questions on the next page.
- For each question **13 – 18**, mark one letter (**A, B, C** or **D**) on your Answer Sheet for the answer you choose.

 TIP Don't choose an option just because you find the same words in the text and the option.

Natural Power

A natural, plant-based energy drink called Natural Power is helping Andy Carlton break into an already crowded market.

Andy Carlton was working as the finance director for drinks manufacturer T&D Beverages two years ago when he started thinking about the fact that although most 'energy' drinks certainly gave consumers an energy boost, they were also full of sugar. After talking to a number of colleagues in the industry, he decided to take the plunge and leave T&D to launch a healthy alternative, despite his limited experience in either marketing or development. He went in search of a suitable recipe, and although the exact proportions of the ingredients remain a closely guarded secret, the resulting drink is a 100% natural, additive-free product, containing plant extracts and minerals. This focus pits the business directly against its synthetic, sugar-laden competitors.

He spent a lot of time conducting market research rather than paying for a service. He visited places in each category where he hoped Natural Power would have a presence – universities, cafés, leisure centres – and gave samples to any willing participants he found. He quickly discovered that this was a great way of getting fast, honest feedback. Just as importantly, he realised that in the cases where people liked his product, being able to include this fact proved a great starting point when pitching to that company or organisation further down the line. It wasn't always easy, of course, and he often wasn't able to get an audience with even an assistant buyer.

Andy is quick to explain to other entrepreneurs that selling a new product is harsh, and says it's essential to be incredibly resilient, both personally and in the way you adapt to market forces and customer feedback. He's also keen to recommend the 'test, learn, iterate' approach adopted by many tech start-ups. This involves launching a minimum viable product (MVP) as soon as possible, and then listening to what people say so that you can work on branding, packaging and so on. In the case of Natural Power, early feedback from customers was that the general design of the can was good, but it could do with having more emphasis on the natural credentials. This resulted in Andy **tweaking** the way the can looked on each new product run until it was just right. He knew that any extra financing he needed to arrange to do this would be worth it.

Andy knows he's up against some huge names in the category, but makes the point that most big drinks brands launched with a product at a time when people weren't so conscious of their health or worried about artificial ingredients. He feels that changing consumer tastes are forcing big players to change their approach, and many flagship products are starting to look out of date. The opportunities are there for start-ups to disrupt markets with products unburdened by history and tradition. 'I can't compete with their budgets, but I can shout about how we're different,' Andy explains.

It's not yet certain whether public sentiment will lump Natural Power in with its competitors. In the energy drinks category, the terms 'unhealthy' and 'energy drink' are almost synonymous, and it's a challenge to separate them. Andy is not really clear on whether this fact will help or hinder his business in the long run. He's less concerned about calls for retailers to ban the sale of energy drinks to younger shoppers, as his brand is marketed at professionals in the 25 to 35-year-old age range. While he admits the drink has a polarising taste – you don't get that sugar hit people have become accustomed to – he's confident about changing people's palates. It can only be good for society to stop drinking all that sweetness.

13 What does the writer say helped Andy make his decision to set up his company?

    A He developed relevant skills in his role at T&D Beverages.
    B He knew the raw materials he wanted in his product.
    C He had a list of contacts from his previous job.
    D He spotted a gap in the existing drinks market.

14 What does Andy give as a benefit of the way he conducted his market research?

    A It gave him a head start when talking about his products at a later date.
    B It was cheaper than sending off samples and waiting for feedback.
    C It was more reliable than using a bespoke market research company.
    D It saved time as he created one focus group of people from various sectors.

15 What advice does Andy have for people wanting to launch a new product?

    A You have to get your product right before you are ready to launch it.
    B Getting your product out into a marketplace is the most important thing.
    C Secure funding beforehand to respond to unforeseen circumstances.
    D Be strong enough to ignore criticism and go with your instinct.

16 What does the word *tweaking* in line 42 mean?

    A adjusting
    B redesigning
    C controlling
    D rejecting

17 What does Andy say about the traditional energy drinks manufacturing sector?

    A The size of many manufacturers means they are reluctant to adapt to changing tastes.
    B It takes huge financial resources to make the necessary changes in a large market.
    C There is room in the marketplace, as consumers are looking for something different.
    D The age of some drinks companies' processing plants is making them less efficient.

18 What concerns Andy about the future of his brand?

    A The fact that it has such a unique taste could limit sales.
    B Changing regulations could affect the people who can buy it.
    C Its market relies on people being willing to pay for a premium brand.
    D Consumers might not appreciate how it is different to other energy drinks.

Advice

13 Read the whole paragraph which describes Andy's background experiences to help you find the best option.

14 Read carefully to discount information which doesn't fully answer the question.

15 Look for the language which gives a piece of advice.

16 Read the whole sentence here for further clues about the meaning of the word in this context.

17 Remember that you are looking for a detail that shows what Andy thinks.

18 Check that you have found a worry or concern, not a general observation.

Training Test 2 — Reading Part 4

REVIEW

1 How many questions do you answer?
2 Is Part 4 mainly a test of vocabulary or grammar?
3 Do the options generally have similar or different meanings?
4 Which of the following would be a good way to prepare for Part 4?
   a Learn verbs and adjectives together with their dependent prepositions, e.g. *depend on, satisfied with*.
   b Memorise the correct participles for verbs, e.g. *report – report<u>ed</u>, keep – ke<u>pt</u>, focus – focus<u>ing</u>*.
   c Make lists of verbs and nouns that commonly go together, e.g. *keep track of, offer support to*.
   d Identify the most formal word in a group, e.g. <u>dispute</u> *argue row disagree*.

USEFUL LANGUAGE: COLLOCATIONS

1 Circle the one option that does *not* collocate with each of the verbs 1 – 6.

		a	b	c	d
1	face	a serious problem	difficulties	long delays	a drawback
2	meet	a client's needs	large orders	an appointment	a deadline
3	deliver	a strategy	results	a speech	on a promise
4	bring	something under control	an impression	to somebody's attention	major changes
5	put	somebody in charge	right	investment	yourself in somebody's position
6	undergo	a change	an application	an investigation	reorganisation

2 Complete the sentences with the correct form of the options in Exercise 1 that did *not* collocate.
   1 We need to **devise** a new .... that will win back our customers from the competition.
   2 To remain in business, we will need to **increase** .... in rebranding our products.
   3 This plan **suffers** from a major .... , which we need to address.
   4 Edwards **submitted** his .... to be transferred to the branch in Sweden.
   5 If you are unable to **keep** your .... , let your client know immediately.
   6 A well designed brochure can **make** a great .... on potential customers.

3 For each sentence 1 – 4, choose the correct answer a – d.
   1 Rumours of the company's financial troubles .... quickly through the industry.
      a increased   b extended   c spread   d developed
   2 Share prices have been .... steady for the past two months.
      a continuing   b holding   c maintaining d standing
   3 The company has .... a number of challenges in the last few years.
      a faced   b dealt   c undergone   d suffered
   4 There are three criteria that your plans for your start-up should ....
      a meet   b submit   c propose   d bring

Exam Practice Test 2 — Reading Part 4

Follow the exam instructions, using the advice to help you.

Questions 19 – 33

- Read the article below about networking.
- Choose the best word (or phrase) to fill each gap from **A, B, C** or **D** on the next page.
- For each question **19 – 33**, mark one letter (**A, B, C** or **D**) on your Answer Sheet.
- There is an example at the beginning (**0**).

TIP The word you need might be a collocation with the surrounding words.

The Benefits of Business Networking

Have you found that networking isn't producing as many chances for your new business as you'd hoped? Then perhaps it's time to rethink your **(0)** ......A...... . For many people, the decision to start networking comes in direct **(19)** .... to low sales figures, in the hope of **(20)** .... up new business by selling to those they happen to meet in a networking situation. But it isn't about just turning up and treating networking as a straightforward **(21)** .... process. In fact, in many cases you have to make a **(22)** .... for between 6 and 12 months to truly benefit from networking. Strategists advise **(23)** .... for networkers who decide to concentrate all their efforts into converting a networking connection into a firm **(24)** .... to do business. Instead, they say, focus on moving into a longer-term relationship, because someone who knows and respects what you do is **(25)** .... likely to buy from you further down the line if they need what you offer. And even if they don't, they might **(26)** .... you to someone else, and if they do this a number of times, there is a very good chance that the **(27)** .... business will be of far greater value than any single **(28)** .... that has been struck.

Understanding the difference between locating new business and networking has a direct and positive effect on your **(29)** .... , because it will save you time in both arenas and therefore make you more productive. Instead of looking for **(30)** .... that could become sales, look for like-minded people to build a relationship with. Seeing everyone as a possible prospect doesn't allow this to develop, so you miss out on the **(31)** .... to grow a powerful network of trusted contacts. It's about selling through your network, rather than to it. What is really **(32)** .... at the end of the day is the **(33)** .... that you're not just talking to one person but, by extension, to everyone they know.

Example:

	A approach	B way	C rationale	D belief

0 [A▪] [B] [C] [D]

19	A	result	B	response	C	answer	D	reply
20	A	setting	B	looking	C	starting	D	picking
21	A	statistical	B	financial	C	practical	D	rational
22	A	promise	B	commitment	C	requirement	D	decision
23	A	attention	B	caution	C	guidance	D	control
24	A	agreement	B	state	C	procedure	D	convention
25	A	evidently	B	highly	C	notably	D	predictably
26	A	advise	B	persuade	C	promote	D	recommend
27	A	improving	B	resulting	C	succeeding	D	advancing
28	A	deal	B	contract	C	arrangement	D	agreement
29	A	dependability	B	efficiency	C	familiarity	D	influence
30	A	indications	B	suggestions	C	leads	D	partners
31	A	opportunity	B	reason	C	development	D	stage
32	A	knowledgeable	B	beneficial	C	understandable	D	realistic
33	A	evaluation	B	convention	C	foundation	D	recognition

Advice

19 Choose the collocation that fits here and has the meaning of taking action.
20 Choose the phrasal verb meaning **finding by chance** to link with **happen to meet**.
21 Choose the word that fits with the theme of commerce in the sentence.
22 Choose the answer that best fits the idea of giving time.
23 Read ahead to make sure you understand the meaning of the text here.
24 Choose the word that has the idea of a future business option.
25 Choose the word which collocates accurately with what follows the gap.
26 Choose the word which expresses an aim of the networking process which would involve **someone else**.
27 Choose the word which expresses the idea of something that might happen based on the networking process.
28 Look ahead in the sentence to find the other part of a phrase meaning **do business**.
29 Choose the word that has the idea of saving time.
30 Choose the word that expresses the idea of a possible source of new business.
31 Choose the word that collocates with the expression to **miss out on**.
32 Choose the word that expresses the idea of the advantage of an approach.
33 Choose the word that explains what a reader should take away from the text.

Training Test 2 — Reading Part 5

REVIEW
1 How many lines of text are you tested on?
2 Is it possible for two errors to occur in the same line? Or in the same sentence?
3 Is it possible that you will be tested on spelling and punctuation?
4 If you think a line is correct, what should you do on the Answer Sheet?

READING THE WHOLE SENTENCE TO FIND UNNECESSARY WORDS

1 Each pair of sentences contains an underlined word. Decide whether this word is incorrect in sentence a or b.

  1 a All this goes to confirm <u>that</u> the company's reputation as a pioneer in technical innovation.
    b All this goes to confirm <u>that</u> the company's reputation as a pioneer in technical innovation is well deserved.
  2 a The meeting should <u>not</u> only deal with items on the agenda, so staff can be well prepared to discuss them.
    b The meeting should <u>not</u> only deal with items on the agenda, but any issue that needs urgent attention.
  3 a Every year thousands of students <u>who</u> head to career fairs say they appreciate the chance to learn more about their options and make contact with potential employers.
    b Every year thousands of students <u>who</u> head to career fairs to learn more about their options and make contact with potential employers.
  4 a The game has become <u>so</u> popular with both younger and older players since its launch earlier this year that retailers are reportedly running out of stock.
    b The game was launched earlier this year, and while it may be <u>so</u> popular with younger players, it has failed to capture the older market.
  5 a <u>Unless</u> targets set by supervisors are achievable, the majority of staff will not even try to reach them.
    b <u>Unless</u> targets set by supervisors should be achievable, so the majority of staff will try to reach them.
  6 a At least 40% of the company's paper waste is sent for recycling in local facilities, with the other 60% being shipped to China and turned <u>it</u> into packaging.
    b At least 40% of the company's paper waste is sent for recycling in local facilities. The other 60% is shipped to China, where factories turn <u>it</u> into packaging.
  7 a If you're planning to merge two separate sales teams, there will certainly be integration issues, no matter <u>how</u> much effort you put in to reduce the risk of that occurring.
    b If you're planning to merge two separate sales teams, there will certainly be integration issues, no matter <u>how</u> the effort you put in to reduce the risk of that occurring.
  8 a Exhibiting your products at a trade fair is an option but always contact the show organiser first because <u>of</u> their knowledge of visitor demographics could make all the difference.
    b Exhibiting your products at a trade fair is an option but always contact the show organiser first because <u>of</u> their knowledge of visitor demographics, something which could make all the difference.

TIP Read the whole sentence before you decide whether a line contains a mistake or not.

TIP Make sure you read any lines at the bottom of a text which are not numbered. Information in the last line may help you identify an error in an earlier part of the same sentence.

TIP If the same word occurs twice in a line, e.g. *the, we, to* it is unlikely to be the unnecessary word.

Exam Practice Test 2 — Reading Part 5

Follow the exam instructions, using the advice to help you.

Questions 34 – 45

- Read the article about business supply chains.
- In most of the lines **34 – 45** there is one extra word. It is either grammatically incorrect or does not fit in with the meaning of the text. Some lines, however, are correct.
- If a line is correct, write **CORRECT** on your Answer Sheet.
- If there is an extra word in the line, write **the extra word** in CAPITAL LETTERS on your Answer Sheet.
- The exercise begins with two examples (0) and (00).

TIP: Remember to write in CAPITAL LETTERS on your Answer Sheet.

Examples:
- 0 | C O R R E C T
- 00 | T H E

MAINTAINING SUPPLY CHAINS

0	A 'pivot' is the term given to a process in which a business decides
00	to make the central changes to its existing business plan. Reasons for
34	these changes can come about from factors such as a desire to expand
35	an existing product lines. Additionally, in the case of a service industry, negative
36	feedback from customers whose needs are not been addressed may lead to a pivot.
37	In all those cases, the process will most likely have an effect on one of the most
38	important aspects of a business: the supply chain. In order to keep the business
39	running as smoothly during what can be a potentially disruptive period, it is
40	essential to maintain such clear communication lines with investors, customers and
41	of suppliers, in addition to your own team. In cases where there are plans to
42	switch products, existing suppliers who are, of course, highly likely to be affected.
43	Keeping them informed of upcoming changes can help protect the trust that
44	has built up throughout a business relationship. If so they will not be in a position
45	to meet new requirements, be sure that you have had your new suppliers in
	place to fulfil orders and avoid disruption.

Advice

- **34** Read carefully to make sure all shorter words are needed.
- **35** Check for accurate language use with plural words.
- **36** Think whether the auxiliary verbs are used correctly here.
- **37** Check for accurate pronoun referencing.
- **38** Read carefully to make sure all shorter words are needed.
- **39** Think whether the idea of comparison is present in this line.
- **40** Check that a reference made to a previous idea is correct.
- **41** Think about the accuracy of preposition use here.
- **42** Check whether a relative pronoun is needed here.
- **43** Read carefully to make sure all shorter words are needed.
- **44** Think about whether a conjunction is used logically here.
- **45** Check the tenses in the line for accuracy.

Training Test 2 — Writing Part 1

USEFUL LANGUAGE: DEALING WITH PROBLEMS AND COMPLAINTS

1 Match the sentences with the correct or appropriate function. The same function can be used more than once.

> apologising   complaining   explaining   informing   offering   requesting

1 The error was caused by a problem with our IT supplier. ....
2 I am very sorry for any inconvenience this may have caused you. ....
3 I am afraid I am very unhappy that the product was delivered so late. ....
4 I would appreciate a reply as soon as possible. ....
5 Would you like me to deal with this matter? ....
6 Please accept my apologies. ....
7 The incident was due to a miscommunication. ....
8 I'd like to take this opportunity to let you know that we were satisfied with the service. ....
9 Please let me know your thoughts. ....
10 This email is to let you know that we are changing our address. ....
11 I was very disappointed with the service I received from your representative. ....
12 Would you prefer a replacement or a refund? ....

USEFUL LANGUAGE: APOLOGISING

2 Complete the sentences with *for* or *to*.
1 I regret .... tell you that I will not be able to attend the meeting.
2 I am sorry .... any inconvenience this may cause.
3 I am sorry .... putting you in this position.
4 I regret .... inform you that we have cancelled next year's conference.
5 I am sorry .... being late when delivering the project.

USEFUL LANGUAGE: AVOIDING ERRORS

3 Correct the mistakes in the sentences.
1 I would like to apologise for not being able to go to meeting.
2 I was very dissatisfied about the information I received.
3 Unfortunately, there were a problem with scheduling.
4 I can to let you know my answer by the end of the week.
5 I would like to know when can you make the payment.
6 Please be returning your comments as soon as possible.

Exam Practice Test 2 — Writing Part 1

1 **Read the exam task below and answer these questions.**
   1 Who are you going to write to in this email?
   2 How could the people you write to affect the register?
   3 What information do the staff need from you?
   4 Can you think of any extra information to include (within the word limit), which is still relevant to the question?

- You work as a project manager in the headquarters of a large company. One of the meeting rooms in your department will be closed on Monday and Tuesday next week.
- Write an **email** to the staff in your department
  - saying why the meeting room has to close
  - telling staff how long the meeting room will be closed
  - apologising for the inconvenience.
- **Write 40 – 50 words.**

2 **Do the exam task.**

TIP Make sure the information in your answer agrees with the information in the question. For example, only one room is closed, not more and it is only closed on Monday and Tuesday.

TIP Use informal email language in your message.

To: All staff
From:
Subject: Room closure

Training Test 2 — Writing Part 2

USEFUL LANGUAGE: WRITING INTRODUCTIONS

1. Choose the correct introduction in each pair and decide if they come from reports, proposals or a piece of business correspondence.

   1. **a** The purpose of this report is to describe the situation in the Research and Development Department.
      b The purpose of this report is describing the situation in the Research and Development Department.
   2. **a** Dear Ms Nelson,
         I am happy to inform you that we would like to place an order with your company for cleaning materials.
      b Dear Ms Nelson,
         I am happy to inform you that we would like to place an order to your company for cleaning materials.
   3. **a** This report sets up the reasons why the company has invested in Silvertone Inc.
      b This report sets out the reasons why the company has invested in Silvertone Inc.
   4. **a** This proposal will show why it is important the company increases investment to training programmes.
      b This proposal will show why it is important the company increases investment in training programmes.
   5. **a** Dear Mr Williams,
         I am writing to apologise to the late payment of your invoice.
      b Dear Mr Williams,
         I am writing to apologise for the late payment of your invoice.
   6. **a** Our working group would like to propose that we recruit new university graduates for the following reasons.
      b Our working group would like to propose that we recruit new university graduates in the following reasons.

USEFUL LANGUAGE: CLOSING

2. Put the words in the right order.
   1. is / recommended / it / that / …
   2. conclusion, / in / can / we / see / …
   3. I / forward / look / hearing / from / to / you / .
   4. if / is / there / anything / need, / you / please / do / to / contact / me / not / hesitate / .
   5. following / the / are / there / recommendations / :
   6. be / it / concluded / can / that / …

Exam Practice Test 2 — Writing Part 2

1 **Read the exam task below and answer these questions.**
   1 Who are you writing this letter to?
   2 Will you write the same amount for each of the handwritten notes?
   3 Will the letter be formal or informal? Why?
   4 How will you begin and end the letter?

- You work in the after sales department of a mobile phone manufacturer. One of your phones has developed a small problem. Your line manager has asked you to write a letter to customers who have bought the phone.
- Look at the information below, on which you have already made some handwritten notes.
- Then, using **all your handwritten notes, write the letter** to customers.
- **Write 120 – 140 words.**

> **TIP** Remember that you are writing to customers who might not be very happy with your company. This will affect the register of your letter.

> **TIP** You don't need to include any addresses in your letter, but you do need to show clearly who the letter is to and from.

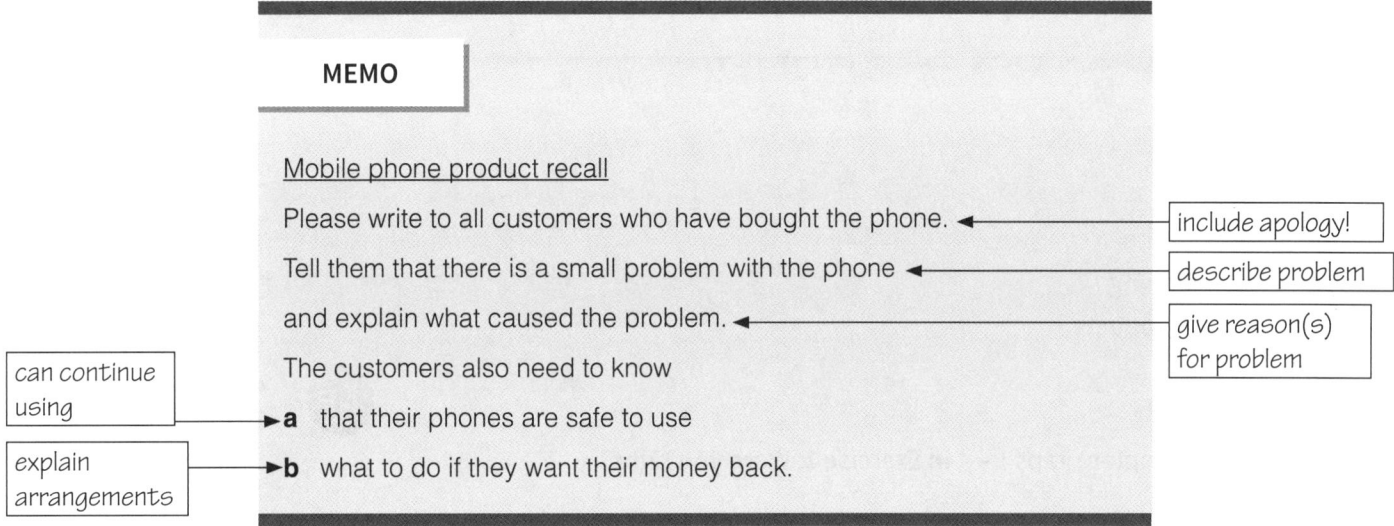

MEMO

Mobile phone product recall

Please write to all customers who have bought the phone. ← include apology!

Tell them that there is a small problem with the phone ← describe problem

and explain what caused the problem. ← give reason(s) for problem

The customers also need to know

→ a that their phones are safe to use — *can continue using*

→ b what to do if they want their money back. — *explain arrangements*

2 **Do the exam task.**

Training Test 2 — Listening Part 1

PROOFREADING AND PREDICTING GRAMMAR

1 Read the instructions and the notes from a recording. Before you listen, decide what kind of information (e.g. a noun, an adjective, a verb, a name or a number, etc.) you will need for each gap. Read the eight options listed, a – h, and decide which two might logically fit each gap.

You will hear two entrepreneurs talking about a client.

Maggie's Problem Client

- got in touch on social media with (1) ....
- with the intention of selling (2) ....
- Maggie's company does (3) ....
- did not check the (4) .... in Maggie's company profile

a pictures
b baby-sitting
c cosmetics
d information
e event planning
f cleaning products
g a request
h a complaint

2 Listen and complete gaps 1 – 4 in Exercise 1. Were you right?

3 You are going to hear the second part of the conversation. Read these notes that a candidate took and correct the forms of the words in the gaps.

Bill's Problem Client
- he wanted free (1) ....*advises*........... unlike the other clients
- Bill didn't immediately (2) ....*saw through*........ it
- it all started when Bill accepted his (3) *contacting request*
- he thought that connecting with Bill meant (4) ....*unlimited excess*.... to him

4 Listen and check your answers. What was wrong with the candidate's answers?

 TIP Try to use your real-life knowledge and vocabulary when preparing to listen. For example, what do people first send each other on social media before they can communicate?

 TIP Check the tense of any verbs and auxiliary verbs in the question. For example, *Bill didn't immediately ...* needs to be followed by an infinitive (i.e. *see*) to be grammatically correct.

Exam Practice Test 2 — Listening Part 1

 Follow the exam instructions, using the advice to help you.

Questions 1 – 12

- You will hear three telephone conversations or messages.
- Write **one or two words or a number** in the numbered spaces on the notes or forms below.
- You will hear each recording twice.

> **TIP** The answers will usually be quite evenly distributed across the material, so if you notice that you haven't caught one in a while, try jumping ahead in the notes. If you think you might have missed a question, don't worry. Focus on what's still coming.

> **TIP** Some words can sound the same in English but belong to different grammatical categories, e.g. nouns or adjectives. Be careful with how a word is used in the recording, e.g. as a noun if the gap you are answering requires one.

Conversation One (Questions 1 – 4)

- Look at the notes below.
- You will hear a consultant on an HR course talking to the participants.

The Gig Economy

- 16.5 million freelance workers in US in 2017
- an increasing **(1)** .... to follow!
- advantages:
  - more authority over your **(2)** ....
  - easier to plan your career
  - more freedom
  - you pick the people you do business with, your customers and **(3)** ....
- most typical in **(4)** .... until now

Conversation Two (Questions 5 – 8)

- Look at the notes below.
- You will hear a customer service operator talking to a potential client.

Your ideal domain

Must go with your **(5)** ....

This will ensure more unified **(6)** ....

Must be memorable and **(7)** ....

Should be **(8)** .... to your company and show what it does

Conversation Three
(Questions 9 – 12)

- Look at the notes below.
- You will hear two colleagues discussing a problem one of them solved.

Sylvia's solution

Reason for change: too many **(9)** ....

Details of new system:

- **(10)** .... software
- colleagues post about their: accomplishments, setbacks, fears and **(11)** ....
- first applied with the **(12)** ....

Advice

1. What might practitioners in any industry want to **follow**? Why?
2. Do you expect to hear a positive or a negative thing in Question 2? And of what word class (e.g. an adjective)?
3. What kind of word do you think might be next after **people** and **customers** in the list?
4. For this question try to catch an answer that comes after the advantages the speaker lists, at the very end of the recording.
5. What synonym can you think of for **go with**?
6. And for **unified**?
7. If the notes say **must be (7)... and memorable**, what type of word (e.g. a noun, adjective) is missing from the gap? (Note: It will be the same as **memorable**.)
8. Can you think of any synonyms of the word **company**?
9. If the **quantity of** something is **overwhelming**, is there too much or too little of it?
10. What is a **widget**? With what synonyms is it expressed in the recording?
11. Notice when the woman starts giving some items from a list, as the answer is going to be the last one on it.
12. If **change trickles down from the top** (= lower-level colleagues follow people higher up in the company's hierarchy) what kind of team should use the system first, so that it takes hold?

Training Test 2 Listening Part 2

DEALING WITH OPPOSITE MEANING AND DOUBLE NEGATIVES

1 Match the opposites from each list.

1	angry	a	wonderful
2	extreme	b	accidentally
3	peacefully	c	calm
4	awful	d	balanced
5	on purpose	e	aggressively

2 Listen to a person talking about what to do when you are angry at work. Write down the double negative expressions you hear.

TIP Sometimes a speaker's opinion is expressed using double negatives (e.g. *I'm not that unhappy in my new job = I like working here*). In these cases, it is especially important to focus on the global meaning of what the speaker is saying, to avoid getting confused.

3 Tick the two options below that contain double negatives.
   A Take your mind off it
   B Don't drink coffee
   C Refrain from using unbalanced language
   D Mind your tone
   E Leave the room
   F Ask a friend for help
   G Communicate neutrally and without criticism
   H Don't assume bad motives

4 You will hear five short recordings, including the speaker from Exercise 2. Five people are talking about what to do when you feel angry at work. For each recording, decide what each speaker is saying. Choose an option (A – H) for each one from above.
   1 ....
   2 ....
   3 ....
   4 ....
   5 ....

Exam Practice Test 2 — Listening Part 2

Follow the exam instructions, using the advice to help you.

Questions 13 – 22

Section One
(Questions 13 – 17)

 TIP Do not expect to hear the same words in the monologues as in the options. Instead, listen out for examples of the concepts mentioned, or explanations connected to them.

- You will hear five short recordings. Five people are talking about what is important when setting up a mentoring programme.
- For each recording, decide what strategy each speaker mentions.
- Write one letter (**A – H**) next to the number of the recording.
- Do not use any letter more than once.
- You will hear the five recordings twice.

 TIP Sometimes you will hear ideas connected to more than one of the options. In such cases always consider which is given more emphasis, e.g. by the speaker talking about it more.

13 ....
14 ....
15 ....
16 ....
17 ....

A creating a positive work environment
B giving clear instructions at the beginning
C running a kick-off mentorship workshop
D not always concentrating on computer skills
E not supervising it at all
F choosing your own specific goals
G pairing the right people up
H considering inviting an external consultant

Advice

13 Be careful. Although the side comment **especially if you bring in an expensive expert from outside** might make you want to choose option H, you should first check what the speaker's main point is. Is he only talking about inviting external consultants?

14 Which of the options A – H is about **match(ing) employees to one another**?

15 What synonym of the key word **guidelines** can you see in which of the options?

16 Two ideas are mentioned by the speaker with a **supportive**, **patient**, **co-operative** atmosphere, and friends **team(ing) up**. Which options talk about these ideas? Which of the two ideas is emphasised more?

17 Can you see a synonym of the word **purpose** in any of the options?

Section Two
(Questions 18 – 22)

- You will hear another five recordings. Five marketing professionals are talking about how to create popular online content.
- For each recording, decide what each speaker recommends.
- Write one letter (**A – H**) next to the number of the recording.
- Do not use any letter more than once.
- You will hear the five recordings twice.

18 ....

19 ....

20 ....

21 ....

22 ....

A put out lengthy content
B consider making it a series
C use narratives
D provoke intense emotions
E team up with another brand
F rely on interaction
G invent a catchy slogan
H provide functional benefits

Advice

18 What's a **'How-to' video**? What kind of content is it?
19 What does the man find surprising?
20 The woman uses the word **narrative**. Can you think of another word for it?
21 Why was the campaign the man describes successful?
22 If your content is **polarising**, how do people react to it?

Listening Part 2   Exam Practice Test 2

Training Test 2 — Listening Part 3

CHOOSING THE RIGHT OPTION

1 You will hear a radio interview with Rebecca Wright, the author of a book titled *Board NOW*, talking about boards of directors. For each question 1 – 8, mark one letter (**A**, **B** or **C**) for the correct answer. You will hear the recording twice.

1 The 'Me, Myself and I' approach
   A describes the attitude of some young board members.
   B is a metaphor to describe young companies.
   C is feasible if the company has already expanded.

2 According to Rebecca, entrepreneurs think boards
   A are too difficult to manage.
   B are only required by venture capitalists.
   C seem to argue too much.

3 Rebecca believes that it is good practice to
   A test the members before hiring them.
   B hire members with no other responsibilities.
   C assemble an advisory board as soon as possible.

4 Rebecca believes it is key that the first board of directors
   A be chosen through recommendations.
   B be practical but keep the founder's main goals in mind.
   C serve only as advisors.

5 Rebecca wouldn't hire family and friends because they
   A won't give their honest advice.
   B are often too obedient.
   C are not financially responsible.

6 According to Rebecca, you shouldn't hire people who
   A know too much about your company.
   B are going to challenge you.
   C are already working for you.

7 The 'CEO's dilemma' is whether to choose
   A members representing the CEO or the investor.
   B internal or external members.
   C members with a legal or marketing background.

8 Rebecca says that it is unfortunate that founders often pick
   A IT experts.
   B advisors that are good at sales.
   C members like themselves.

2 Read questions 1 – 4 again and look at audioscript 18 on page 176. Compare your answers with a partner and discuss why the other two options were incorrect.

3 Read questions 5 – 8 in Exercise 1 again. Compare your answers, then underline the answers and cross out the distractions in audioscript 18 on page 176.

TIP Remember: for an option to be correct it is not enough that the same words are used. The whole sentence has to mean the same as what the speaker is saying.

Exam Practice Test 2 — Listening Part 3

 Follow the exam instructions, using the advice to help you.

Questions 23 – 30

- You will hear a radio interview with a business consultant talking about product launch strategies.
- For each question, **23 – 30**, mark one letter (**A**, **B** or **C**) for the correct answer.
- You will hear the recording twice.

 TIP Phrases at the beginning of the questions such as *According to ...* can orientate you to whose ideas you should listen out for. Also, if the same idea is expressed as stated in an option but by the other person in the conversation, this option should be eliminated. Pay attention to who a statement is connected to if it's not a general one about the topic.

TIP Sometimes meaning is 'co-constructed' between the two speakers, both using incomplete sentences. Make sure you notice these 'turns' and only answer a question after the last turn has been said about the subject.

23 Heather believes that selling anything nowadays

    A is impossible without traditional marketing techniques.
    B needs to be rooted in honesty.
    C has to be based on product launches.

24 According to Heather, advertisers no longer

    A try to control the client's mind.
    B avoid live launches.
    C disapprove of manipulation.

25 What temporary advantage do live launches have?

    A a lot of incoming ad revenue
    B new partnerships
    C immediate engagement with your audience

26 According to Heather, what tends to happen after a live launch?

    A subsequent ones tend to be less profitable
    B subscribers opt out of receiving your emails
    C your ads become more expensive

27 'Evergreen' launches are safer because

    A they do not leave you drained.
    B they require less advertising.
    C you are not dependent on a single revenue.

28 How does an 'evergreen' strategy help you to optimise?

    A by helping your customers find you online
    B by making you improve your videos
    C by allowing you to keep revising your technology

29 According to Heather, companies should respect their clients by

    A allowing them to shop when best for them.
    B highlighting the importance of timing to them.
    C having fewer assumptions about their problems.

30 Heather thinks live launches will

    A experience a major change in their business model.
    B disappear completely.
    C need to be built on trust.

Advice

23 *How is the idea of **selling anything nowadays** expressed? You will hear the answer to question 23 right after the expression paraphrasing this.*

24 *When do you hear the two speakers start talking about **advertising**? Do they use the same word?*

25 *Can you catch when the **temporary advantages** of live launches are discussed? Heather mentions a few examples. Are they all focused on **ad revenue**, **partnerships** or **engagement**?*

26 *What synonym does Heather use to express **after (a live launch)**?*

27 *If you are **at the mercy of** something, are you **safe**? What is not ideal to be **at the mercy of**, according to Heather? Why?*

28 *What do you think is the key word in the first part of the question? Can you catch it being introduced in the recording?*

29 *What does Heather say about **respect**?*

30 *If you hear or read the auxiliary word **will**, what do you typically expect to hear about: the present, past or future? When do the speakers use it?*

Training Test 2 — Speaking Part 1

USEFUL LANGUAGE: ASKING FOR CLARIFICATION

1 Put the words in the right order.
  1 the / question/ could / I'm / repeat / sorry, / you / ?
  2 you / catch / could / didn't / quite / again, / say / it / please / that. / I / ?
  3 please / that, / you / repeating / would / mind / ?
  4 do / mean / by / what / you / ...?
  5 you / could / more / please / be / specific, / ?
  6 that, / you / elaborate / on / would / please / ?
  7 you / mean / do / ...?
  8 example, / you / could / give / me / an / please / ?

TIP It is all right to check something with your partner if you don't understand.

USEFUL LANGUAGE: LINKING IDEAS

2 Put the words and phrases in the box in the appropriate column.

such as   as well as   like   so   and   because   then   also   for example

Linking ideas	Giving an example	Giving a reason

3 Listen to three people answering some questions from Part 1 of the test. Which of the words and phrases from Exercises 1 and 2 do you hear?

USEFUL LANGUAGE: AVOIDING MISTAKES

4 Correct the common mistakes in these sentences.
  1 I am studying publicity at university for the last two years.
  2 I am responsible for create advertising campaigns.
  3 After my studies, I would like to working in a management position.
  4 I study Business Administration when I was at university.
  5 In my sort of work, patience and communication is the two most important soft skills.
  6 The thing I like about my job it is developing other people in my team.
  7 The most big challenge I face is balancing my working life with my family life.
  8 I first become interested in logistics when I was working as an intern.
  9 You have to be able to understand a lot of informations very quickly in my job.
  10 I very like the fact that every day is different at my company.

TIP Give full answers to the questions, not just *yes* / *no*. Also, try to give a reason or example for your answers.

5 Rewrite the sentences in Exercise 4 so they are true about you.

Exam Practice Test 2 — Speaking Part 1

Part 1 3 minutes (5 minutes for groups of three)

1 Work in pairs. One of you takes the role of the interlocutor and asks the questions, while the other answers the questions. Then swap roles.

> **Interlocutor:** Good morning / afternoon / evening.
> - What's your name?
> - And where are you from?
> - Do you work, or are you a student?
> - What do you like most about your work or studies?

> **Thank you. Now I'm going to ask you some questions about working with colleagues.**
> - Do you think it's necessary to get on well with work colleagues? (Why? / Why not?)
> - Do you think companies should organise social events so that staff can get to know each other? (Why? / Why not?)
> - Do you think that it is easier to work with a large or a small group of colleagues? (Why?)
>
> **Thank you.**

 TIP If you can't think of the right word, it's better to be open about it, rather than pausing for a long time while you try to remember it. Say *I can't remember the exact word for this, but it's something like … .* Then use other words to describe what you mean.

TIP Don't worry about being right or wrong, just say what you think and give a reason why you think that. There are no right or wrong answers in the B2 Business Vantage Speaking test.

2 Now swap roles.

> **Interlocutor:** Good morning / afternoon / evening.
> - What's your name?
> - And where are you from?
> - Do you work, or are you a student?
> - What do you like most about your work or studies?

> **Thank you. Now I'm going to ask you some questions about working with colleagues.**
> - Do you think it's necessary to get on well with work colleagues? (Why? / Why not?)
> - Do you think companies should organise social events so that staff can get to know each other? (Why? / Why not?)
> - Do you think it's a good idea to be friends with colleagues outside work? (Why? / Why not?)
>
> **Thank you.**

Training Test 2 — Speaking Part 2

UNDERSTANDING THE TASK

1 Read the advice for Part 2 of the Speaking test. Which one is *not* a good piece of advice?

1 Before the test, practise talking for a minute.
2 Prepare a standard sentence for starting your talk.
3 In the exam, decide very quickly which topic you want to talk about.
4 Make sure you clearly show the examiner when you are moving on to another point.
5 If you don't have a lot to say about the two bullet points on the card, you can add your own ideas.
6 Ask the examiner when you can finish talking.
7 Give examples from your own experience.
8 When your partner is talking, make sure you pay attention so you can ask a relevant question at the end.

> **TIP** It's a good idea to make notes when preparing for your talk.

USEFUL LANGUAGE: ASKING AND RESPONDING TO QUESTIONS

2 Match the question halves.

1 Do you think a pay rise
2 Would you prefer to start work earlier
3 Is it true that accountants earn less money
4 Wouldn't it be better for the government to lower taxation
5 Why is a university degree more important
6 Is it better for you to do your own market research

a or later?
b is better than longer holidays?
c than lawyers?
d than on-the-job training?
e or contract a specialist company?
f than increase subsidies?

> **TIP** Asking a question with two options is a good strategy, as it is easy for your partner to answer it. This helps you to build a good relationship with your partner for the next part of the test.

3 Complete the sentences with the words or phrases from the box.

| I suppose   would prefer   I would choose   you could say   I'm not really sure   it depends |

a Personally, ……………………… to start work earlier so I could get home and spend time with my family in the evenings.
b Most people I know ……………………… a pay rise because they can decide what to do with the money.
c Yes, I think on average ……………………… it's true, they do earn more.
d ……………………… which one is better in the long term.
e ……………………… because traditionally universities were seen as having a high status.
f I think ……………………… on how much research I would have to do, but I would usually do it myself.

4 Match each question in Exercise 2 with a sentence in Exercise 3.

Exam Practice Test 2 — Speaking Part 2

Part 2 6 minutes (8 minutes for groups of three)

1. Work in pairs, A and B. One of you should take the role of the examiner and give the instructions below.

> **Interlocutor:** Now, in this part of the test, I'm going to give each of you a choice of three different topics. I'd like you to select one of the topics and give a short presentation on it for about a minute. You will have a minute to prepare this and you can make notes if you want. After you have finished your talk, your partner will ask you a question.
>
> All right? Here are your topics on page 163 *(A)* and page 165 *(B)*.

[1 minute – A and B should now choose their topic and prepare their presentation]

 TIP If possible, choose the topic which you have personal experience of, perhaps at work if you have a job or something you've done as a student. Use that experience as the basis of your talk.

 TIP Make sure that you keep your answer relevant to the question. For example, if the question is about staff meetings at work, don't talk about other types of meeting unless you are trying to show how staff meetings are different. That keeps it relevant.

2. One of you takes the role of the examiner and gives the instructions, while the other follows the instructions. Then swap roles.

> **Interlocutor:** Now, *(A)*, which topic have you chosen, A, B or C?
>
> Would you like to talk about what you think is important when *[state A's chosen topic]*?
>
> *(B)*, please listen carefully to *(A)*'s talk, and then ask him/her a question about it.

[1 minute – A speaks about the chosen topic]

> **Interlocutor:** Thank you. Now *(B)*, please ask *(A)* a question about his/her talk.

3. Now swap roles.

> **Interlocutor:** Now, *(B)*, which topic have you chosen, A, B or C?
>
> Would you like to talk about what you think is important when *[state B's chosen topic]*?
>
> *(A)*, please listen carefully to *(B)*'s talk, and then ask him/her a question about it.

[1 minute – B speaks about the chosen topic]

> **Interlocutor:** Thank you. Now *(A)*, please ask *(B)* a question about his/her talk.

Training Test 2 — Speaking Part 3

UNDERSTANDING THE TASK

1 Read the task and take 30 seconds to think of some things you might talk about.

> **Organising an Open Day**
>
> The food and drink factory you work for is planning to organise an Open Day for local college students to visit and discover more about the world of work, as well as job opportunities within the company.
>
> You have been asked to help organise the Open Day.
>
> Discuss the situation together and decide:
>
> - what you should show to the students
> - who in the company to involve during the Open Day

TIP If you have a quiet partner, ask them questions to encourage them to speak. The examiner will notice and you will not be penalised if your partner does not contribute.

TIP You are not assessed on your business knowledge, just on the quality of your English when talking about business topics.

2 Listen to two candidates answering the question in Exercise 1. Mark the statements T (true) or F (false).
   1 They give reasons for their opinions.   ....
   2 They discuss both ideas from the question.   ....
   3 When they disagree, they do it politely.   ....
   4 They don't encourage each other to speak.   ....
   5 They listen and respond to each other.   ....

USEFUL LANGUAGE: BUYING TIME

3 What questions do you think the examiner might ask as a follow-up to the task in Exercise 1?

4 Listen and write the three questions the examiner asked.
   1 ....
   2 ....
   3 ....

5 Complete the phrases that the candidates use at the beginning of their answers so they have time to think.
   1 .... a good question.
   2 I have .... thought of that.
   3 .... , I would say that ...

6 Prepare some short answers of your own in response to the examiner's questions.

Exam Practice Test 2 — Speaking Part 3

Part 3 5 minutes (7 minutes for groups of three)
Phase 1

Interlocutor: Now, in this part of the test, you are going to discuss something together. You will have 30 seconds to read this task carefully and then about three minutes to discuss and decide about it together. You should give reasons for your decisions and opinions. You don't need to write anything. Is that clear?

[30 seconds – Candidates look at the task on page 167]

Interlocutor: I'm just going to listen and then ask you to stop after about three minutes. Please speak so that we can hear you.

[3 minutes – Candidates discuss the situation in the task]

Interlocutor: Thank you.

Phase 2
Take it in turns to ask these questions.

- How do you think competition can be a good thing for a company?
- Do you think competition always benefits customers? Why? / Why not?
- What do you think customers look for most in a retail store? Why?
- Do you think all retailers benefit from having high street stores? Why? / Why not?
- Do you think companies should try to attract older or younger customers? Why? / Why not?

> **TIP** This task is where you get most marks for interaction, so make sure that the examiners can clearly see you interacting. You need to have a proper discussion which means giving and reacting to each other's opinions.

> **TIP** Try to use a variety of expressions when you give your opinions. Don't just say *I think* or *I agree with you*. Try *It seems to me that ...* or *That's a very good point (but)... .* This shows the examiner that you have a good range of language.

> **TIP** If you need to, give yourself time to think by using phrases such as *Well, I'm not sure, let me think about that.*

Test 3 Reading Part 1

Questions 1 – 7

- Look at the statements below and the article given on the next page about advice to managers for keeping staff motivated.
- Which section (**A, B, C** or **D**) does each statement **1 – 7** refer to?
- For each statement **1 – 7**, mark one letter (**A, B, C** or **D**) on your Answer Sheet.
- You will need to use some of these letters more than once.

Example:

0   Employers have to consider a range of situations in order to ensure workers' happiness.

1   Workers are more likely to stay at a company if they agree with its aims.

2   Managers may employ a strategy in the workplace which is not especially effective.

3   Companies should try to ensure that what they offer is appealing to a wide audience.

4   It costs a lot to find new staff when people leave a company.

5   Workers need to know that their managers are concerned about the way they feel.

6   When specific essentials are provided, workers are more likely to stay at a company.

7   Managers should comment on workers' performance allowing them to understand their role.

A	In order for employees to really enjoy their work, they must not only feel that their jobs are secure, but that their managers care about their well-being. The happier a workforce is, the more productive it is. It's, therefore, crucial for employers to keep staff engaged. There are, of course, multiple factors to take into account, which not only include adequate levels of pay and a pleasant and comfortable physical environment, but also ensuring that workers are aware of their responsibilities. Additionally, staff should be fully included and relationships with co-workers and risk factors, such as stress, should be managed well.
B	Some managers may assume that keeping workers happy means trying to make the workplace fun. However, people come to work in order to work, and do not necessarily wish to be distracted from the task at hand by having to break off to celebrate someone's birthday, or have to engage in social activities outside working hours. Managers should, instead, focus their attention on providing supportive and timely feedback, and ensuring employees have a sense of purpose about their work. This is not to say, however, that a relaxed and pleasant atmosphere does not contribute to staff well-being: it does.
C	If employees do not fully understand what they are doing for a company, the results can be significant: productivity and morale can drop and, worse, the chance of quitting increases. People are expensive to replace, so looking after your workforce is of major importance. When workers know what they're doing and why, and have empathy for the company's objectives, this creates loyalty and job satisfaction, and ensures that workers give their best. This, in turn, increases business success and leads to greater rewards – financial and otherwise – for everyone involved.
D	Although it may have been overlooked in the past, employers now recognise that workers react in an emotional way to work, and if certain needs are not fulfilled, they may well look elsewhere. A supportive atmosphere, clear goals, reasonable working hours and a decent pay packet are necessities. Companies have to be aware not only of what makes their company attractive to their customers, but to potential employees too, who seek inspiring roles to engage with. Brand reputation not only relates to products and services, but to people as well.

Test 3 Reading Part 2

Questions 8 – 12

- Read the article below about managing major changes within a company.
- Choose the best sentence from the next page to fill each of the gaps.
- For each gap **8 – 12**, mark one letter (**A – G**) on your Answer Sheet.
- Do not use any letter more than once.
- There is an example at the beginning, (**0**).

Change Management

For large companies in the global marketplace, change is inevitable. In the past, it was enough for businesses to concentrate on plans and strategies, and the human element of change management was overlooked. **(0)** ....G.... It is, after all, people – individuals – who make a company what it is, and by ignoring this, plans, however well made, may not work out.

Change can affect an entire company or only part of it, to a greater or lesser degree. **(8)** .... Different factors may be more or less important in the overall scheme of things, especially when the process lasts for such a long time. Without getting individuals on board, rewards will be hard to come by. This is something that many managers are all too aware of. Their concerns include the reactions of the workforce to the proposed changes, how they can ensure teams work together, and their own leadership abilities. All this is in addition to making sure the company's unique values and identity are retained, along with a committed workforce.

So, how *should* change be managed? Experts suggest a range of practices which can be adapted to suit individual companies. The first of these is to deal with the human element head on. Any big change can make employees feel uneasy. **(9)** .... While this may be the case, their worry is not without grounds: they may need to acquire new skills, or find that their job role will change. It is vital to deal with 'people issues' as early as possible in the process, being transparent about what is happening, and available to answer queries and concerns.

Change is of concern to everyone involved in a company, including workers, managers, shareholders and other stakeholders. **(10)** .... Such leaders must embrace the new approaches and be able to motivate those around them. They must also understand that individuals may feel stressed and, therefore, be able to provide the right encouragement and information.

Change must be managed throughout the company, with plans for who will take charge of each part of the process, and clear responsibilities. **(11)** .... In addition to ensuring this trouble-free transition, leaders must also be motivated to make the change happen, be in agreement with the company's vision and well-equipped to implement their individual mission.

Leaders must also be prepared to answer questions: 'Do we really need to change the way we do things?', 'What's the point of all this change?'. They should have a convincing case for the change and be able to communicate their vision. It is also important to demonstrate that the company has a viable future and the right people to lead the company in that future. **(12)** .... This is because each and every person within the company needs to know what new behaviours are expected and understand the systems which will be put in place.

In sum, taking the time to talk to individuals and address their concerns is of vital importance to the success of any transformation.

Example:

A This is because they are happy with the way things are and fear change, often overlooking the possibility that they will be better off in the long run.

B That kind of preparation is, if course, crucial at this stage of the process.

C These leaders must also be able to communicate clearly the changes which will occur to individuals.

D Those in charge of change must, therefore, provide strong and confident guidance to interested parties, providing support and direction throughout the process of change.

E It can last for months and, in some cases, years.

F This is so that change occurs as smoothly as possible at every level within the organisation.

G But for any company to manage change effectively, it must consider its culture and values, people and behaviours.

Test 3 Reading Part 3

Questions 13 – 18

- Read the article below about the different roles in a team and the questions on the next page.
- For each question **13 – 18**, mark one letter (**A, B, C** or **D**) on your Answer Sheet for the answer you choose.

THE DIFFERENT ROLES WITHIN A TEAM

In every team there are different people, different personal characteristics and different functions or roles. Some teams work brilliantly, whereas others fail, having an enormous impact on the people involved and the project at hand.

Researchers who have studied teams in operation have identified distinct personality traits and characteristics, using psychometric tests, in order to find out more about the roles people play within a team. Psychometrics is a field of study concerned with the objective measurement of skills and knowledge, abilities, attitudes, personality traits and educational achievement. Psychometric tests are often used by HR departments to build up a picture of their employees, and may be used as part of the recruitment process to ascertain whether a candidate is suitable for the job they have applied for.

During a personality-type test, a participant will answer a series of questions which identify their skills, knowledge and personality. A question may focus on, for example, whether someone is an extrovert or an introvert, how they prefer to take in new information, or what kind of decision-maker they are. A limited set of options is provided for test takers to choose from. The results indicate how an individual's attributes can be useful to and have an impact on a team.

Experts discovered that how successful a team was depended not so much on factors like intellect but on the way people act instead. Different behaviour types were categorised, and distinct 'roles' identified. These roles were defined as the way an individual conducts him- or herself, contributes to the team, and interacts with others. Most people are not confined to one particular role but, instead, display different elements to a greater or lesser extent.

So, what are the roles that make a successful team? Firstly, there are creative people who can think outside the box and solve problems in less conventional ways. Then there are the logical thinkers, who are able to **weigh up** all the options which are available and decide which might be best without getting emotionally involved. Others are goal-orientated, able to draw on the strengths of other team members and delegate tasks. And there are those with specialist knowledge, who bring expertise to the table.

At times, teams can become so absorbed in the task at hand that they forget to look beyond the team and at whether what they are doing will work in the long run. This is where the people able to provide outside knowledge come in, as do those who are good at planning – coming up with practical strategies which can be implemented smoothly. There are also those who are good at getting the team to work together to get the task done, and others who drive the team forwards, making sure momentum is not lost. And once a project is completed, there are those who check it for errors and ensure the work is of high quality.

For a team to work effectively, it is crucial to have a balance of each of these roles, which may be no easy feat. If a team has no one with a creative spark, for example, it may be difficult to get the ball rolling. With no one to motivate the team, stages of the work may not get completed on time, resulting not only in a loss of productivity, but a drop in morale too. Simply put, it is individual differences and strengths which make all the difference between a team which works well and one which doesn't.

13 According to the second paragraph, psychometric testing

    A is used to determine which people would work well together.
    B can help employers measure what their staff have achieved.
    C can be useful in the early stages of employing someone.
    D is used to find out how well a team is getting on with each other.

14 In the third paragraph, the writer claims that a personality test will

    A allow candidates to answer questions in any way they like.
    B highlight how a candidate is likely to perform at work.
    C give candidates an extensive list of options to choose from.
    D help a candidate find out more about themselves.

15 The fourth paragraph says that a team is more likely to do well if

    A a range of abilities is covered by its members.
    B each person in the team is given a specific role.
    C team members are more intelligent than average.
    D the people in the team communicate well with each other.

16 What does *weigh up* in line 39 mean?

    A measure
    B consider
    C select
    D deliver

17 What is said about teams in the sixth paragraph?

    A They rely on a small number of people to do specific tasks.
    B They often fail to ensure that work is carried out properly.
    C They are keen to seek advice from outside sources.
    D They sometimes lose sight of the wider picture.

18 What is the general conclusion of the article as a whole?

    A Individuals with strong personalities may not be especially effective in teams.
    B Teams should draw on available tools to ensure they recruit the right people.
    C It can be tricky to maintain the right mix of required skills in a single team.
    D Companies should seek to employ people to fulfil specific team roles.

Test 3 Reading Part 4

Questions 19 – 33

- Read the article below about improving company performance.
- Choose the best word to fill each gap from **A, B, C** or **D** on the next page.
- For each question **19 – 33**, mark one letter (**A, B, C** or **D**) on your Answer Sheet.
- There is an example at the beginning, (**0**).

IMPROVING COMPANY PERFORMANCE

There are several (**0**) ......*A*...... which can be taken in order to improve and grow a company. The first of these is to check that you know your numbers. These include your cash (**19**) .... , in addition to gross and net profit, which help you (**20**) .... how well your company is performing. These will tell you whether goods and services are being sold at a price which (**21**) .... production costs and whether your (**22**) .... align with profits from sales. They will also provide information about whether the company is (**23**) .... over time. Keeping a close eye on these (**24**) .... of financial performance will allow managers to deal with potential problems before they become serious.

It is also important to take a look at your processes. Profit will take a (**25**) .... if operations are not effective and efficient; for example, if your product or service is not of a (**26**) .... enough quality or delivered on time and within (**27**) .... It is, therefore, crucial that procedures are (**28**) .... integrated and carried out without error or waste.

Thirdly, it is important to assess the performance of employees. As companies (**29**) ...., it is vital to look at how individual job roles will adapt. Staff may have to acquire new skills and expertise, and your company should (**30**) .... these needs are met.

Finally, strategic planning is crucial. Plans do not need to be particularly sophisticated, but should (**31**) .... into account the long-term development of the company (**32**) .... on providing value to customers and shareholders. Planning strategically should allow a company to be flexible and (**33**) .... to change.

Example:

	A steps	B moves	C stages	D acts
0	■ A	□ B	□ C	□ D

19	A course	B run	C flow	D movement
20	A determine	B settle	C diagnose	D master
21	A extends	B covers	C spreads	D reaches
22	A payments	B amounts	C figures	D expenses
23	A capable	B sustainable	C reasonable	D passable
24	A dimensions	B totals	C measurements	D calculations
25	A beat	B strike	C bang	D hit
26	A high	B large	C full	D top
27	A money	B estimate	C number	D budget
28	A certainly	B seriously	C fully	D dearly
29	A enlarge	B expand	C increase	D stretch
30	A ensure	B reassure	C secure	D assure
31	A have	B make	C take	D get
32	A founded	B built	C formed	D based
33	A answer	B respond	C reply	D act

Test 3 Reading Part 5

Questions 34 – 45

- Read the text below about delegating work.
- In most of the lines **34 – 45** there is one extra word. It is either grammatically incorrect or does not fit in with the meaning of the text. Some lines, however, are correct.
- If a line is correct, write **CORRECT** on your Answer Sheet.
- If there is an extra word in the line, write **the extra word** in CAPITAL LETTERS on your Answer Sheet.
- The exercise begins with two examples, (0) and (00).

Examples:
0 | C | O | R | R | E | C | T
00 | D | O

WHAT IS COST CONTROL?

0	Cost control is the process or activity of reducing costs associated with an activity,
00	process or company. Businesses must identify their expenses before aiming to do
34	cut them and increase its profits. This begins with the budgeting process. Business
35	owners compare what is actually happening with the planned costs outlined in to the
36	budget. If costs are shown to be higher than expected, managers must then take
37	action. One way to do this is to find out if whether services and their products can be
38	acquired even more cheaply from other suppliers and then seek to lower costs.
39	Businesses must employ cost-control methods in order to maximise their profits.
40	Outsourcing is not a common way to control costs, as it can be less expensive to pay for the
41	services of a third party to carry out particular tasks than it may be to keep the work
42	in-house. One such an area where this is done is payroll: tax laws frequently change,
43	and staff turnover, especially when high, as it is the case for temporary and seasonal
44	jobs, can require constant changes to payroll records. Companies which are specialise in
45	payroll can make up the necessary calculations for tax and net pay for individuals, which
	can save an employer not only money, but time too.

Test 3 Writing Part 1

- You are the sales director for a mobile phone company. The sales of your company's main mobile phone product are beginning to fall.
- Write a short **email** to all staff:
  - saying which model is having falling sales
  - explaining why this is a problem for the company
  - telling staff about a new advertising campaign to improve sales.
- **Write 40 – 50 words**.

Test 3 Writing Part 2

- The department where you work recently had a new IT system installed by a company called Target IT Ltd. Your new Managing Director has asked you to write a report for her about the new system.
- Look at the information below, on which you have already made some handwritten notes.
- Then, using **all** your handwritten notes, write your **report** for the Managing Director.
- **Write 120 – 140 words.**

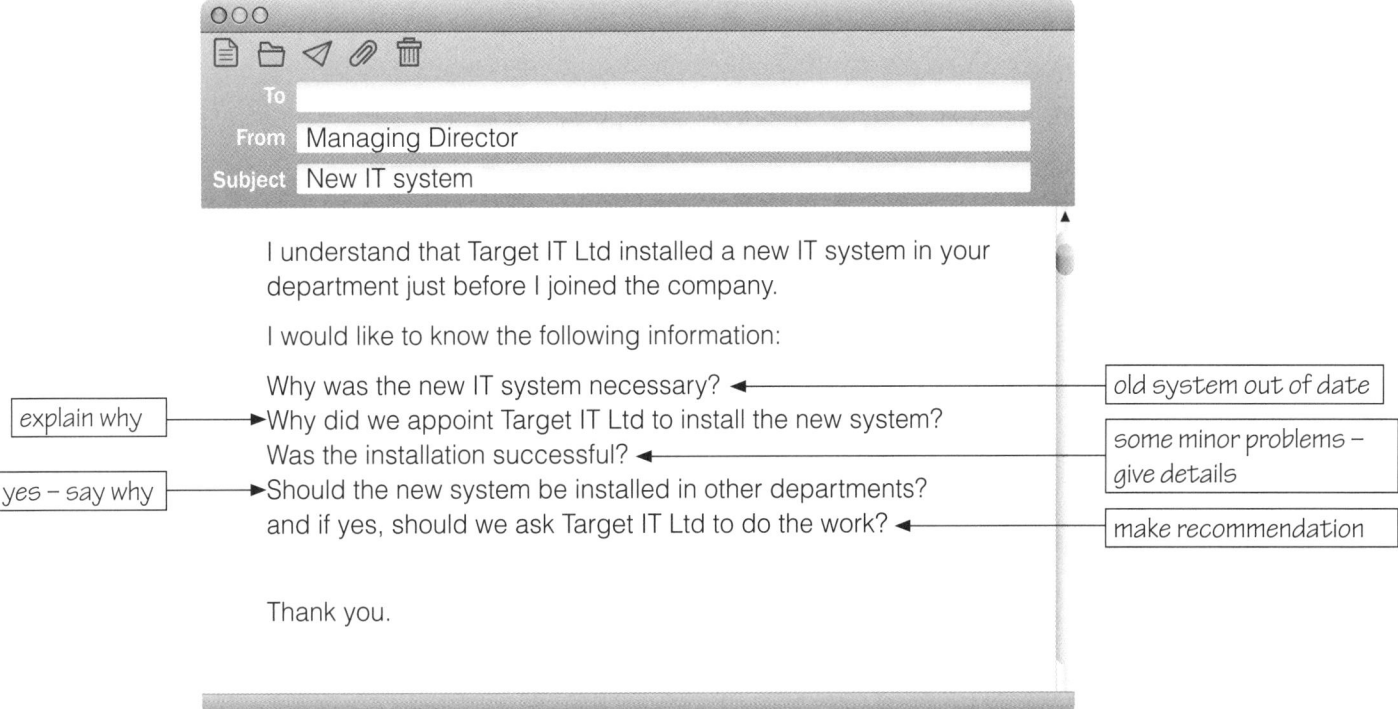

Test 3 Listening Part 1

 Questions 1 – 12

- You will hear three telephone conversations or messages.
- Write **one or two words or a number** in the numbered spaces on the notes or forms below.
- You will hear each recording twice.

Conversation One
(Questions 1 – 4)

- Look at the notes below.
- You will hear a boss talking to one of her staff about an important upcoming presentation.

Tomorrow's presentation

Begin with short (1) .... of firm

Don't overcrowd (2) .... !

Include vivid (3) ....

Avoid using (4) .... when changing slides

Conversation Two
(Questions 5 – 8)

- Look at the notes below.
- You will hear a business analyst called Miley talking to the managing director of a clothing company about a new trend.

Athleisure

- a new (5) .... in clothing
- items for exercising and for general use
- contributing to a massive (6) .... in society
- customers want more (7) .... from their clothes
- frequently advertised by micro (8) .... (= people doing certain sports as a hobby)

Conversation Three
(Questions 9 – 12)

- Look at the notes below.
- You will hear the head of a PR firm talking to employees of a company about having a press kit.

Press Kits

Must include a (9) .... about your firm that describes
- you
- partners
- company
- market

Should be (10) .... to avoid further enquiry
Possible extra info to include:
- year of foundation
- founders
- place of foundation
- where it operates now
- number of (11) ....

Visuals:
- photos (e.g. some (12) ....)
- videos (e.g. short interviews with owners)

Test 3 Listening Part 2

Section One
(Questions 13 – 17)

- You will hear five short recordings. Five company owners are talking about what they look for in candidates applying for jobs at their firms.
- For each recording, decide what each speaker looks for.
- Write one letter (**A – H**) next to the number of the recording.
- Do not use any letter more than once.
- You will hear the five recordings twice.

13 ....
14 ....
15 ....
16 ....
17 ....

A above-standard IT skills
B not afraid to disagree with customers
C taking responsibility
D a client-focused perspective
E being brave enough to try things
F conflict management skills
G the willingness to invent and simplify
H management experience at university

Section Two
(Questions 18 – 22)

- You will hear another five recordings.
- For each recording, decide what each speaker's advice is for improving brand credibility.
- Write one letter (**A – H**) next to the number of the recording.
- Do not use any letter more than once.
- You will hear the five recordings twice.

18 ....
19 ....
20 ....
21 ....
22 ....

A Humanise your brand
B Keep your language simple
C Have a website
D Have a physical location
E Create your own app
F Mention concrete achievements
G Have a testimonials page
H Choose the right colours

Test 3 Listening Part 3

Questions 23 – 30

- You will hear a radio interview with the CEO of a company talking about how he reformed its meetings culture.
- For each question, **23 – 30**, mark one letter (**A**, **B** or **C**) for the correct answer.
- You will hear the recording twice.

23 Dan believes meetings do not need to be a drain if

    A the presenters use a clear checklist.
    B they are more precisely described.
    C there is more dialogue about them.

24 It is important that a meeting's agenda

    A mentions who is calling the meeting.
    B includes how long every item will be discussed.
    C states why the meeting is inevitable.

25 Starting a meeting with silence allows employees to

    A come up with some relevant questions.
    B review the other participants' summaries.
    C do some research about the topic.

26 According to Dan, trivial matters are often discussed longer

    A because more employees can say something about them.
    B when these are most important at an organisation.
    C if not enough people really understand them.

27 Dan says consensus is

    A important when deciding who is in charge.
    B not always necessary.
    C hard for some people to adapt to.

28 Despite the 'two-pizza rule', Dan says it is essential that

　　A some old default topics be discarded.
　　B all participants understand the topics.
　　C the principal participants be present.

29 According to Dan, how did meetings use to be scheduled?

　　A they tended to disrupt employee focus
　　B without checking when employees were free
　　C interfering with other meetings

30 What is Dan's theory about meetings?

　　A they make people anxious
　　B they raise people's curiosity about authority figures
　　C they are representative of a company's culture

> You now have 10 minutes to transfer your answers to your Answer Sheet.

Test 3 Speaking Part 1

Part 1 3 minutes (5 minutes for groups of three)

1 Work in pairs. One of you takes the role of the interlocutor and asks the questions, while the other answers the questions. Then swap roles.

Interlocutor: Good morning / afternoon / evening.
- What's your name?
- And where are you from?
- Do you work, or are you a student?
- What do you like most about your work or studies?

Thank you. Now I'm going to ask you some questions about selling products online.
- Do you think online selling is suitable for all products? (Why? / Why not?)
- Do you think online selling will continue to grow in importance in the future? (Why? / Why not?)
- Do you think there are any disadvantages for companies which only sell products online? (Why? / Why not?)

Thank you.

2 Now swap roles.

Interlocutor: Good morning / afternoon / evening.
- What's your name?
- And where are you from?
- Do you work, or are you a student?
- What do you like most about your work or studies?

Thank you. Now I'm going to ask you some questions about selling products online.
- Do you think online selling is suitable for all products? (Why? / Why not?)
- Do you think online selling will continue to grow in importance in the future? (Why? / Why not?)
- Why do you think that many customers still prefer to shop in-store instead of online?

Thank you.

Test 3 Speaking Part 2

Part 2 6 minutes (8 minutes for groups of three)

1 Work in pairs, A and B. One of you should take the role of the examiner and give the instructions below.

Interlocutor: Now, in this part of the test, I'm going to give each of you a choice of three different topics. I'd like you to select one of the topics and give a short presentation on it for about a minute. You will have a minute to prepare this and you can make notes if you want. After you have finished your talk, your partner will ask you a question.

All right? Here are your topics on page 163 *(A)* and page 165 *(B)*.

[1 minute – A and B should now choose their topic and prepare their presentation]

2 One of you takes the role of the examiner and gives the instructions, while the other follows the instructions. Then swap roles.

Interlocutor: Now, *(A)*, which topic have you chosen, A, B or C?

Would you like to talk about what you think is important when *[state A's chosen topic]*?

(B), please listen carefully to *(A)*'s talk, and then ask him/her a question about it.

[1 minute – A speaks about the chosen topic]

Interlocutor: Thank you. Now *(B)*, please ask *(A)* a question about his/her talk.

3 Now swap roles.

Interlocutor: Now, *(B)*, which topic have you chosen, A, B or C?

Would you like to talk about what you think is important when *[state B's chosen topic]*?

(A), please listen carefully to *(B)*'s talk, and then ask him/her a question about it.

[1 minute – B speaks about the chosen topic]

Interlocutor: Thank you. Now *(A)*, please ask *(B)* a question about his/her talk.

Test 3 Speaking Part 3

Part 3 5 minutes (7 minutes for groups of three)
Phase 1

Interlocutor: Now, in this part of the test, you are going to discuss something together. You will have 30 seconds to read this task carefully and then about three minutes to discuss and decide about it together. You should give reasons for your decisions and opinions. You don't need to write anything. Is that clear?

[30 seconds – Candidates look at the task on page 167]

Interlocutor: I'm just going to listen and then ask you to stop after about three minutes. Please speak so that we can hear you.

[3 minutes – Candidates discuss the situation in the task]

Interlocutor: Thank you.

Phase 2
Take it in turns to ask these questions.

- Would you be interested in attending a company open day? Why? / Why not?
- Do you think all companies would benefit from holding open days? Why? / Why not?
- Which parts of a company do you think are most interesting for visitors to see? Why?
- Do you think staff should be asked about how to organise an open day? Why? / Why not?
- What kind of information do you think visitors could be given about the company on an open day? Why?

Test 4 Reading Part 1

Questions 1 – 7

- Look at the statements below and the article given on the opposite page about a strategy for expanding a company.
- Which section (**A, B, C** or **D**) does each statement **1 – 7** refer to?
- For each statement **1 – 7**, mark one letter (**A, B, C** or **D**) on your Answer Sheet.
- You will need to use some of these letters more than once.

Example:

0 Companies may believe they will be better off financially if they join with another business.

1 It can cost less to promote products which are similar to others in the range.

2 Merging with another company must be organised meticulously.

3 One advantage of merging with a company elsewhere is having established contacts.

4 Companies often merge in order to make sure there are fewer competitors.

5 Companies offer different justifications for horizontal integration.

6 Growing too quickly can create problems for the companies involved.

7 There can be financial benefits of increasing the number of goods offered.

Growing a business through horizontal integration

A Horizontal integration is one way of growing a business, by acquiring another company in the same, or a different, industry. Reasons given for doing so are numerous and may include a desire to increase in size, widening the range of products and services on offer, achieving economies of scale, and accessing new customers or markets. The competitive strategy of merging two companies is often done in order to create higher income than either company would have been able to achieve on its own. However, it is important to get it right: this means not creating either an oligopoly (where a small group of companies control the market) or a monopoly (where a single company has a dominant share of the market).

B The advantages of horizontal integration include savings in operating costs, such as in marketing, research and development, production and distribution. And, in addition to economies of scale, where costs are saved when production is increased, there may be economies of scope. This is where making different products at the same time can result in reduced costs. Companies which merge, say, different health and beauty products, will be able to lower their marketing and product development costs per product. Synergies can also occur through combining products or markets. This provides opportunities for selling different products to existing customers and increases the market for each business.

C Synergies, or the interaction between organisations to produce a combined effect greater than the sum of their separate effects, allow companies to diversify their products. An example of this is a sports clothing company which then chooses to offer accessories, such as watches or backpacks. Merging with a similar company which is located in a different market, such as another country, helps to avoid having to start from nothing there to build up a distribution network.

D The main reason that companies merge horizontally is to reduce opposition, which may be in the form of new companies entering the market, substitutes or established rivals. But, as with anything, there are, of course, disadvantages. Synergies may *not* be created and added value may not occur as hoped. There is even a danger of negative synergies, which reduce the value of the business as a whole. This can happen when companies become too big to manage well, or when the merger is unsuccessful because of different leadership styles and company cultures.

Test 4 Reading Part 2

Questions 8 – 12

- Read the article below about the importance of training and education throughout a person's career.
- Choose the best sentence from the opposite page to fill each of the gaps.
- For each gap **8 – 12**, mark one letter (**A – G**) on your Answer Sheet.
- Do not use any letter more than once.
- There is an example at the beginning, (**0**).

Continuing professional development

As a new recruit straight out of university, it may be tempting to think that once you've gained the relevant qualifications and got a great job in your chosen field, you don't need to worry about doing any more learning. You would be wrong. Continuing professional development, or CPD, should be viewed not as an extra, but as an obligation.

CPD is crucial if you want to stay ahead in your profession. And it isn't just those new to a field who need to think about it, but experienced professionals, too. **(0)** ....*G*.... It isn't just that CPD helps employees develop professionally, but it can help the company's development and, in certain fields, the public's, too.

So, what exactly are the benefits of CPD? In any profession there are standards to maintain, as well as a range of skills and knowledge required to provide clients with a professional service. By being involved in CPD, your skills and knowledge stay current. You also gain information about industry trends and changes. **(8)** .... For example, it could allow competitors to leave you behind.

On a personal level, undertaking CPD allows you to make useful contributions to team projects, and makes you a skilled and effective worker. Perhaps you dream of moving upwards or taking on a new managerial or training role. If this is the case, it is vital to gain all the knowledge and skills you can. **(9)** .... It's, therefore, crucial to acquire new approaches, and CPD opens up such possibilities.

Additionally, CPD can help you understand better what it is you are aiming for in your chosen field, and help you appreciate the impact your industry has on other people. **(10)** .... This can then be fed back to your colleagues. The better each team performs, the better the company does, and the greater the public confidence in the business.

In certain professions, CPD can be crucial to quality of life and the environment, sustainability or the economy. One example of this is the field of medicine, where it is imperative to keep up with advances and safety procedures. **(11)** .... Employees in high-risk fields should see it as a personal responsibility to keep their skills as up to date as possible, in order to safeguard the interests of the public, and to meet the expectations of customers.

So, what makes good CPD? It may sound as though it is nothing but hard work. **(12)** .... This ensures that those involved in the training stay motivated, take in what they need to know and understand why what they are learning is relevant to what they do. It also helps them to be able to assess what they have learnt and put it to good use, so they can apply their new skills and knowledge to their job in the right way.

Example:

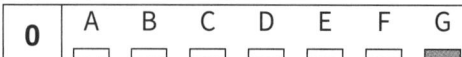

A   Indeed, professional organisations or codes of conduct or ethics in professions such as this may demand that CPD is carried out.

B   But it should keep employees engaged too.

C   This is not to say that certain employees don't benefit from CPD.

D   Not keeping up with these would be foolish for a company.

E   You should aim to know as much as possible about the venture you're currently involved in.

F   This is because it can be easy to keep doing things the way you've always done them.

G   In reality, it is something employees should do throughout their career in order to make sure they stay good at their jobs.

Test 4 Reading Part 3

Questions 13 – 18

- Read the article below about how to learn from business mistakes and the questions on the opposite page.
- For each question **13 – 18**, mark one letter (**A, B, C** or **D**) on your Answer Sheet for the answer you choose.

How to Learn from Business Mistakes

You don't become a millionaire by ignoring the things you did wrong in business. In fact, highly successful entrepreneurs seem to be particularly good at working out what went wrong and why, and making sure they don't do the same thing again. What's more, they also look at their successes and analyse what went right.

When something goes wrong – or right – in business, it's easy to move on without looking back. But failing to invest time and effort in examining what happened could mean missing out on useful information, which will help business owners discover solutions to problems and advance the business more effectively.

Talk to any entrepreneur and they will no doubt have lots to tell you about their poor business decisions, investments that didn't work out, and choosing bad business partners. They will tell you that they probably already had an idea that things weren't right at the time, but they went ahead anyway without listening to their instinct. They almost set themselves up to fail. But they'll also tell you what they learnt from those failures, and how they were determined not to let the situation repeat itself.

Business experts suggest a seven-step approach to learning from mistakes. The steps depend on the nature of the business and may need to be adapted to the situation at hand. The first step is to review aspirations. This means being clear about what you want to achieve when you go into a new business venture. Secondly, it is important to keep a record of what's happening in the venture: if things have already started to go wrong, look at these failures, decide how bad they are, and think about what outcome you would like.

The third point is to identify **discrepancies**. What this means is being able to quantify the gaps between your expectations for a venture and what has actually occurred. This is closely linked to the fourth step: make a list of the mistakes that have been made which led to the discrepancies. The most beneficial way to do this is not to say whose fault it was or who to make responsible for it, but to look carefully at how the same mistakes may have resulted in several discrepancies.

Once you have recorded what's happened, you can start to think about what you need to learn from the mistakes which have been made. Look at the cause of inconsistencies. This will enable you to see where you misjudged things and provide you with a wider perspective. The conclusions you make from doing **this** will teach you what not to do next time round, so that the same mistakes are not repeated.

The sixth step is to look across all business ventures where things have gone wrong. Evaluating a single project is less likely to provide you with the information you need to be more successful in the future. Looking at the bigger picture will highlight where you keep going wrong. And this takes us to the final step – use the knowledge you've gained to learn lessons and develop better judgement. You will still make mistakes, but they will be new ones, and provide further opportunities to become ever more successful.

13 What does the writer say about business mistakes in the first paragraph?

    A Too many people focus only on the mistakes they have made.
    B Successful businesspeople are unlikely to make many mistakes.
    C Making mistakes is a necessary part of developing a business.
    D It is helpful to consider things that have gone well in addition to mistakes.

14 What does the writer suggest about entrepreneurs in the third paragraph?

    A They are optimistic that things will always turn out for the best.
    B They sometimes ignore their natural sense of what is right.
    C They get satisfaction from talking about their successes and failures.
    D They are unhappy when they are unable to resolve their mistakes.

15 When the writer introduces the seven-step process to learning from mistakes, he says that the steps

    A are suitable for every kind of business.
    B only work for certain kinds of problem.
    C can be changed to fit individual circumstances.
    D have been tried and tested by business owners.

16 What does *discrepancies* in line 34 mean?

    A errors of judgement
    B differences between things
    C variations in approaches
    D conflicting theories

17 What does *this* in line 49 refer to?

    A being provided with a wider perspective
    B the conclusions you make
    C misjudging things
    D looking at the cause of inconsistencies

18 What is the writer doing in the final paragraph?

    A advising business owners to make the most of information they have gathered
    B encouraging business owners to consider any new projects carefully
    C expressing regret that not all errors can be avoided in business
    D criticising those who fail to learn from their business mistakes

Test 4 Reading Part 4

Questions 19 – 33

- Read the article below about research and development.
- Choose the best word to fill each gap from **A, B, C** or **D** on the opposite page.
- For each question **19 – 33**, mark one letter (**A, B, C** or **D**) on your Answer Sheet.
- There is an example at the beginning, **(0)**.

THE ROLE OF RESEARCH AND DEVELOPMENT

Research and development (R&D) is an important part of business, and **(0)** ....A.... businesses to be creative and innovative. Without it, businesses are in danger of standing **(19)** .... or worse, falling behind the competition.

R&D is particularly important in the current business **(20)** ...., with customers keen to **(21)** .... rapid advances in technology. **(22)** .... one step ahead is vital in order to remain competitive and **(23)** .... market share. R&D plans ahead of the rest of a business and must have a clear **(24)** ...., with solutions to possible challenges immediately available. R&D may incur costs financially, but these costs should be viewed as worthwhile investment. Patience and foresight are required, particularly as it can take time for a **(25)** .... on investment to occur. Once it has, it can be substantial. This is often the **(26)** .... for the pharmaceutical and automotive industries, for instance, which **(27)** .... considerable investments in R&D.

Such companies become leaders in technology because their **(28)** .... to get new products onto the market quickly can make other products held in stock **(29)** .... almost as soon as they're on sale. Products which are the **(30)** .... of successful R&D include many modern inventions, such as mobile phones, laptops and tablets, music technology and washing machines. The technological revolution made **(31)** .... cameras, typewriters and letters redundant.

R&D helps businesses **(32)** .... on by predicting future trends and preparing for them. But for R&D to **(33)** .... to business success, it must bring products to market as quickly as it can.

Example:

	A allows	B permits	C lets	D gives

0 A B C D

19	A quiet	B stopped	C fixed	D still
20	A climate	B situation	C position	D condition
21	A agree	B attempt	C acquire	D adopt
22	A Doing	B Holding	C Keeping	D Having
23	A collect	B maintain	C reserve	D continue
24	A vision	B sight	C view	D image
25	A refund	B return	C repayment	D replacement
26	A cause	B point	C case	D state
27	A form	B create	C produce	D make
28	A technique	B skill	C ability	D facility
29	A outdated	B ancient	C aged	D past
30	A reaction	B effect	C result	D end
31	A standard	B traditional	C historical	D established
32	A take	B go	C run	D move
33	A contribute	B apply	C donate	D present

Test 4 Reading Part 5

Questions 34 – 45

- Read the text below about health and well-being at work.
- In most of the lines **34 – 45** there is one extra word. It is either grammatically incorrect or does not fit in with the meaning of the text. Some lines, however, are correct.
- If a line is correct, write **CORRECT** on your Answer Sheet.
- If there is an extra word in the line, write **the extra word** in CAPITAL LETTERS on your Answer Sheet.
- The exercise begins with two examples, (**0**) and (**00**).

Examples: 0 C O R R E C T   00 D O

Health and Well-Being at Work

0	In the past, 'health' in the workplace almost always meant 'health and safety'. This is
00	still something that companies do take very seriously. But they are also considering
34	other aspects of the health not related to, for example, dirt, noise or physical danger.
35	Most of us are very aware of the need for a good work-life balance, and we are
36	starting to think about the impact of our jobs not only on to our physical well-being but also
37	our psychological and well-being. Clearly, there are benefits to employees of
38	being so happy and healthy at work, but there are just as many advantages for
39	employers, who lose a lot of money through staff taking their time off because of
40	physical illnesses like flu, but also such things as stress, which should be avoided.
41	What is it that makes a healthy workplace, then? First and foremost there are
42	effective policies in place to look out after workers. There are also trusting relationships
43	between managers and employees. An example of this is that involving staff in the
44	decision-making process. People skills are at a must for successful managers and,
45	above all, staff should feel appreciated for what they do, with stress reduced to a minimum.

Test 4 — Writing Part 1

- You are the HR manager of your company. There is a job vacancy in the marketing department.
- Write an **email** to all staff:
  - explaining what the job is
  - saying which department of the company has the vacancy
  - telling staff what to do if they would like to apply for the job.
- **Write 40 – 50 words.**

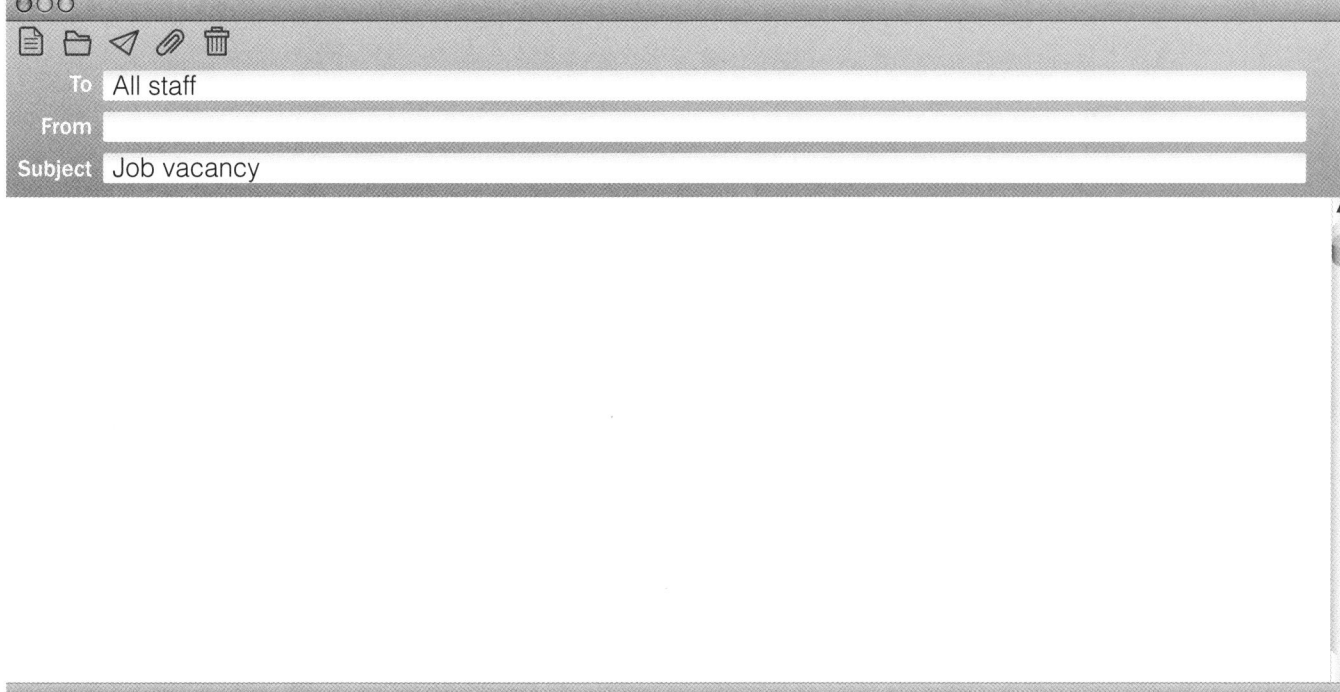

Test 4 Writing Part 2

- The department store you work for is considering opening another store in Wigston, a nearby town. Your line manager has asked you to write a proposal for the new store.
- Look at the information below, on which you have already made some handwritten notes.
- Then, using **all** your handwritten notes, write a **proposal** for your line manager.
- **Write 120 – 140 words.**

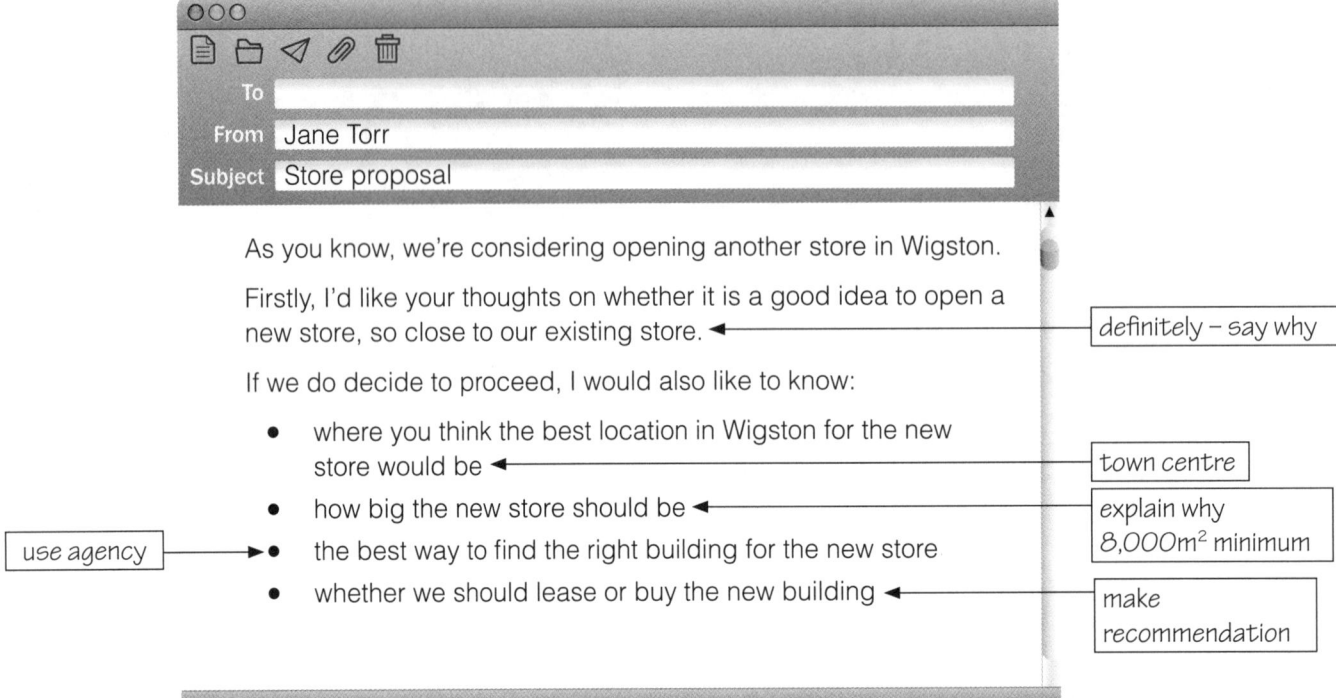

Test 4 Listening Part 1

Questions 1 – 12

- You will hear three telephone conversations or messages.
- Write **one or two words or a number** in the numbered spaces on the notes or forms below.
- You will hear each recording twice.

Conversation One
(Questions 1 – 4)

- Look at the notes below.
- You will hear a CEO talking to his assistant about a new plan he has.

Weekly CEO videos

A new way to keep in touch with employees

Will replace

- meetings
- video-conferencing
- weekly **(1)** ....

To address colleagues from all departments and **(2)** ....

Goals:

- to share company news
- to exchange **(3)** ....

Production:

- shouldn't take much time
- can be done anywhere
- **(4)** .... and visual aspects won't be edited

Conversation Two
(Questions 5 – 8)

- Look at the notes below.
- You will hear a software engineer and her boss talking about developing a new application for buying furniture.

Our new VR app

- may improve our numbers for the **(5)** ....
- will help clients visualise our items in their **(6)** ....
- currently 22% of clients buy the wrong product!
- should make measuring easier
- provides **(7)** .... inspiration
- assists with colours
- **(8)** .... by November

Conversation Three
(Questions 9 – 12)

- Look at the notes below.
- You will hear a market researcher talking about ways to get to know your customer.

Get to know your customer!

Customers don't say what they mean!

(9) .... is better than any info provided by customer

(10) .... are problematic:

— resource intensive

— results not representative

— number of replies doesn't ensure **(11)** ....

— can't predict future customer behaviour

Better sources of feedback:

— customer support calls / emails

— subscribing to a **(12)** .... service

Test 4 — Listening Part 2

Section One
(Questions 13 – 17)

- You will hear five short recordings. Five HR professionals are talking about different ways to keep high performers.
- For each recording, decide what each speaker's recommendation is.
- Write one letter (**A – H**) next to the number of the recording.
- Do not use any letter more than once.
- You will hear the five recordings twice.

13 ....

14 ....

15 ....

16 ....

17 ....

A Make sure their pay beats the competition's.
B Consider remote and flexible work.
C Notice their lack of cooperation in time.
D Publicly recognise their accomplishments.
E Offer them fairly calculated bonuses.
F Reduce their workload.
G Involve them in interesting upcoming tasks.
H Provide opportunities for growth.

Section Two
(Questions 18 – 22)

- You will hear another five recordings.
- For each recording, decide what strategy each speaker describes for getting recipients to read emails.
- Write one letter (**A – H**) next to the number of the recording.
- Do not use any letter more than once.
- You will hear the five recordings twice.

18 ....

19 ....

20 ....

21 ....

22 ....

A wording it as a reminder
B proofreading your writing
C including some numbers
D respecting the characteristics of your trade
E offering a discount
F using leading vocabulary
G personalising your message
H not using capital letters

Test 4 Listening Part 3

Questions 23 – 30

- You will hear a radio interview with a journalist talking about how to get media coverage.
- For each question, 23 – 30, mark one letter (**A, B** or **C**) for the correct answer.
- You will hear the recording twice.

23 When choosing your target media, Ashley recommends

    A approaching a journalist through social media.
    B becoming familiar with their topics and staff.
    C avoiding being too secretive on social media.

24 A successful pitch

    A is always sent via email.
    B raises the journalist's interest immediately.
    C is subtle.

25 Some amazing pitches Ashley receives also

    A provide stories about funny misunderstandings.
    B contain information about the company's past mistakes.
    C give tips on how to feature the story.

26 Regarding the timing of a pitch, Ashley says that it should be

    A tied to the news.
    B useful throughout the year.
    C about a new product or service.

27 A company's crisis plan

    A should be compiled when a major event occurs.
    B will depend on its industry.
    C could contain some of its old publications.

28 The term 'hijacking' is used to refer to

    A forcing journalists to run your story.
    B trying to connect your story to any big news.
    C journalists ignoring a pitch because of the news.

29 'HARO' is

    A a platform providing entrepreneurs with expert insight.
    B a media outlet only for start-up experts.
    C a useful tool to gain media exposure.

30 The media like a pitch containing an infographic because

    A it tends to be shared more.
    B it needs no translation.
    C it is appealing outreach bait for their customers.

You now have 10 minutes to transfer your answers to your Answer Sheet.

Test 4 Speaking Part 1

Part 1 3 minutes (5 minutes for groups of three)

1 Work in pairs. One of you takes the role of the interlocutor and asks the questions, while the other answers the questions. Then swap roles.

Interlocutor: Good morning / afternoon / evening.
- What's your name?
- And where are you from?
- Do you work, or are you a student?
- What do you like most about your work or studies?

Thank you. Now I'm going to ask you some questions about communicating with colleagues.
- Do you think technology has improved communication between colleagues? (Why? / Why not?)
- Do you think having online meetings with colleagues is as effective as meeting them face to face? (Why? / Why not?)
- What communication skills are needed when working with colleagues?

Thank you.

2 Now swap roles.

Interlocutor: Good morning / afternoon / evening.
- What's your name?
- And where are you from?
- Do you work, or are you a student?
- What do you like most about your work or studies?

Thank you. Now I'm going to ask you some questions about communicating with colleagues.
- Do you think technology has improved communication between colleagues? (Why? / Why not?)
- Do you think having online meetings with colleagues is as effective as meeting them face to face? (Why? / Why not?)
- Do you think there are any disadvantages of relying on technology to communicate with colleagues? (Why? / Why not?)

Thank you.

Test 4 Speaking Part 2

Part 2 6 minutes (8 minutes for groups of three)

1 Work in pairs, A and B. One of you should take the role of the examiner and give the instructions below.

Interlocutor: Now, in this part of the test, I'm going to give each of you a choice of three different topics. I'd like you to select one of the topics and give a short presentation on it for about a minute. You will have a minute to prepare this and you can make notes if you want. After you have finished your talk, your partner will ask you a question.

All right? Here are your topics on page 164 *(A)* and page 166 *(B)*.

[1 minute – A and B should now choose their topic and prepare their presentation]

2 One of you takes the role of the examiner and gives the instructions, while the other follows the instructions. Then swap roles.

Interlocutor: Now, *(A)*, which topic have you chosen, A, B or C?

Would you like to talk about what you think is important when *[state A's chosen topic]*?

(B), please listen carefully to *(A)*'s talk, and then ask him/her a question about it.

[1 minute – A speaks about the chosen topic]

Interlocutor: Thank you. Now *(B)*, please ask *(A)* a question about his/her talk.

3 Now swap roles.

Interlocutor: Now, *(B)*, which topic have you chosen, A, B or C?

Would you like to talk about what you think is important when *[state B's chosen topic]*?

(A), please listen carefully to *(B)*'s talk, and then ask him/her a question about it.

[1 minute – B speaks about the chosen topic]

Interlocutor: Thank you. Now *(A)*, please ask *(B)* a question about his/her talk.

Test 4 Speaking Part 3

Part 3 5 minutes (7 minutes for groups of three)
Phase 1

Interlocutor: Now, in this part of the test, you are going to discuss something together. You will have 30 seconds to read this task carefully and then about three minutes to discuss and decide about it together. You should give reasons for your decisions and opinions. You don't need to write anything. Is that clear?

[30 seconds – Candidates look at the task on page 168]

Interlocutor: I'm just going to listen and then ask you to stop after about three minutes. Please speak so that we can hear you.

[3 minutes – Candidates discuss the situation in the task]

Interlocutor: Thank you.

Phase 2
Take it in turns to ask these questions.

- Do you think some staff are always more motivated than others in a company? Why? / Why not?
- Do you think companies need to think about the motivation of all types of staff? Why? / Why not?
- Do you think managers should meet staff regularly to discuss how they are feeling about work? Why? / Why not?
- Do you think people should change jobs frequently in order to stay motivated? Why? / Why not?
- Do you think some reasons for poor staff motivation are outside a company's control? Why? / Why not?

Test 5 Reading Part 1

Questions 1 – 7

- Look at the statements below and the text given on the next page about the importance of technology in business.
- Which section (**A, B, C** or **D**) does each statement **1 – 7** refer to?
- For each statement **1 – 7**, mark one letter (**A, B, C** or **D**) on your Answer Sheet.
- You will need to use some of these letters more than once.

Example:

  0 the size of a company being unimportant to the benefits it receives

1 the reduction in the amount of face-to-face interaction required

2 the advantage companies can take of not being the only ones that use the internet

3 the way responding to existing customers quickly may catch others' attention

4 the latest product innovations in their field helping companies stay up to date

5 the competitiveness companies can have through using better technology

6 the way technology enables processes to be carried out faster and without mistakes

7 the way useful technology is available in every business sector

The importance of technology in business

A The need to embrace new technologies is greater than ever before. And innovation in technology allows companies to *do* more than ever before. Whether a company is a small to medium-sized enterprise (SME) or a global organisation making billions, technology has an impact on all its operations, making these more efficient, and making the business an effective player in the marketplace. Technology saves time and resources, keeps track of cash flow and helps manage every aspect of daily business activities. Without it, a company will probably fail.

B One of the greatest advantages of technology is its ability to ensure accuracy. Software, such as spreadsheets or accounting programs, enables companies to keep track of stock, record sales, and pay bills and employees. What once took hours can now be achieved in a matter of minutes. This allows a company to remain competitive. The internet has been an incredible driver of business: it enables companies to promote themselves via an online presence, target customers and sell to a wide audience. And, of course, there is the added advantage of being able to keep an eye on competitors.

C Another benefit of technology is super-fast communication. Instead of having to walk the length of the office or go up a flight of stairs to talk to a colleague, it is possible to message them instantly. Instead of having to get on a plane to visit counterparts in other countries, it is possible to set up video calls. Technology not only speeds up interactions between companies but with clients too. Thoughtful, timely communication can even build reputation and attract new business.

D Whatever the industry or profession, there is technology to make its activities easier. In manufacturing, machines are fast and efficient; in healthcare, technology can help save lives; in farming, engineering helps maintain crops and improve the harvest; in education, there are multiple tools which teachers can employ; in music, there are digital enhancements. It is crucial that a company, regardless of what it does, invests in advanced technologies to enable it to produce cutting edge goods and, therefore, stay relevant, increase productivity and succeed in today's highly competitive business world.

Test 5 Reading Part 2

Questions 8 – 12

- Read the article below about hiring the right candidate.
- Choose the best sentence from the next page to fill each of the gaps.
- For each gap **8 – 12**, mark one letter (**A – G**) on your Answer Sheet.
- Do not use any letter more than once.
- There is an example at the beginning, (**0**).

Hiring the Right Candidate

Business changes, and the rate of change is faster than ever before. Therefore, employers need to be even more careful to take on staff who can respond to change rapidly and help move a business forward.

Some candidates look great on paper: they have all the right qualifications and experience. **(0)** ...G... This includes not only being adaptable, but qualities such as flexibility and being keen to learn. Having a broad knowledge of business also helps. Employers can find out whether the candidate in front of them is right for the job by asking the right questions, which offers candidates the opportunity to prove, for instance, their ability to adapt, by providing examples of how they have grown and developed in previous roles.

One would hope that every candidate does some research into a company before they attend their interview. But it is also important that they ask thoughtful questions during the interview process in response to what they learn. **(8)** .... If they can, they will also have the capacity to deal with potential problems as they occur.

The right candidate will also be curious and able to cope with uncertainty. **(9)** .... If a candidate is curious, he or she is probably a great learner too, and this can lead to greater productivity and the generation of solutions. Often candidates who are curious about work are curious about everything. They have interests they are passionate about and can extend this passion to their job.

From receptionist to senior manager, today's employees must be able to deal with vast amounts of information. **(10)** .... It is no longer enough to react to what is happening, they must additionally be able to spot what is likely to happen in a market and communicate that to colleagues. These skills are required across the board, regardless of position.

A good candidate will also understand that the best way forward is by collaborating with others. Great team players should not be overlooked in favour of another employee who may seem brilliant but is only in it for personal gain. **(11)** .... It is not necessarily important to have it all when working in a team. Indeed, knowing how to deal with limitations can be very useful in business, as can being able to own up to mistakes. A candidate with a mature approach to work knows that mistakes do not have to indicate a lack of ability. They also know that lessons can be learnt from mistakes, and progress can be made.

Above all, it can be helpful to remember that it is the person who is being hired, not their skill set. Can they communicate well? Would they fit into the culture of the workplace? **(12)** .... After all, positive people spread positive feelings, and this can generate the energy required to get things done.

Example:

A   Doing so indicates how the candidate thinks and whether or not they will be able to assess what is happening in an industry.

B   They should have the capacity to find patterns in this data and determine trends.

C   Rather than the latter, someone who adds to a collective set of skills and also understands their weaknesses is ideal.

D   It is definitely an advantage to recruit people who are enthusiastic and likeable.

E   Attributes like these are very useful in a world where things change quickly and constantly.

F   Bear in mind that no one will perfectly qualify for this.

G   But do they also possess the right personality?

Test 5 Reading Part 3

Questions 13 – 18

- Read the article below about management styles and the questions on the next page.
- For each question 13 – 18, mark one letter (**A, B, C or D**) on your Answer Sheet for the answer you choose.

Different Management Styles

While most managers have their own distinct style, the most successful are flexible, shifting the way they do things as the need arises, depending on the situation. Possessing a comprehensive set of skills can be crucial to success as a manager. The main commonly recognised styles are autocratic, consultative, persuasive, democratic, chaotic and laissez-faire. As their names may suggest, some of these have significant downsides, while others are generally more positive in their effects.

The autocratic manager tells employees what to do. Employees who do not conform may have to deal with being disciplined. Autocratic managers do not wish to get employee feedback, and this means that employees have to trust that these managers are doing their jobs well. There are drawbacks to this management style: it does not encourage workers to be creative, but even worse, things continue to be done in the same way, not always with the best results. This is not to say that there are no positives of this style. Employees understand what their individual role is, and decision-making is clear and straightforward. This can be helpful when there is a crisis and decisions must be made quickly. However, on the whole, this style of management results in a less contented workforce.

The consultative management style encourages employees to offer their opinions and ideas, which creates positive relationships between managers and workers. Feeling valued and heard, employees with consultative managers are more likely to stick around and remain loyal to the company, knowing that they can approach their managers to discuss issues or concerns in the workplace. The drawback is that this style is still top-down. Employees are encouraged to give their opinions, but decisions are ultimately made at the top.

With the persuasive management style, managers are still in charge of the decision-making process, but they take time to explain their decisions, and highlight their importance to the company. This helps employees commit to the decisions made, but the style can leave employees feeling un-listened to, with managers focusing on explaining why their decisions are right.

The democratic management style appears to work well, and it certainly has its advantages for employees. Decisions are made by a majority and this works well for important decisions which will have a long-term effect. This style certainly means that employees are on board with the decisions made and will be committed to making sure they work in practice. It also encourages good working relationships between managers and employees. Together, they can create a strong vision for the company, and communication between parties is strong. It can mean that roles are less defined than they are for people working under autocratic managers, but is generally a good fall-back position for many managers.

Managers who employ the chaotic style allow employees to make decisions. This means the decision-making process lacks structure and the style is associated with flat companies. This style can be useful for certain kinds of project, but it can be inefficient and confusing.

The final management style is laissez-faire, which roughly translates as 'leave alone'. Here, the manager plays the role of mentor rather than leader, not getting too involved in what workers are doing. Employees make their own decisions and consult the manager only when necessary. This means they may lack direction, but it allows them plenty of opportunity to be creative.

13 What is the writer doing in the first paragraph?

　　A suggesting a combination of styles which managers should use
　　B pointing out what makes some managers good at what they do
　　C criticising some managers for their choice of management style
　　D explaining the pros and cons of different management styles

14 What, according to the writer, is the main disadvantage of the autocratic management style?

　　A Management may keep making unsuccessful decisions.
　　B Employees' attempts to be imaginative are ignored.
　　C Managers do not respond well to what employees have to say.
　　D Workers are unsure whether they are doing their job correctly.

15 What does the writer suggest about the consultative management style?

　　A It shares few similarities with other management styles.
　　B It makes managers more likely to remain loyal to a company.
　　C It inspires employees to take an interest in what is happening.
　　D It allows employees to make final decisions about what affects them.

16 What is the shared characteristic of consultative and persuasive styles?

　　A Managers are keen to get on well with employees.
　　B Employees are encouraged to offer their views.
　　C Managers maintain control of decision making.
　　D Employees feel that managers listen to them.

17 The writer thinks that the democratic management style

　　A is not as positive as it might initially sound.
　　B helps companies to develop a clear direction.
　　C works better in some situations than in others.
　　D should be adopted by managers whenever possible.

18 The text says that both the chaotic and laissez-faire management styles

　　A allow employees a high level of freedom in their work.
　　B leave employees without someone to go to for advice.
　　C give employees too little chance to explore their own ideas.
　　D encourage employees to share possible solutions with each other.

Test 5 Reading Part 4

Questions 19 – 33

- Read the article below about social-media marketing.
- Choose the best word to fill each gap from **A, B, C** or **D** on the next page.
- For each question **19 – 33**, mark one letter (**A, B, C** or **D**) on your Answer Sheet.
- There is an example at the beginning, (**0**).

SOCIAL-MEDIA MARKETING

Social media is everywhere, but this does not automatically mean it is the best marketing (**0**) ....C.... Before deciding whether or not to (**19**) .... and advertise your products and services on social media platforms, it is essential to weigh (**20**) .... the pros and cons.

The pros: Social media works via sharing, tagging and blogging. The (**21**) .... for finding new leads is almost inexhaustible, as is the opportunity to (**22**) .... your brand. Once your brand is built, you can start to build loyalty too. (**23**) .... on a personal level with customers, by replying to their comments and feedback, shows them you are (**24**) .... to them and builds a relationship between you. The same feedback can help you improve not only your goods but customer service too. This extends to other marketing (**25**) .... you may have, such as direct mail. Last but not (**26**) .... , social-media marketing is (**27**) .... cost-effective.

The cons: Creating content is (**28**) .... Any content you create must be checked and edited before it is (**29**) .... Pages must be updated on a regular (**30**) .... and it can be challenging to keep thinking up content that is (**31**) .... to your readers and will keep them interested. But while you have control over what you create, you don't have much control over how people (**32**) .... to it. Once you've been publicly criticised, it can be difficult to turn things around. It also takes time to build loyalty, and many customers spend so much time browsing online that they may almost (**33**) .... forget about what they've just been looking at.

Example:

      A route   **B** avenue   **C** channel   **D** course

0   A ☐   B ☐   C ■   D ☐

19	**A** go ahead	**B** set off	**C** come along	**D** reach up
20	**A** out	**B** in	**C** on	**D** up
21	**A** capacity	**B** potential	**C** ability	**D** possibility
22	**A** increase	**B** spread	**C** grow	**D** raise
23	**A** Interacting	**B** Speaking	**C** Discussing	**D** Exchanging
24	**A** motivated	**B** committed	**C** obliged	**D** inspired
25	**A** attacks	**B** functions	**C** appeals	**D** campaigns
26	**A** less	**B** lowest	**C** least	**D** little
27	**A** greatly	**B** widely	**C** deeply	**D** highly
28	**A** risk-taking	**B** time-consuming	**C** long-acting	**D** eye-catching
29	**A** broadcast	**B** printed	**C** published	**D** advertised
30	**A** basis	**B** system	**C** manner	**D** way
31	**A** related	**B** relevant	**C** reasonable	**D** right
32	**A** reply	**B** behave	**C** respond	**D** answer
33	**A** instantly	**B** directly	**C** presently	**D** currently

Test 5 Reading Part 5

Questions 34 – 45

- Read the article below about the role of transportation management.
- In most of the lines **34 – 45** there is one extra word. It is either grammatically incorrect or does not fit in with the meaning of the text. Some lines, however, are correct.
- If a line is correct, write **CORRECT** on your Answer Sheet.
- If there is an extra word in the line, write **the extra word** in CAPITAL LETTERS on your Answer Sheet.
- The exercise begins with two examples, (**0**) and (**00**).

Examples:

| 0 | C | O | R | R | E | C | T |
| 00 | O | N | | | | | |

THE ROLE OF TRANSPORTATION MANAGEMENT

0	Without effective transportation, it would be much more difficult to conduct business
00	and go on about our lives. Goods are transported to retail outlets or straight to us at
34	home or the office. How so well a system works is down to the transportation manager,
35	who has to make sure things work smoothly, regardless of the heavy traffic, breakdowns
36	or staff shortages, so that the customer is not negatively affected. It is easy for customers
37	to overlook what it takes to ensure deliveries arrive on time and at not too high of
38	a cost. Transportation management is a challenging role, with a wide range of its skills
39	required and responsibilities to accept. If people who undertake this role may work in
40	diverse areas, such as the public or private sectors, freight or passenger transportation,
41	or in planning or at operations. Each area of expertise has its own challenges. The skills
42	required of the transportation manager are too many and varied. Not only should they be
43	knowledgeable about transportation and have their good geographical knowledge, but they
44	should, among other things, excel at planning and scheduling, and have a good
45	understanding of vehicle technologies, remain up to date on transport trends and have an
	awareness of health, safety and environmental effects.

Test 5 Writing Part 1

- A new project manager will be joining your department next week.
- You are the managing director of the company. Write an **email** to all staff:
  - saying who the new manager is
  - explaining what the new manager will do
  - giving details about when staff can meet the new manager.
- **Write 40 – 50 words.**

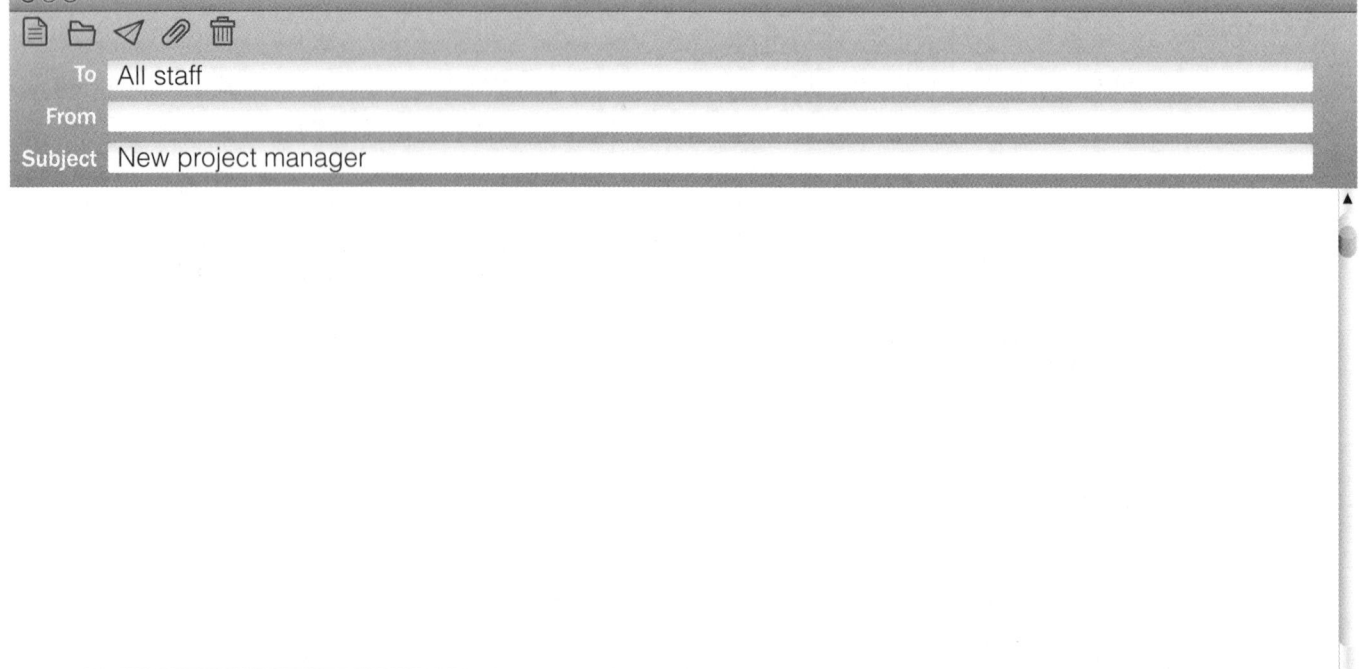

Test 5 — Writing Part 2

- Wyford Construction, the company you work for, needs a company to supply equipment. You have seen the advertisement below for a possible supplier. Write a letter to Mr Fellowes, of Quadrant Equipment Supplies, asking about the services his company provides.
- Look at the information below, on which you have already made some handwritten notes.
- Then, using **all** your handwritten notes, write a **letter** to Mr Fellowes.
- **Write 120 – 140 words.**

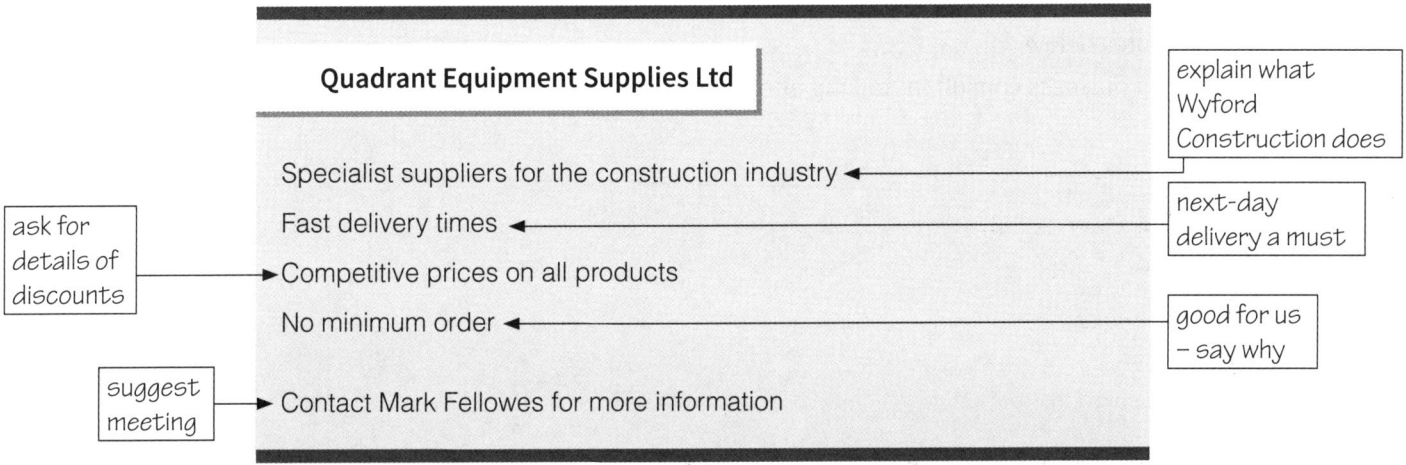

Test 5 Listening Part 1

 Questions 1 – 12

- You will hear three telephone conversations or messages.
- Write **one or two words or a number** in the numbered spaces on the notes or forms below.
- You will hear each recording twice.

Conversation One
(Questions 1 – 4)

- Look at the notes below.
- You will hear a business consultant talking about what members of Generation Z are like.

Generation Z

- born after 1995
- 1/4 of US population
- contribute $44 billion to the US economy
- more efficient **(1)** .... than previous age groups
- are **(2)** '............................': they begin working as teenagers
- might choose not to take part in conventional **(3)** ....
- are very entrepreneurial
- their **(4)** .... is dramatically changing

Conversation Two
(Questions 5 – 8)

- Look at the notes below.
- You will hear two leaders discussing how they inform their teams of bad news.

How to give bad news

1st step: share the (5) .... for the change

(6) .... to hire them back later

Give generous (7) ....

Help leaving staff with (8) .... in the field

Conversation Three
(Questions 9 – 12)

- Look at the notes below.
- You will hear two business partners talking about delegating.

How to delegate

Leaders often can't (9) .... their employees.

This affects the (10) .... of the company.

It is OK to be scared when changing your fixed (11) ....

Begin by delegating some (12) ....

Listening Part 1

Test 5

Test 5 Listening Part 2

Section One
(Questions 13 – 17)

- You will hear five short recordings. Five people are talking about why they quit their jobs.
- For each recording, decide why each speaker quit.
- Write one letter (**A – H**) next to the number of the recording.
- Do not use any letter more than once.
- You will hear the five recordings twice.

13	**A** relocation
	B career change
14	**C** scheduling problems
	D difficult colleagues
15	**E** found a permanent position
	F illness
16	**G** going back to studying
17	**H** better benefits

Section Two
(Questions 18 – 22)

- You will hear another five recordings.
- For each recording, decide what recruitment mistake each speaker mentions.
- Write one letter (**A – H**) next to the number of the recording.
- Do not use any letter more than once.
- You will hear the five recordings twice.

18	**A** being impatient
	B not defining your ideal candidate
19	**C** sending generic emails
	D hiding things
20	**E** being thrifty
21	**F** not tracking your performance
	G using social media badly
22	**H** being inattentive

Test 5 Listening Part 3

Questions 23 – 30

- You will hear a radio interview with a business leader talking about martial arts.
- For each question, 23 – 30, mark one letter (**A**, **B** or **C**) for the correct answer.
- You will hear the recording twice.

23 The most important lesson Ryan learnt is

    A how to handle complaining customers.

    B about quality control.

    C to be mentally ready for unpleasant circumstances.

24 Ryan now believes failure

    A cannot be avoided.

    B is a necessary part of good training.

    C is especially important for certain characters.

25 What does Ryan mean by being 'complete'?

    A knowing how to stand up when you fall

    B qualifying for a competition

    C being prepared for many different situations

26 According to Ryan, mastery

    A is crucial if you want to save time.

    B requires perseverance.

    C is about being able to change tactics.

27 What does Ryan think about being a beginner?

    A that you should not hurry it

    B that it is exciting

    C that many people never master the basics

28 What is the 'shiny-object syndrome'?

    A a new approach to entrepreneurship
    B the practice of unnecessarily changing tactics
    C an implementation strategy

29 What does Ryan say about teams?

    A they might betray you if you are weak
    B they always need a highly trained manager
    C they add to your strength

30 Ryan believes challenges

    A might be leveraged by your opponent.
    B need to be exploited.
    C create opportunities for survival.

 You now have 10 minutes to transfer your answers to your Answer Sheet.

Test 5 — Speaking Part 1

Part 1 3 minutes (5 minutes for groups of three)

1 Work in pairs. One of you takes the role of the interlocutor and asks the questions, while the other answers the questions. Then swap roles.

Interlocutor: Good morning / afternoon / evening.
- What's your name?
- And where are you from?
- Do you work, or are you a student?
- What do you like most about your work or studies?

Thank you. Now I'm going to ask you some questions about keeping up to date with business news.
- What do you think are the advantages of keeping up to date with business news?
- What do you think are the best ways of keeping up to date with business news?
- Do you think that technology is making it easier or more difficult to keep up to date with business news? (Why?)

Thank you.

2 Now swap roles.

Interlocutor: Good morning / afternoon / evening.
- What's your name?
- And where are you from?
- Do you work, or are you a student?
- What do you like most about your work or studies?

Thank you. Now I'm going to ask you some questions about keeping up to date with business news.
- What do you think are the advantages of keeping up to date with business news?
- What do you think are the best ways of keeping up to date with business news?
- How interested do you think the general public are in business news?

Thank you.

Test 5 Speaking Part 2

Part 2   6 minutes (8 minutes for groups of three)

1 Work in pairs, A and B. One of you should take the role of the examiner and give the instructions below.

Interlocutor: Now, in this part of the test, I'm going to give each of you a choice of three different topics. I'd like you to select one of the topics and give a short presentation on it for about a minute. You will have a minute to prepare this and you can make notes if you want. After you have finished your talk, your partner will ask you a question.

All right? Here are your topics on page 164 *(A)* and page 166 *(B)*.

[1 minute – A and B should now choose their topic and prepare their presentation]

2 One of you takes the role of the examiner and gives the instructions, while the other follows the instructions. Then swap roles.

Interlocutor: Now, *(A)*, which topic have you chosen, A, B or C?

Would you like to talk about what you think is important when *[state A's chosen topic]*?

(B), please listen carefully to *(A)*'s talk, and then ask him/her a question about it.

[1 minute – A speaks about the chosen topic]

Interlocutor: Thank you. Now *(B)*, please ask *(A)* a question about his/her talk.

3 Now swap roles.

Interlocutor: Now, *(B)*, which topic have you chosen, A, B or C?

Would you like to talk about what you think is important when *[state B's chosen topic]*?

(A), please listen carefully *to (B)*'s talk, and then ask him/her a question about it.

[1 minute – B speaks about the chosen topic]

Interlocutor: Thank you. Now *(A)*, please ask *(B)* a question about his/her talk.

Test 5 Speaking Part 3

Part 3   5 minutes (7 minutes for groups of three)
Phase 1

Interlocutor: Now, in this part of the test, you are going to discuss something together. You will have 30 seconds to read this task carefully and then about three minutes to discuss and decide about it together. You should give reasons for your decisions and opinions. You don't need to write anything. Is that clear?

[30 seconds – Candidates look at the task on page 168]

Interlocutor: I'm just going to listen and then ask you to stop after about three minutes. Please speak so that we can hear you.

[3 minutes – Candidates discuss the situation in the task]

Interlocutor: Thank you.

Phase 2
Take it in turns to ask these questions.

- Do you think all companies need to become greener? Why? / Why not?
- Do you think cost is the most important consideration when deciding which steps to take to make a company greener? Why? / Why not?
- Who do you think benefits most from a more environmentally friendly business sector?
- Do you think companies should use information about how green they are in their marketing? Why? / Why not?
- Do you think there should be government support for companies that want to become greener? Why? / Why not?

Test 6 Reading Part 1

Questions 1 – 7

- Look at the statements below and the article given on the opposite page about how to name a company.
- Which section (**A, B, C** or **D**) does each statement **1 – 7** refer to?
- For each statement **1 – 7**, mark one letter (**A, B, C** or **D**) on your Answer Sheet.
- You will need to use some of these letters more than once.

Example:

0 the costs of not making an effort to find a good name for a business

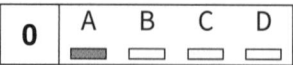

1 the importance of recognising developments in naming which have taken place

2 the inclusion of a location in a name being an advantage

3 the value of doing research to confirm the current existence of a name

4 the importance of a name in representing business activities

5 the avoidance of attaching personal elements to company names

6 the official steps which can be taken to ensure a name remains unique to a company

7 the way combining several elements in a name can provide useful information

How to name a company

A One of the things that often goes unconsidered until the last minute when starting a business is the selection of an appropriate name. This is a poor decision, as taking the time to come up with the right name can make every difference to how well a business performs. There are several things to take into consideration when evaluating how effective a name is. First off, does it sound good when it is said aloud? It not only needs to be easy to pronounce but have some significance too. People who hear the name should have an immediate understanding of what the business does.

B A common error made when naming a business, especially smaller, family-run ones, is to involve your surname. While 'Johnson's' may carry meaning within the family, it conveys nothing to customers about the goods or services on offer. 'Johnson's Cakes' goes somewhere to addressing the issue, though the 'Johnson's' part of the name is still redundant. Replace this with the name of the area in which it operates – 'London Cakes' – and some headway is made. Staying away from initials is also advisable. IBM may now be a household name, but start-ups do not have the benefit of experience and reputation that giants of industry such as IBM possess.

C Remember that naming conventions change. For example, until recently, names which used 'u' for 'you' and '4' for 'for' were on trend. But it isn't helpful for a customer who's only heard the name to have to wonder how to search for 'Cakes for you' online. Numbers *can* have some purpose if they help to describe what a business does: 'Ten-min Thai Takeaway' tells you not only that its meals will be ready in ten minutes, but what kind of food it is and where it will be consumed.

D Depending how big a brand will be, it may be worth considering trademarking its name. This not only aids customers with the identification of the source of goods and services, but it also prevents others from operating under the same name. This means it's also important to check out whether a name is already in use before adopting it. Finally, test a new name out online: find out how often people carry out a search on particular keywords and which businesses will be competitors.

Test 6 Reading Part 2

Questions 8 – 12

- Read the article below about how people learn at work.
- Choose the best sentence from the opposite page to fill each of the gaps.
- For each gap **8 – 12**, mark one letter (**A – G**) on your Answer Sheet.
- Do not use any letter more than once.
- There is an example at the beginning, (**0**).

UNDERSTANDING LEARNING STYLES

Just as there are different management styles, so too are there different learning styles. A good manager needs to take these into account when dealing with individuals in a team, in order to help them fulfil their potential. Whatever the management style employed, it is important for managers to create a working environment where every member of the team is able to carry out the work they have been tasked to do. **(0)** ...... *G* ...... .They also know how to get the most out of individuals.

The visual-verbal learner works best when they are able to listen and see information simultaneously. **(8)** .... Visual-verbal learners enjoy quiet working environments, so it is helpful to provide calm spaces for these people to work in. They also tend to be good problem-solvers and proficient researchers.

Visual-nonverbal learners also prefer a quiet learning environment. **(9)** .... They work well on their own and jobs particularly suited to this kind of learner include those in the creative arts, or those working alone at the computer. They may have a natural dislike of meetings and discussions, though they appreciate having someone they can ask questions of when necessary.

Auditory-verbal learners will learn best through hearing and talking. If they have a problem, they will want to discuss their ideas and go over what they are learning. In addition to taking in what they hear, these learners have good writing skills, such as the ability to compile reports. **(10)** .... In fact, they benefit from, and indeed enjoy, having music on while they work. But what if they are sharing a room with visual-verbal or visual-nonverbal learners who prefer silence? This is where headphones come in. And, of course, the best way to check whether this learner has grasped what they are learning is to talk to them about it.

Tactile-kinaesthetic employees learn by doing. This kind of learner has a need for mutual respect between themselves and their manager. It is important to make this learner feel valued by providing the right kind of environment. While they like calm working conditions, tactile-kinaesthetic learners like the opportunity to move about while they learn. This kind of learner is in a minority. **(11)** .... It can, therefore, be easy to misunderstand their movements as nervousness or disruption, when it is these very movements which help them to process information.

Once an employee's learning style has been identified, it becomes easier for a manager to understand an individual's strengths and weaknesses, and make the most of what each person has to offer during the learning process and beyond. **(12)** .... .Instead, managers can aim to incorporate elements of each style in their materials. They may choose to deliver information in a variety of ways: perhaps all that is needed to help an employee grasp a new concept is a simple diagram or brief explanation.

Example:

A Indeed, only around 5 per cent of people learn in this way.

B Time can easily be wasted by using the wrong approach during such sessions.

C A presentation which would suit such a learner would involve both slides and explanations of the slides.

D Background noise is not a problem for such learners.

E However, they will only acquire new information through diagrams and charts rather than listening.

F It is not necessary to provide different training programmes for different kinds of learner, though.

G The most successful managers understand that different people process information in different ways.

Test 6 Reading Part 3

Questions 13 – 18

- Read the article below about company culture and the questions on the opposite page.
- For each question 13 – 18, mark one letter (**A, B, C** or **D**) on your Answer Sheet for the answer you choose.

Why Company Culture Matters

When you're looking for a new job, it can be worthwhile investing time and energy in finding out whether there's a good fit between you and the company in question. Understanding a company's culture will help you determine whether your personality and that of the company's match. Culture describes the working environment, which includes the company mission, values and ethics, aims and expectations. Cultures can be team-based or have more formal structures; they may take a casual and relaxed approach or require strict adherence to rules and regulations.

Company culture is important because if you don't fit in, your time at work will be less enjoyable. If your needs and values are reflected in the culture of the company you're working for, you will feel more comfortable with what you're trying to achieve and will have better working relationships too – all of which leads to a productive atmosphere. For example, if you prefer to work quietly away on your own, but the company has large, open-plan offices and encourages discussion, you may find it difficult to be as efficient as you would like to be.

In smaller or more casual companies, you may have the opportunity to sink your teeth into a range of interesting projects and roles, whereas in a company which is more traditional in its approach, you will be more likely to have a defined role, with few opportunities to try something new unless you progress formally through the ranks. This is an important consideration when looking for the right place to work, and should certainly feature strongly in the decision-making process. It is, therefore, crucial to find out as much as you can about potential employers if, like the majority of people, you intend to find a job where you will stay for a long period. Employers who offer a strong company culture benefit from low staff turnover and higher productivity as a result.

How can you find out about a company's culture before you work there? A good place to start is the company's website. The 'About us' page will fill you in on what the company is about: what its mission is and what the core values are. Employee testimonials can give you a flavour of what it's like to work there. But the company's website is not the only source of information available online about a company. It is also possible to find reviews written by employees past and present, and access information about highly rated places to work based on their culture.

It may be that you already know someone who works for the company – or you have connections on business social media. If so, talk to them and learn about the company. If you are still at university, your careers service may be able to put you in touch with former students who have gone on to work there. These people will be able to give you a good idea of what it might be like to be employed at the company. Hearing as many people's experiences as possible will ensure you are not just getting a single, possibly biased, point of view.

If you do decide to go ahead with an application and get to the interview stage, don't be afraid to ask questions about what you really want to know, such as the schedule or teamwork expectations. This will help you find out whether the 'fit' is right.

13 In the first paragraph, the writer advises job seekers to

   A think carefully about what they want to achieve in a job.
   B find out what will be required of them in a particular role.
   C make sure the job they're applying for suits their character.
   D find out as much as possible about company working conditions.

14 In the second paragraph, the writer says that

   A employees should not be too focused on gaining pleasure from their work.
   B certain work environments can be less favourable for some employees.
   C companies should take into consideration what employees hope to gain from work.
   D many believe that the most important element of a job is the people they work with.

15 What is the writer referring to when he says 'This is an important consideration' in the third paragraph?

   A meeting potential employers
   B progressing through the ranks
   C looking for the right place to work
   D knowing about the opportunities available

16 In the third paragraph, the writer suggests that many job seekers prefer

   A looking for a company where they can be promoted.
   B finding permanent jobs than short-term ones.
   C working at conventional kinds of companies.
   D having a varied job and a less defined role.

17 What point is the writer making about using the internet in the fourth paragraph?

   A it is not difficult to find relevant data about companies
   B being cautious about personal opinions is advisable
   C research does not need to be especially thorough
   D it provides an option to contact a company for details

18 In the fifth paragraph, the writer says that potential job applicants should

   A research suitable jobs before leaving education.
   B try not to listen to too many different opinions.
   C take advantage of the contacts they have.
   D save questions for the interview stage.

Test 6 Reading Part 4

Questions 19 – 33

- Read the article below about setting up a business without much money.
- Choose the best word to fill each gap from **A, B, C** or **D** on the opposite page.
- For each question **19 – 33**, mark one letter (**A, B, C** or **D**) on your Answer Sheet.
- There is an example at the beginning, (**0**).

STARTING A BUSINESS WITH LITTLE MONEY

People often have brilliant ideas for businesses, but never (**0**) ....C.... for it because they don't have the money. But starting a business may not (**19**) .... the huge financial investments that people think. It is perfectly possible to grow a business from (**20**) .... nothing, if you have the know-how.

Businesses need cash injections when they start out. (**21**) .... out how much you need during the (**22**) .... stages is important if you are to find (**23**) .... round this obstacle. This depends on the kind of business you are hoping to (**24**) .... up. If you're a carpenter, you'll need tools and wood (**25**) .... ; if you're a freelance writer, you'll need a laptop; if you're a hairdresser, you'll need equipment. And whatever you do, you'll need a base: somewhere to work from. You may also need to splash out on licences or permits, subscriptions or memberships. You may need to pay legal (**26**) .... or have operating expenses, such as promoting your goods and services. You may even need to pay a member of staff if you can't do the job (**27**) ....–handed.

If you have (**28**) .... funds available, you will need to reduce your needs: work from home, be a sole trader, find cheaper materials, (**29**) .... out unnecessary processes. It will be impossible to avoid *all* expenses, so if (**30**) .... out a loan doesn't appeal and you don't want to (**31**) .... people you know for help, you will need to start small. This might mean using social media as your only marketing (**32**) .... , or sitting at the kitchen table instead of renting office space. But if you want to avoid huge costs from the start, you will need to (**33**) .... your business brick by brick.

Example:

	A call	B run	C go	D send

0	A	B	C	D
	☐	☐	▓	☐

19	A depend	B require	C desire	D want
20	A virtually	B barely	C hardly	D roughly
21	A Counting	B Making	C Deciding	D Working
22	A primary	B initial	C original	D leading
23	A ways	B methods	C plans	D means
24	A do	B lay	C put	D set
25	A produce	B materials	C supplies	D goods
26	A prices	B fees	C rates	D figures
27	A single	B one	C only	D open
28	A controlled	B regulated	C limited	D tight
29	A chop	B block	C slice	D cut
30	A having	B taking	C bringing	D carrying
31	A approach	B propose	C question	D advance
32	A system	B scheme	C strategy	D style
33	A form	B base	C order	D build

Reading Part 4 Test 6 151

Test 6 Reading Part 5

Questions 34 – 45

- Read the article below about the value of policies and procedures.
- In most of the lines **34 – 45** there is one extra word. It is either grammatically incorrect or does not fit in with the meaning of the text. Some lines, however, are correct.
- If a line is correct, write **CORRECT** on your Answer Sheet.
- If there is an extra word in the line, write **the extra word** in CAPITAL LETTERS on your Answer Sheet.
- The exercise begins with two examples, (0) and (00).

Examples:
| 0 | C | O | R | R | E | C | T |
| 00 | T | O | | | | | |

POLICIES AND PROCEDURES

0	Policies and procedures are put in place for important reasons. They make sure that
00	a company complies with laws and regulations, aid to decision-making and help
34	business operations run so smoothly. Although there may be some resistance to these
35	'rules', staff need to understand why they must have to follow them. To begin with, they keep
36	things running well. If anything goes wrong, it can be quickly identified and dealt with.
37	This frees up a time which can be spent on achieving business aims instead of sorting
38	out problems. It is also helpful for employees to work in to a consistent environment, so
39	they know what to expect and what is expected from them in the return. Policies and
40	procedures make staff feel confident both in the company and their individual roles, and
41	allow them to focus on the real purpose of their job. The result is of higher quality
42	work which also leads to an enhanced reputation for the company. One of the most
43	important reasons for policies and procedures to be in place is to protect the staff
44	themselves. Highlighting this is, therefore, a good way which to exemplify why such
45	rules exist, and aid an understanding of what their overall purpose in any kind of workplace.

Test 6 — Writing Part 1

- You are the assistant manager in the sales department and you will be away from the office for the early part of next week to attend a sales conference in Berlin.
- Write an **email** to all staff in the department:
  - explaining why you need to be away from the office
  - saying when you will be back in the office
  - telling staff what to do if they need to contact you while you are away.
- **Write 40 – 50 words.**

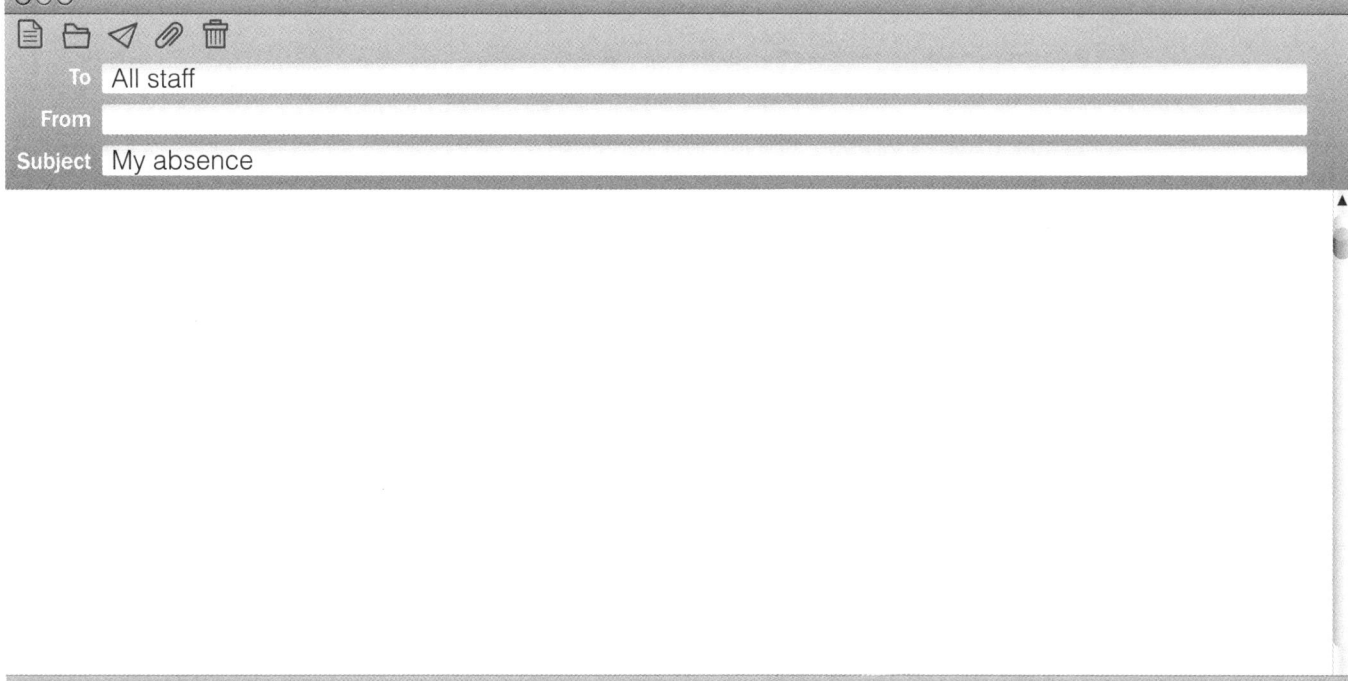

To: All staff
From:
Subject: My absence

Test 6 — Writing Part 2

- You work for a retail company. The company has received a large number of complaints from customers in the last month. The Customer Services Manager has asked you to write a report on the situation.
- Look at the information below, on which you have already made some handwritten notes.
- Then, using **all** your handwritten notes, write a **report** for the Customer Services Manager.
- **Write 120 – 140 words.**

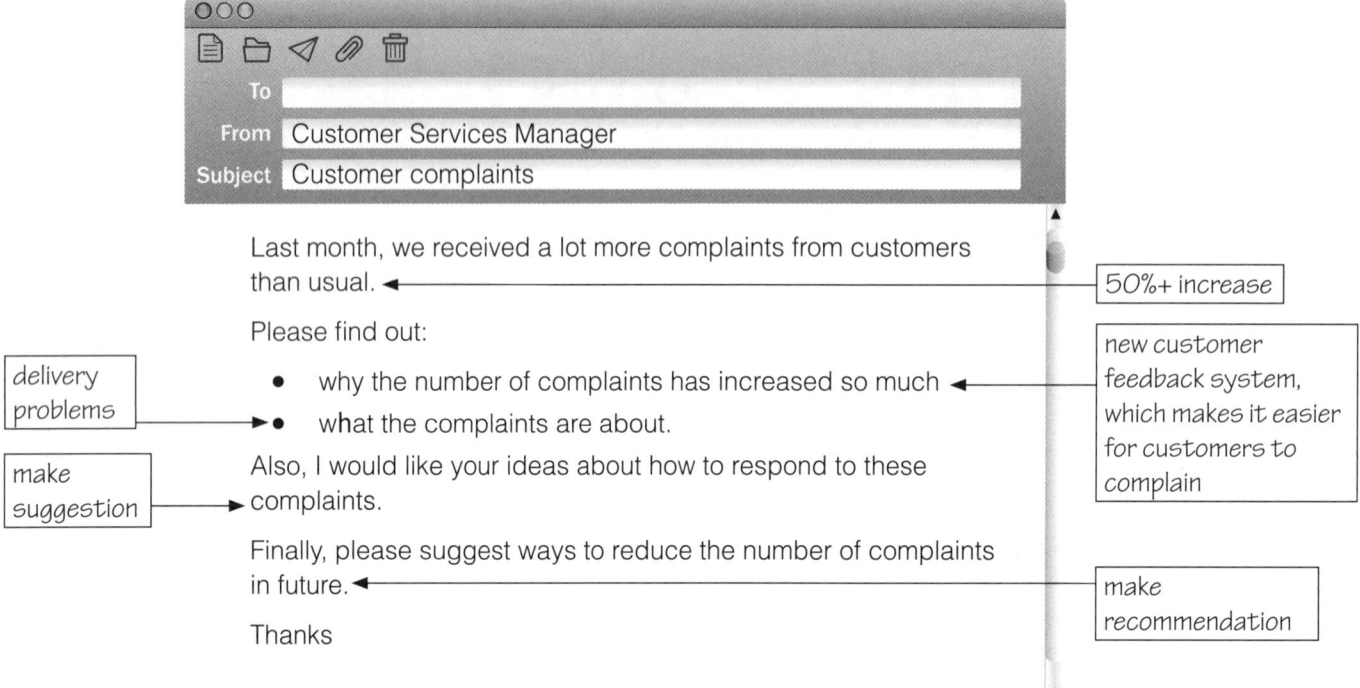

From: Customer Services Manager
Subject: Customer complaints

Last month, we received a lot more complaints from customers than usual. ← *50%+ increase*

Please find out:

- why the number of complaints has increased so much ← *new customer feedback system, which makes it easier for customers to complain*
- what the complaints are about. ← *delivery problems*

Also, I would like your ideas about how to respond to these complaints. ← *make suggestion*

Finally, please suggest ways to reduce the number of complaints in future. ← *make recommendation*

Thanks

Test 6 Listening Part 1

Questions 1 – 12

- You will hear three telephone conversations or messages.
- Write **one or two words or a number** in the numbered spaces on the notes or forms below.
- You will hear each recording twice.

**Conversation One
(Questions 1 – 4)**

- Look at the notes below.
- You will hear the sales director of a company talking to a new member of her team.

Tips for building relations with customers

- try to **(1)** .... different features / uses of our products

- become a subject-matter expert of our oils (home, hygiene, health)

- go to conferences and **(2)** ....

- subscribe to **(3)** .... , research reports, blogs

- become a **(4)** .... in their eyes

Conversation Two
(Questions 5 – 8)

- Look at the notes below.
- You will hear an HR consultant talking to a client about how to get promoted.

How to get promoted

- Behave like a (5) ....
- Inspire your co-workers
- Propose new (6) .... on your own
- Don't abandon your current tasks
- (7) .... to track your achievements
- Don't participate in (8) ....

Conversation Three
(Questions 9 – 12)

- Look at the notes below.
- You will hear a PR consultant talking about rebranding.

How to rebrand

Protect your brand equity!

Notify all (9) .... before starting

Check if

- chosen URL meets the (10) .... you had in mind
- (11) .... is available

Switch social media profiles

Set up (12) .... before changing your website and promotional materials

Test 6 — Listening Part 2

Section One
(Questions 13 – 17)

- You will hear five short recordings. Five people are talking about changing part of their websites.
- For each recording, decide what change each speaker found necessary.
- Write one letter (**A – H**) next to the number of the recording.
- Do not use any letter more than once.
- You will hear the five recordings twice.

13 ....

14 ....

15 ....

16 ....

17 ....

A   blog should feature industry experts
B   *Frequently Asked Questions* not up to date
C   *About Us* section not detailed enough
D   *Testimonials* and *Case Studies* too concealed
E   *How We Work* section not polished enough
F   *Contact* page to include social media
G   user accounts login to be simplified
H   *Products* page too short

Section Two
(Questions 18 – 22)

- You will hear another five recordings.
- For each recording decide what aspect of business culture surprised each speaker.
- Write one letter (**A – H**) next to the number of the recording.
- Do not use any letter more than once.
- You will hear the five recordings twice.

18 ....

19 ....

20 ....

21 ....

22 ....

A   small talk
B   eating lunch at your desk
C   holidays
D   language problems
E   socialising after work
F   work habits
G   self-promotion
H   paid parental leave

Test 6 Listening Part 3

Questions 23 – 30

- You will hear an interview with a business coach talking about what distinguishes business owners from entrepreneurs.
- For each question, 23 – 30, mark one letter (**A**, **B** or **C**) for the correct answer.
- You will hear the recording twice.

23 Which of the following is a way of life, according to Adam?

    A being an entrepreneur
    B being a business owner
    C both, if you have the right mindset

24 Adam says business owners often start out

    A by inheriting a company.
    B as entrepreneurs before taking over a company.
    C in innovative industries.

25 When he works with a client for the first time, Adam

    A tells them about the differences between entrepreneurs and owners.
    B asks them which entrepreneurs they are following.
    C first tries to understand how they lead.

26 What point does Adam make about the day-to-day activities of business owners?

    A they have unrealistic expectations of their workers
    B they concentrate mostly on resolving operational issues
    C they prioritise their customers over their equipment

27 Adam says that the bravest entrepreneurs

    A even question how their software is designed.
    B know how to handle even reactive customers.
    C might establish entirely new fields.

28 According to Adam, business owners' view of the future

  A tends not to be well-defined.
  B focuses on training their employees.
  C revolves around delegating and outsourcing more.

29 Entrepreneurs' future plans often include

  A merging their identities with their company's.
  B leaving their business behind.
  C changing their company's name.

30 Entrepreneurs try to avoid

  A that their employees become too involved.
  B actively participating in running their firms.
  C delegating too much.

You now have 10 minutes to transfer your answers to your Answer Sheet.

Test 6 Speaking Part 1

Part 1 3 minutes (5 minutes for groups of three)

1 Work in pairs. One of you takes the role of the interlocutor and asks the questions, while the other answers the questions. Then swap roles.

Interlocutor: Good morning / afternoon / evening.
- What's your name?
- And where are you from?
- Do you work, or are you a student?
- What do you like most about your work or studies?
- How important to you is free time from your job or studies?

Thank you. Now I'm going to ask you some questions about time management.
- Do you think you are a well organised person at work or in your studies? (Why? / Why not?)
- Do you think being well organised is a necessary skill in the workplace? (Why? / Why not?)
- Do you think companies can train staff to be well organised at work? (Why? / Why not?)

Thank you.

2 Now swap roles.

Interlocutor: Good morning / afternoon / evening.
- What's your name?
- And where are you from?
- Do you work, or are you a student?
- How important to you is free time from your job or studies?

Thank you. Now I'm going to ask you some questions about time management.
- Do you think you are a well organised person at work or in your studies? (Why? / Why not?)
- Do you think being well organised is a necessary skill in the workplace? (Why? / Why not?)
- What do you think staff can do every day to manage their time effectively?

Thank you.

Test 6 Speaking Part 2

Part 2 6 minutes (8 minutes for groups of three)

1. Work in pairs, A and B. One of you should take the role of the examiner and give the instructions below.

> **Interlocutor:** Now, in this part of the test, I'm going to give each of you a choice of three different topics. I'd like you to select one of the topics and give a short presentation on it for about a minute. You will have a minute to prepare this and you can make notes if you want. After you have finished your talk, your partner will ask you a question.
>
> All right? Here are your topics on page 164 *(A)* and page 166 *(B)*.

[1 minute – A and B should now choose their topic and prepare their presentation]

2. One of you takes the role of the examiner and gives the instructions, while the other follows the instructions. Then swap roles.

> **Interlocutor:** Now, *(A)*, which topic have you chosen, A, B or C?
>
> Would you like to talk about what you think is important when *[state A's chosen topic]*?
>
> *(B)*, please listen carefully to *(A)*'s talk, and then ask him/her a question about it.

[1 minute – A speaks about the chosen topic]

> **Interlocutor:** Thank you. Now *(B)*, please ask *(A)* a question about his/her talk.

3. Now swap roles.

> **Interlocutor:** Now, *(B)*, which topic have you chosen, A, B or C?
>
> Would you like to talk about what you think is important when *[state B's chosen topic]*?
>
> *(A)*, please listen carefully to *(B)*'s talk, and then ask him/her a question about it.

[1 minute – B speaks about the chosen topic]

> **Interlocutor:** Thank you. Now *(A)*, please ask *(B)* a question about his/her talk.

Test 6 Speaking Part 3

Part 3 5 minutes (7 minutes for groups of three)
Phase 1

Interlocutor: Now, in this part of the test, you are going to discuss something together. You will have 30 seconds to read this task carefully and then about three minutes to discuss and decide about it together. You should give reasons for your decisions and opinions. You don't need to write anything. Is that clear?

[30 seconds – Candidates look at the task on page 168]

Interlocutor: I'm just going to listen and then ask you to stop after about three minutes. Please speak so that we can hear you.

[3 minutes – Candidates discuss the situation in the task]

Interlocutor: Thank you.

Phase 2
Take it in turns to ask these questions.

- Do you think social-media marketing works for most products and services? Why? / Why not?
- Do you think that companies which change to social-media marketing have to recruit new staff? Why? / Why not?
- Do you think traditional marketing such as TV will survive in the future? Why? / Why not?
- Do you think customers usually trust the information in advertisements? Why? / Why not?
- How do you think customers feel about the amount of advertising they see online? Why?

Exam Practice Test 1 — Speaking Part 2

CANDIDATE A TASK CARDS

A: What is important when …?

Buying new equipment
- Price
- Benefit to company
- …
- …

B: What is important when …?

Choosing a hotel for a business trip
- Location
- Comfort
- …
- …

C: What is important when …?

Selling products abroad
- Arranging deliveries
- Dealing with language differences
- …
- …

Exam Practice Test 2 — Speaking Part 2

CANDIDATE A TASK CARDS

A: What is important when …?

Arranging a business meeting
- Having a clear agenda
- Inviting the right participants
- …
- …

B: What is important when …?

Choosing the best location for a new retail store
- Transport links
- Size of retail store
- …
- …

C: What is important when …?

Sponsoring a cultural event
- Type of event
- Other sponsors
- …
- …

Test 3 — Speaking Part 2

CANDIDATE A TASK CARDS

A: What is important when …?

Writing a business email
- Reason for writing
- Clear language
- …
- …

B: What is important when …?

Buying new business software
- Keeping it up to date
- Cost
- …
- …

C: What is important when …?

Choosing a business bank for a company
- Reputation of the bank
- Fees charged
- …
- …

Test 4 Speaking Part 2

CANDIDATE A TASK CARDS

A: What is important when ...?

Launching a new food product
- Market research
- Studying competitors
- ...
- ...

B: What is important when ...?

Chairing a meeting
- Preparing an agenda
- Involving all participants
- ...
- ...

C: What is important when ...?

Improving a business website
- Potential users
- Ease of updating
- ...
- ...

Test 5 Speaking Part 2

CANDIDATE A TASK CARDS

A: What is important when ...?

Deciding how to advertise a new product
- Target customer
- Advertising budget
- ...
- ...

B: What is important when ...?

Attending a business conference
- Choosing which sessions to attend
- Making new contacts
- ...
- ...

C: What is important when ...?

Buying new computer hardware for a business
- Choosing a brand name
- Negotiating a discount
- ...
- ...

Test 6 Speaking Part 2

CANDIDATE A TASK CARDS

A: What is important when ...?

Doing market research
- Target market
- Using social media
- ...
- ...

B: What is important when ...?

Writing a letter of complaint
- Having clear aims
- Including relevant detail
- ...
- ...

C: What is important when ...?

Providing staff with company cars
- Type of car
- Costs involved
- ...
- ...

Exam Practice Test 1 — Speaking Part 2

CANDIDATE B TASK CARDS

A: What is important when …?
Advertising a new product
- Choosing where to advertise
- Deciding on an advertising budget
- …
- …

B: What is important when …?
Preparing for a job interview
- Doing research
- Deciding what to wear
- …
- …

C: What is important when …?
Managing a busy office
- Leadership skills
- Regular meetings
- …
- …

Exam Practice Test 2 — Speaking Part 2

CANDIDATE B TASK CARDS

A: What is important when …?
Giving a presentation
- Audience
- Opportunity to practise
- …
- …

B: What is important when …?
Choosing a new supplier
- Terms of contract
- Reliable deliveries
- …
- …

C: What is important when …?
Deciding on a training budget
- Benefit for company
- Staff needs
- …
- …

Test 3 — Speaking Part 2

CANDIDATE B TASK CARDS

A: What is important when …?
Appointing a new member of staff
- Experience
- Personal qualities
- …
- …

B: What is important when …?
Deciding on a marketing budget
- Company priorities
- Type of product to be marketed
- …
- …

C: What is important when …?
Changing the design of a product
- Customer feedback
- Cost to the company
- …
- …

Test 4 | Speaking Part 2

CANDIDATE B TASK CARD

A: What is important when ...?

Making new business contacts
- Attending business events
- Using social media
- ...
- ...

B: What is important when ...?

Designing packaging for a product
- Type of packaging material
- Information to include
- ...
- ...

C: What is important when ...?

Applying for a business loan
- Preparing a business plan
- Interest charges
- ...
- ...

Test 5 | Speaking Part 2

CANDIDATE B TASK CARDS

A: What is important when ...?

Giving a product presentation to customers
- Product knowledge
- Free samples
- ...
- ...

B: What is important when ...?

Deciding whether to rent or buy office space
- Flexibility
- Costs
- ...
- ...

C: What is important when ...?

Interviewing a candidate for a job
- Length of interview
- Setting the job candidate a task
- ...
- ...

Test 6 | Speaking Part 2

CANDIDATE B TASK CARDS

A: What is important when ...?

Preparing to negotiate a sales contract
- Choosing a negotiating team
- Doing careful research
- ...
- ...

B: What is important when ...?

Organising business travel abroad
- Planning the schedule
- Having cultural knowledge of the country
- ...
- ...

C: What is important when ...?

Responding to negative feedback from a customer
- Replying to the customer immediately
- Being polite
- ...
- ...

Exam Practice Test 1 — Speaking Part 3

TASK CARD

Increasing production

The car manufacturer you work for would like to increase production of one of its models.

You have been asked for your ideas on how best to do this.

Discuss the situation together and decide:
- what extra resources will be needed
- what the risks are of increasing production

Exam Practice Test 2 — Speaking Part 3

TASK CARD

A new competitor

The chain of clothing stores you work for is facing competition from a new company in the market.

You have been asked for your suggestions on how best to deal with the situation.

Discuss the situation together and decide:
- how best to keep your existing customers
- what you could do to win new customers in the future

Test 3 — Speaking Part 3

TASK CARD

Organising an open day

The manufacturing company you work for is considering whether to hold an open day, so that students from a local business college can see what the company does and meet some of the staff.

You have been asked for your ideas on how best to do this.

Discuss the situation together and decide:
- what the advantages and disadvantages are of holding a company open day
- how to make the open day interesting and enjoyable for the students

Test 4 | Speaking Part 3

TASK CARD

Motivating sales staff

You have been asked for your ideas on what the company can do to improve the situation.

Discuss the situation together and decide:
- why having highly motivated staff is important for a company
- what could motivate staff to sell more products

Test 5 | Speaking Part 3

TASK CARD

A green company

The company you work for is interested in becoming more environmentally friendly.

You have been asked for your suggestions on how the company could become greener.

Discuss the situation together and decide:
- what the advantages and disadvantages of becoming more environmentally friendly are for the company
- how the company could most easily reduce its environmental impact

Test 6 | Speaking Part 3

TASK CARD

Marketing strategy

The retail company you work for is considering whether it should stop using newspaper and TV advertising and focus on social-media marketing instead.

You have been asked to make recommendations about marketing strategy.

Discuss the situation together and decide:
- what the advantages for the company are of using traditional marketing methods
- how effective social-media marketing might be

Audioscripts

Test 1

LISTENING PART 1

 Training Exercise 2

01 **Woman:** Pete, can you do me a favour, please?
Man: Sure. What is it?
Woman: Could you please call the woman again, to confirm the day of our move with her? You know, Mrs Lipton, the estate agent?
Man: Oh, yes. Will do in a minute.
Woman: If you do get hold of her, check again if the deposit is really only going to be £700, will you? It just sounds too good to be true …
Man: It does indeed. Anything else?
Woman: Yes, we need to know the exact address for the accountant. Ask her if it's really 34 Willow Street, TS17 5PJ. I was given this address by her colleague, but it's worth checking this too.

 Training Exercise 4

 1

Woman: I think this time we'll really have to do something about Peter.
Man: Peter McCarthy? What has he done now?
Woman: I've just received another email from his line manager. Apparently, since the first client complaint about him in September, on 9th September to be exact, he has missed the deadline on yet another quarterly report.
Man: Oh, no. Jason needs that on time!
Woman: I know. He also came to the office wearing sandals and shorts last week, on 4th October. It was a sunny day, but still … Jason even sent me a picture of it. He knows our dress code, but doesn't seem to care much, unfortunately.
Man: I also heard that his lack of punctuality has been causing delays with some clients? Is that true?
Woman: Yes, that's true as well. I think this time he really needs to go. So what ideas do we have for his replacement?

2

Man: So? Are you excited? You've been dreaming about working for this company for ages, Cheryl!
Woman: I have, haven't I? …
Man: But you seem confused now, is everything OK?

Woman: I guess … It's just that it's so hard to know how to make the best impression at the interview to actually get hired! The clothes, for example!
Man: I hear you. Haven't you got a friend who works there? Maybe you could call her and ask about the dress code? Or even the recruiter who got you the interview?
Woman: Good idea! I also thought I'd scan some of their social media to see if I can find any pictures of company events, etc.
Man: Yes, do that. You really don't want to give the impression that you don't understand your environment.
Woman: Exactly. I'll ask my friend if people generally wear a suit for work, for example. Or what kinds of shoes are acceptable.
Man: Yes, but don't worry too much about it. And remember, if in doubt, just go with smart business casual.

3

Hello everyone and thank you for showing up. Before we begin, I have a few questions. Do you like routine? How many decisions do you make in a day? Do you enjoy making them? I'm asking these because today we're talking about 'decision fatigue', which simply means that the more decisions we make in a day, the worse they will be. In other words, our daily decision-making power is limited. In one of the most important studies on this, researchers looked into the decisions made by judges. It was found that their decisions in the morning were much better than in the afternoon, because by then they had grown tired. The implications for business owners are that they should restrict themselves to focusing on the bigger decisions that really matter too. One effective strategy is to eliminate the smaller daily decisions, including what to eat or what clothes to wear. Those of you who don't like eating the same things and wearing the same clothes every day might want to try making those decisions the night before. Devising a morning routine can also help.

 EXAM PRACTICE

03 **Conversation 1**

Man: Mosaic Marketing, Oliver Murray, how can I help you?
Woman: Hi, I'm Amanda Wallace and I'm interested in your next course on writing effective business content.
Man: Hi, Amanda. I see. Do you mean the one coming up in April, or the one we just started last week?

Woman: I think maybe the one that's starting soon? I'd like to attend the whole thing, you see. But isn't it in May?
Man: Well, the first workshop will be on 30th April. May I ask what you might find most useful to learn about during the course? Besides keyword optimisation, obviously. The course will deal with that a lot!
Woman: I'm not sure, really. Typically, what topics do other participants find interesting? I'm new to the whole thing – content writing, I mean.
Man: Well, other popular issues include if you should have one or multiple bloggers. Or if you should seek out experts in their fields, rather than just online content writing ...
Woman: Perfect, just what I need. Sign me up please.

Conversation 2

Good morning, and thank you for taking the time to come and listen to the details of our new building project, *Urban Cow*. As you might already know, construction is to begin early next year and we are still looking for investors. Due to the recent opening of yet another university in our town, the demand for more, modern co-living spaces has grown exponentially. To meet this need, we hope to offer fully furnished apartments to students and young professionals in the city centre for rent as of September. The building complex is going to be right next to the Cathedral, behind the old mill, and the apartments will typically cost about €900 per month and come with utilities and WiFi, and even housekeeping. If you are familiar with the market you may notice that this is much cheaper than renting a studio apartment in the area, which is usually around €1,500. Another competitive advantage we will have is that tenants will be able to rent for as little as three months, and also nearly all of the apartments will have washers and dryers.

Conversation 3

Man: Research and Invest, Chris Johnson speaking, how can I help you?
Woman: Hello, I'm Margaret Ashwood and I read about your report on IoT, *The Internet of Things*. I'm calling because I'm considering buying it.
Man: Certainly. Well, we created the report because we believe that *The Internet of Things* is an ongoing revolution. Our annual survey, which we've just released, provides the reader with critical insights into the new developments in the field. We project that there will be more than 55 billion IoT devices by 2025. This is impressive, as this is way higher than the 9 billion in 2017. We also expect the wearables market to grow.
Woman: Wearables?
Man: Yes; smart watches, fitness trackers, etc.
Woman: You mean the devices used by consumers to record their exercise and health statistics and progress?

Man: Yes, and hospitals, med-tech and pharmaceutical companies, as well as insurance firms, have all started to utilise these devices. IoT is going to seriously impact the healthcare industry as well!
Woman: OK, I think I'd like to buy your document. Where can I get hold of it?

LISTENING PART 2

Training Exercise 4

1

I don't mind working with so many introverts, really. I mean, unlike extroverts who are more easily motivated by external rewards and are, therefore, happier to take risks, my colleagues like to have a more careful approach. This is why, while you will have sales employees jump on board straightaway, introverts will always prefer to ask some questions first. And I don't mind this one bit. Maybe because I am one too.

2

So I had this boss at my previous workplace ... I didn't appreciate it then, but man, was he good at listening! I miss having a line manager like him now. No superficial chit-chat with him, ever. He would always want to process what he was hearing before deciding to speak and only then make a decision, as it should be. My current team leader is already thinking what he will say while the other person is still talking!

3

When I look for a new employee, I need to always bear in mind that we're all scattered across the globe, you know? In practice, this means that each one of us spends a lot of their time focusing on their own tasks. If I find colleagues who can't stand being so isolated, they'll be miserable and lose their motivation. We've had this happen before, actually. I need people who prefer working on their own, so that both they and our projects can thrive.

4

We've recently had a minor crisis at the company. We lost an important client and had to restructure some of our key processes as a result. What I noticed during all this turmoil is that the more reserved employees seemed more able to persist in finding the necessary solutions. The ability to keep calm is so key in unclear times or critical moments of a difficult project! The last thing you need in situations like these is to have to soothe your staff too.

5

Not to say that extroverts can never be humble, but introverts tend to have a more accurate sense of their true abilities and achievements, I think. They often have a better ability to acknowledge their mistakes and imperfections, or if they have any knowledge gaps or limitations. This is an amazing quality because being humble also often indicates an openness to new ideas or even to receiving contradictory information.

EXAM PRACTICE

 Section 1

05 **13**

Nothing is worse than trying to give a presentation on a topic you are not fully confident about. What personally helps me combat presentation nerves is reminding myself from time to time why I am the authority on the subject. If I remember that I do have new insights to share with my audience, I usually feel much calmer because I feel that what I am sharing couldn't easily be provided by just anybody.

14

The more familiar you are with it, the more naturally you will be able to pace and deliver your presentation. If I feel that I have prepared enough, I can usually deliver my content more naturally. My sentences are somehow more organically connected, and my side comments are more naturally linked to the topic. For this to happen, I always make sure I memorise the order of my slides too, before the day.

15

Besides knowing what to say and being kind and welcoming, I think it is crucial to prepare for the practical aspects of the delivery as well. I always check the room and the technology ahead of a presentation if I can, and make sure I have anticipated any unexpected technical or logistical problems. What calms me a lot is when I know that I have back-up plans and all kinds of contingency plans in place in case of, for example, equipment failure or if there is no internet connection.

16

In my career, I have had to sit through many presentations that were just not right for the participants in question. Either the material was way too advanced or the delivery was too slow, simplified or the opposite: extremely complicated to the people present, with the speaker frantically walking around. What I have learnt from all this is to always be sensitive and identify the participants' concerns, biases and questions about the subject and cater to these carefully.

17

I organise my presentations by giving myself reminders about the upcoming material further along. I find that memorising some key phrases helps me move from one part onto the next more smoothly and breathe better as well. I often even write these expressions into the notes below each slide, to be honest. Also, the visuals you include can be exploited to grab your audience's attention throughout and help you remember what you want to say next.

Section 2

06 **18**

With my team, what helps when introducing any major change is to approach it by talking together about a problem we've been struggling with, and to which the change is a necessary response. It seems that it also helps if I talk them through any other changes we've so far implemented that have already helped us as a team. After this, what often follows is where I tell them what is hopefully going to be accomplished with the change.

19

When I need to implement any major change in policy or even just some minor HR processes, such as onboarding, I often lead by highlighting that I am completely aware that for a while things may be annoying or confusing. Typically, I also remind them that my door is always open if they want to further discuss the details of the shift. In my experience, just by acknowledging that change is tough, you can avoid employees getting defensive or uncooperative.

20

Getting some of your team on board before making a significant change can prevent lots of problems down the road. This is why I tend to approach any senior team members with news of the change and some details in advance. I often tell them why I believe the adjustments are necessary and that I need their help to sell it to the rest of the team. We also go through their questions and concerns together, which is useful too.

21

Right after any change has been announced. I think it is key to keep discreetly checking for signs that everybody is more or less on board and cooperating. It is predictable that there will always be workers who disagree with any major new procedures being put into practice for one reason or another, and they may even decide to sabotage it. It's important to catch these behaviours fast and talk to the employee in private about them.

22

A few days after any main change, I make sure I schedule to meet up with my direct reports to discuss how they are doing. Often they only use these opportunities to vent about any temporary problems they're encountering, but I don't mind this at all. I'm just happy they're telling *me* their opinions and not their own subordinates. I also get more feedback about how we're doing this way.

LISTENING PART 3

Training Exercise 4

07 **Man:** Good morning everyone, this is your host, Justin Middleton. With me in the studio today is business owner Angela Kemp, and she's going to discuss what it takes to become a full-time entrepreneur. So many of you requested her opinion about the subject that we decided to invite her back in to talk to us again. Angela, welcome.
Woman: Hi Justin, thank you.
Man: Angela, I think the main question on everybody's mind is: Should one just take the leap, say from a leadership position, and go ahead and do it, or prepare a bit more thoroughly and then jump?
Woman: Yes, I agree this is the most common dilemma about the transition and, not surprisingly, my answer is: it depends. There are a few things that need to be considered before someone decides either way.
Man: And what are those?
Woman: Well, the first issue is time. If you decide to leave your day job, you must be prepared for the fact that while part of your time will be spent on paid projects, you'll also need to dedicate some of it to networking and meeting potential clients, and the latter has to gradually take priority.
Man: Fair enough, that is probably to be expected, yes. What else?
Woman: You should also honestly ask yourself if you're OK with the idea of not being able to take a proper holiday any more, as clients might at times need things from you and you should try to be available even while you're away from home.
Man: This is a confusing one for me. Does this mean you must always jump to fulfil their every wish, really?
Woman: I'd say only within reason. And it's exactly one of the new things that requires practice.
Man: What do you mean?
Woman: Knowing how to set boundaries between your work and personal life.
Man: And what about autonomy? Would you say entrepreneurs are really that much freer than employees?
Woman: No, I personally would not, although I realise many entrepreneurs might disagree with me about this. I believe that you might start enjoying more autonomy as you start creating the direction for your business. Parallel to this, however, you should also always carefully consider how your decisions affect your clients, suppliers or employees.
Man: That's so true. It's not all about the freedom, people! It's just different freedom, perhaps.

Woman: Exactly. You also need to be willing to go to lots of business networking events to make new contacts and friends, following up diligently whenever possible and being as helpful as you can be.
Man: And what about sales? How good does someone have to be at sales before taking the plunge?
Woman: Excellent question! In my experience it really helps if you at least have faith in yourself. Sales can have a bad reputation as an activity, but they really shouldn't.
Man: And how can someone achieve this shift in their mindset?
Woman: In my experience, by thinking through what they think the value is in what they are doing or producing for the client.
Man: Awesome. That should create some confidence, yes.
Woman: It also helps if you have two to three months of living expenses saved up. While having the desire to make money is a good thing because you need that hunger and fear to keep going, you also need to be sensible; especially if you have a family.
Man: I guess! Anything else you think is also key?
Woman: Maybe just that you should make sure you have a portfolio with at least five projects in it. Also, very importantly: start practising charging for your work!
Man: That's such a great point! I know it can be very tricky for some. Any tips how?
Woman: Yes. Start paying attention to the language needed to be honest but firm with prospective clients. Show that you are enthusiastic about their project, but make sure you establish clear payment terms beforehand.
Man: Angela Kemp, thank you!

EXAM PRACTICE

08 **Man:** Good morning and welcome to *Enterprise Now*. Our guest on the show today is Vanessa Campbell, who is here to tell us about monetising a podcast. Vanessa, thank you for coming in.
Woman: My pleasure.
Man: I'd like to start by clarifying our key concepts here, for the sake of our less tech-savvy listeners. Podcasts? Monetising? ...
Woman: Sure. So, a podcast is audio or video content produced by, well, almost anybody coming from any sector and made available on the internet for downloading to a computer or mobile device. Podcasts often come in a series nowadays, new instalments of which can be received by subscribers automatically. Monetising is finding ways to make it earn you some money.
Man: Which is necessary because a lot of this content is available free of charge for the listener, if I'm not mistaken?
Woman: That's correct. Small businesses, or even individual experts in various fields, may decide to start producing

their own audio content because there are several ways to generate income from it.

Man: So I heard, yes. It's just so hard for the average listener to imagine this while accessing content that is sometimes of top quality, without having to pay for an episode or a subscription.

Woman: I know! Isn't this amazing? One of my favourite options to earn from it as a creator is by producing my own online courses that teach similar content or a skill to what I talk about on my show. Other podcasters frequently do this too. They show that they're an expert on their topic, which tends to make it much easier to get clients without having to advertise to them on any other platform. This is an increasingly popular method across industries, in fact.

Man: Nice. What else?

Woman: Well, there's affiliate marketing or, as it is also sometimes called, performance marketing. This is when you get a commission when you refer people to other companies on your show. You will earn money only when someone makes an actual purchase. In other words, following this model the online retailer only pays a commission to the external website, the podcaster, for any sales that have been generated.

Man: This sounds a bit dishonest with your audience though. Can these recommendations ever be authentic, in your opinion?

Woman: Great question! The small start-up owners and individual entrepreneurs that I coach often ask me just this. My opinion is that affiliate marketing works best when you promote products or services that you also happily use and are familiar with, so you can honestly endorse them.

Man: And then there's the more traditional advertising model as well, right? How does that work in practice? I mean, typically, who seeks out whom?

Woman: That varies. However you come across your sponsors though, you should be ready to show them what they will get for their money. Sponsorship is often calculated based on 'Cost Per Mile', which means that you receive a fee for every thousand downloads or views, even if no purchase has been made by the listeners.

Man: I imagine for sponsorship to be effective, you need a large, engaged audience then?

Woman: Indeed.

Man: And which model do beginner podcasters prefer, typically?

Woman: Well, exactly because of this, affiliate marketing. It's a great way for beginner podcasters to get started because they don't need to have a minimum number of listeners.

Man: And what's the process like in practice? I mean, how does the online retailer pay the commission?

Woman: What podcasters often do is that they include a link in the show's notes, which can be downloaded, or on their own website, that listeners are told to use. This usually offers a temporary discount to the listener. You might also hear the host say something like, 'This episode is brought to you by XYZ company', or 'Visit www.xyz.com to claim your free €25 sign-up voucher by using promo code Tom', if the podcaster happens to be called Tom, for example.

Man: A whole new platform for advertising! Vanessa, thank you for coming to talk to us today.

SPEAKING PART 1

Training Exercise 4

09 **Question a:** Where are you from?
One: Rio de Janeiro.
Two: I come from Rio de Janeiro in Brazil.
Three: I was born in Curitiba in the south of Brazil, but I have been living in Rio for the last five years since there are more job opportunities here.

Question b: Do you work or are you a student?
One: I am a Personal Assistant.
Two: I am the Personal Assistant for the Chairman of the Board at a large multinational company.
Three: I am the PA for the Chairman of a large multinational company. I am responsible for organising her diary, all of her correspondence and anything else she wants me to do. I have been doing this job for two years and I love it.

Question c: What do you like most about your work or studies?
One: I like being able to choose my own hours.
Two: I have a lot of freedom to choose when I start and finish my day, so this gives me some flexibility to organise things.
Three: There are lots of things about my job that I like, but I think the best thing is having the freedom to choose my own hours. If I want to start early or finish late, I can. I can even work at the weekend if I need to. This gives me the flexibility I need to organise my life.

SPEAKING PART 2

Training Exercise 2

10 *I'd like to talk about* what is important when deciding on packaging for products. *First of all*, probably the most important factor is the cost. I don't mean that the packaging needs to be as cheap as possible, but it does need to offer value for money. It is sometimes worth paying a bit more for packaging if it can meet a goal, for example, if it is unique or looks great. *This brings me on to my next point*, which is the image of the packaging. Ideally, the packaging will be attractive and encourage people to buy the product. However, if we are worried about cost, we might not be able to afford the best-looking product and so have to use something

else instead. *My final point* is something that has become important in recent years, which is the environment. In my country, people are worried about plastic and recycling, so it might be useful to think about not using plastic or using very little packaging. *In conclusion*, I'd say all of these points are important, but it all comes back to cost, in my opinion.

Test 2

LISTENING PART 1

🎧 Training Exercise 2

11 *Woman:* I'm sorry I'm late, Bill. I just ended a call with a problematic client.
Man: That doesn't sound good, Maggie. How problematic? Are they late with a payment or something?
Woman: I wish. You know the type of 'prospective' client that finds you and always leads with what *they* want?
Man: Yes, unfortunately all too well.
Woman: Well, this lady first approached me on social media a couple of months ago, and she immediately started with a request.
Man: Not a good start. What did she ask you to do?
Woman: She wanted me to buy something from her, but to this day I'm still not sure what she is actually selling, to be honest. Some cosmetics, I believe.
Man: That's funny. Your profile is not even close. Event planning and cosmetics?! I don't see how those two combine at all.
Woman: That's right! She didn't even do much research before writing to me. And it wouldn't have been too hard as my company profile is full of pictures of our events!
Man: Anyway, I say just ignore her.

🎧 Training Exercise 4

12 *Woman:* How about you, Bill? Any funny client stories of late? They always make me laugh.
Man: Glad you enjoy my misery at least. But yes, I had to be firm with a 'prospective' client yesterday as well, actually.
Woman: Oh, really? What happened?
Man: The usual. He wanted to get the advice my clients pay for, but for free.
Woman: But you saw right through it?
Man: Not at first, surprisingly. He was very good.
Woman: So what happened?
Man: I accepted his contact request and he started messaging me with his questions. He thought he could, just because we're connected.
Woman: Right.
Man: But then he was asking more and more questions and I realised I needed to put an end to this.

Woman: Well done. Connection doesn't mean unlimited access to you.
Man: I don't think so, no. If someone is ready to buy from you, they won't make you waste your time, you know? They will have already made a decision based on other factors.
Woman: Absolutely.

🎧 EXAM PRACTICE

13 **Conversation 1**

Many of you wanted to know more about the report I mentioned last time, about the latest trends in HR. Well, it focuses on people working in this growing segment of the workforce now loosely known as the 'gig economy'. The document says that in the US alone about 16.5 million people were working in some kind of 'alternative work arrangement' in 2017, so this is clearly a growing trend that is worth paying attention to. The people interviewed for the report stated that becoming independent contractors in this new economic landscape gives them more control over the work they do, and over the planning of their professional lives overall. They also seem to enjoy building their careers with greater independence, while having the freedom to choose business partners, clients and vendors whose values agree with their own. Many said that working for someone else cannot possibly match that level of autonomy. So far it is mostly the creative occupations that constitute the largest part of the freelance economy.

Conversation 2

Man: Good afternoon, WebHost 101, Jim speaking. How can I help you?
Woman: Hi Jim! I need some help picking the right domain name for my business.
Man: Sure. Do you already have a business?
Woman: Sort of ...
Man: OK. So what matters is that your domain name matches your business name.
Woman: Why is that?
Man: Because that way you have a far better chance of being remembered and keeping your branding cohesive.
Woman: Yeah, OK, that makes sense.
Man: You should also make your domain name memorable.
Woman: How?
Man: By making sure it's unique.
Woman: I see. Anything else?
Man: It should also be short, simple and relevant to your business. By this I mean that it should reflect what your company is about.
Woman: And is there anything I should avoid?
Man: Yes. Numbers, ambiguous words and too creative spellings. Oh, and another thing. Make sure it is ordered as well.

Woman: What do you mean?
Man: For example, 'sellyourcar' would count as ordered, while 'yourcarsell' wouldn't; that sort of thing.
Woman: Got it, OK. Then I'd like to register www …

Conversation 3

Man: Hi Sylvia! How are you?
Woman: Hey Nick! Not too bad, you?
Man: So-so. I just feel I'll never get to the end of my to-do list for the week.
Woman: I know what you mean! Have I told you about our new system of information sharing? It might help you too.
Man: What's it like?
Woman: Well, as our team grew, I realised that we would need a new model to communicate effectively. The quantity of emails especially got overwhelming. To combat this, we created a system that encourages us to write our updates, connect with our colleagues and regularly reflect on our work.
Man: Sounds great! What does it look like in practice?
Woman: We use an online project management programme where everyone inputs four significant points from the previous week under these categories: achievements, disappointments, worries and goals.
Man: And does it really work? Is everybody using it?
Woman: Yes, but change trickles down from the top, so to achieve a critical mass I introduced it to our senior team first.

LISTENING PART 2

Training Exercise 2

When I was younger, I'd always get into trouble with my colleagues due to my temper. Then I learnt that reframing my way of thinking to de-escalate any negative emotions is actually not a bad way to calm myself down. Now, I'm more conscious about communicating less extremely. Few people are consistently awful and few things are terrible all the time, after all. Feeling angry isn't uncommon when you feel hurt, but I should always question my own perspective before I speak.

Training Exercise 4

1

When I was younger, I'd always get into trouble with my colleagues due to my temper. Then I learnt that reframing my way of thinking to de-escalate any negative emotions is actually not a bad way to calm myself down. Now, I'm more conscious about communicating less extremely. Few people are consistently awful and few things are terrible all the time, after all. Feeling angry isn't uncommon when you feel hurt, but I should always question my own perspective before I speak.

2

… then I had to explain to him again over coffee that the problem with his anger is that it fires up the emotion centres of his brain, making it challenging for him to think or speak in a logical way, and that he can't behave like this in front of our clients. We agreed that next time he'll try to do something else for a while before returning to the situation. He should really calm down a little bit beforehand!

3

My boss asked his HR expert friend to come and talk to us about anger management, to see if that could help. He was talking about how if you feel yourself starting to get upset, you should temporarily and peacefully 'remove yourself from the situation'; you know, to calm down. His tone made me laugh out loud. I mean I can't just stand up and walk out in the middle of a meeting, now can I? Although sometimes I'd really love to …

4

It took me a long time to understand that when a supplier does this, they probably don't realise what they're doing, you know? We're talking about very different cultures and company cultures too, in many cases. They probably have no idea that I'm not happy when they do this. They tend not to know the consequences of these situations at our end, that's all. After all, most of us don't run around with evil intentions, just upset others accidentally.

5

My advice to you then, is that if you want to preserve your professional reputation and relationships, always try to discuss your frustrations without blaming the other person. In my experience, the best way to express negative emotions is by being as positive as possible and avoiding blaming the other person on purpose. Using 'I' statements and speaking about your own perspective and needs, rather than what the other person did wrong in your opinion, is very useful.

EXAM PRACTICE

Section 1

13

It is essential to realise that there's so much more to be learnt at any workplace than just technological tricks and the like. All these fancy mentoring programmes today, focusing on the latest apps, for example, are just way out of proportion; especially if you bring in an expensive expert from outside to conduct them. A successful mentoring programme will find a way to exploit in-house talent in other areas such as sales, marketing or customer support as well.

14

When you decide to ask a young colleague to mentor an older one in a kind of reverse mentoring programme, what really matters is that you actually match employees to one another in an intentional manner. I've seen so many failed mentoring systems where people are assigned to one another in a quick meeting, usually at the beginning of the year or a new quarter, based on some random factor like age or seniority, instead of a team's skill set.

15

Our first mentoring programme ever, the one we ran in 2004, was a bit of a disaster, to be honest. Besides the fact that nobody really had the necessary IT knowledge to benefit from it at the time, we also forgot to provide some key guidelines from the outset. You can imagine the rest of the story after that. Now I know that even the best programme ideas can fail, if different employees interpret your vision in diverse ways.

16

If the atmosphere at your firm is less than supportive and helpful on a day-to-day basis, I don't think you should suddenly expect co-workers to be patient and co-operative within any mentoring programme set up either. I believe that company culture can make or break any mentoring programme. Do make sure you emphasise the importance of all these basic teamworking skills before launching your programme and don't allow, for example, that only friends team up in it.

17

In the typical corporate mentoring system, the purpose tends to be bridging any generational gaps between older and younger employees, or encouraging innovation and new product or service ideas by more actively engaging younger workers. This does not have to mean, however, that this is the only purpose you can give to your programme. It should be defined more by your company's needs and the characteristics of your current staff.

Section 2

18

I noticed that our customers respond very well to anything that is of practical value to them concerning our products. Our 'How-to' videos particularly have been liked many times on social media, so we're planning to keep these. People appreciate them not only because they learn new tricks for themselves, but because they like to feel helpful for others when they share them. This makes them look good and we get to advertise our brand, so it's a win-win situation.

19

What I just found out recently, and I have to say it surprised me quite a lot, is that writing longer blog entries, even if they're not connected to one another in their topic, is actually a winning strategy. I used to think that the shorter the better when it comes to online content, but apparently this is not the case, necessarily. What matters more is if your article is relevant, well researched and well thought out, and if it stands out enough.

20

You want to draw people in. And you know what doesn't do that any more? Traditional, complicated ads. These actually push people away, because they feel … fake and fail to provoke any strong, positive feelings in us. What people need today is authenticity, and there's nothing more original than telling and listening to stories. It's some kind of an ancient need in all of us, I think; perhaps because it allows us to connect with each other.

21

Whenever people can engage with something, it tends to make the experience more memorable. And a memorable video or post increases the probability that it will be discussed or shared too. This is why we like to create material that invites our customers to do something in response to our ads. Last month, we asked them to share their best summer pictures on our site, and we got 7,000 engagements with this campaign that we had simply called *My Summer*!

22

I know it is sort of a risky strategy, but trust me, your material should be brave enough even to the extent of being polarising. The era of trying to sell to everybody is over. Today, probably the first rule if you want your content to go 'viral', as we say, is to make sure it evokes some kind of strong reaction. Ideally, this should be a positive one, but really, what matters is that your narrative doesn't create indifference.

LISTENING PART 3

Training Exercise 1

Man: Good morning everyone. With me in the studio today is Rebecca Wright, the author of a new book, *Board NOW*. She is here to talk to us about assembling your first board of directors. Rebecca, welcome to *Business Talk*.

Woman: Thank you, Corey.
Man: Let's start by talking about what boards are and why they are needed.
Woman: Well, many entrepreneurs, especially of young companies, use what I call the 'Me, Myself and I' approach to their corporate governance, as in: *I am the sole shareholder. I vote myself to be the sole board member and as a board member, I hire myself to be the CEO.* Now, while this approach certainly provides the ultimate control over the company's affairs, after a certain point it is just not feasible any more. If your company has expanded, it's time to assemble a board of directors to help protect, govern and manage all you've built.
Man: And when do companies make this transition?
Woman: Good question. Many entrepreneurs seem confused about this. Some don't use a board because they think it's only useful for big companies or it seems too complicated to administer. As you might know, an official, more formal board of directors is only required when going public or upon the interest of venture capital investors, but in my book I argue that hiring an advisory board, even before that, is normally recommendable.
Man: Yes, as a 'test drive' for later, right?
Woman: Indeed. These advisory boards are voluntary and have no legal and financial responsibilities.
Man: What are some of the rules or recommendations to bear in mind when someone is selecting their first board of directors, even if only advisory?
Woman: Perhaps the biggest goal should be that the members serve your company on a day-to-day basis well, while still respecting your vision as its founder.
Man: And who should you not hire?
Woman: Now this is key. My main rule is not to invite family or friends, because they tend to become 'yes people'. Plus, they're going to give you advice whether you want it or not, so that's a given.
Man: Any other common mistakes?
Woman: I also wouldn't include such people as your accountant, legal or marketing consultant on your board.
Man: Why not? They might actually know a lot about your company!
Woman: Yes, and you already pay those people to advise you. You should be looking for people external to your company instead who are going to challenge you, who may have gone through the same issues you have and will bring a different perspective.
Man: Yes, but in your book you mention the 'CEO's dilemma'. Can you tell our listeners what it is and how to avoid it?
Woman: The short-term desires of shareholders, and consequently your board, can be in direct opposition to the long-term vision of the CEO, especially a founding CEO. When the two interests diverge too greatly, conflicts may arise. The dilemma is who to hire, because picking idolising followers reduces the perspective the board can offer the leader. However, a board too easily influenced by investors and their desire for short-term profit can be in conflict with the CEO's mission.
Man: So the best way to avoid this is by picking members who are very similar to you, right?
Woman: Actually, that isn't entirely true. You need to choose members who counterbalance your weaknesses. Many founders are tempted to choose board members who possess the same skills set as their own, but the best boards are those that bring strengths that are important to the company but aren't possessed by the founders. If you're an IT expert, bring on advisors that are good at sales. If you're a sales expert, include a product development or technical advisor, and so on.
Man: Rebecca, thank you for your time.

🎧 EXAM PRACTICE

19 *Man:* Good afternoon everyone, and thank you for accepting our invitation, Heather. Everyone, Heather Middleton, our star consultant on the show, is in the studio with me today, to talk to us about successful product launches.
Woman: Hi Jon! Thanks for the invitation.
Man: Let's dive straight in, shall we? What one thing is key, in your opinion, when talking about product launches?
Woman: So, essentially I think that success in sales today all comes down to how genuine you are. I know this goes against traditional marketing wisdom, but the era of manipulating the customer is over.
Man: I thought all advertising and marketing was built on this, to some extent?
Woman: Yes, *was* being the operative word here. In my opinion, live product launches create a scarcity mindset, that is, a feeling that what is on offer is limited and you will miss out if you don't act immediately. This manipulates the customer and should be avoided.
Man: Interesting. So you disapprove of live launches?
Woman: Yes, yes, I do. While a live product launch strategy to sell online courses and programmes, for example, often results in amazing sales on the day, the fundamental problem is that it only gives you short-term success with no long-term gain.
Man: So why do so many entrepreneurs use live launches these days?
Woman: Well, a live product launch strategy creates a lot of money, attention, instant exposure, traffic and many exciting leads right away, as well as a lot of opportunities for partnerships.
Man: But?

Woman: But you realise afterwards that it was all a lot of work and left you totally exhausted; that it was not that profitable after all, if you take into account your expenses on ads, for example; that <u>most of your new leads have since unsubscribed from your mailing list, etc.</u>
Man: Plus, when it's over, you have to think where your next massive income will come from, so you can start setting up the entire process again soon, right? What's the alternative then?
Woman: What I call an 'evergreen' product launch strategy; that is selling 'around the clock', as opposed to short 'bursts' like this. <u>It is simply not ideal to be at the mercy of your product launches, if these are your only sources of income.</u>
Man: Is this the only key difference between the two ways?
Woman: It is an important one, but so is the fact that an evergreen launch strategy allows you to optimise.
Man: What do you mean by that?
Woman: Well, with a live launch, you have no idea how effective your conversion funnel is.
Man: Your conversion what? Could you explain that?
Woman: Of course – it's the track your consumer takes through the internet and your website, which eventually converts to a sale.
Man: Oh, I see.
Woman: <u>You might not know whether your video works. You're unsure if your emails and social media ads are on point.</u> You don't know much of anything, really. You're basing your entire product launch strategy on assumptions. But what if your sales page, message or webinar is off, for example? Also, I think it's time companies really started to respect their customers more.
Man: How so?
Woman: By highlighting their problems, so <u>they buy your product at a time relevant to them, even if that's not right now.</u>
Man: That's such a great point! And do you think live launches will be more or less popular in the future?
Woman: <u>I predict they will entirely go out of fashion,</u> because they really do not help build trust with your clients, or create a robust business model, for that matter.
Man: Heather, thank you for your time.

SPEAKING PART 1

Training Exercise 3

a

Examiner: How important is access to training for you in your job?
Candidate: I'm sorry, could you repeat the question?
Examiner: Yes. How important is access to training for you in your job?
Candidate: Erm, I'd say it's extremely important. I want to feel that I am improving as a person and in my career, so I would definitely want an employer to give me some training. As well as that, I think it's useful for the employer, as it means they would get better workers.

b

Examiner: What qualities are important when working in a team?
Candidate: I didn't quite catch that. Could you say it again, please?
Examiner: Yes. What qualities are important when working in a team?
Candidate: Oh, I think the ability to listen is essential because you need to know what the other people in your team are thinking and doing. Communication skills are also important because you need to be clear about what you want and how you are going to do it.

c

Examiner: Would you like to have the opportunity to travel in your career?
Candidate: Would you mind repeating that, please?
Examiner: Yes. Would you like to have the opportunity to travel in your career?
Candidate: Mmm, I think so. I don't want to live in a different city or country because I have family at home and I don't think they would want to move. However, I would like to travel to different places on short trips, like for a week or two.

SPEAKING PART 3

Training Exercise 2

Candidate A: OK, are you ready to start?
Candidate B: Yes, OK. Right, well, I think this is an excellent idea and that the students will learn a lot.
Candidate A: Yes, I agree. What do you think about using the canteen as a kind of reception space?
Candidate B: <u>Absolutely! It's a big space and we could have a place for people to meet and show maps and information and stuff.</u>
Candidate A: <u>OK. I was thinking we could take the students around the business in small groups</u> because it would be better than having one big group trying to get into some of the offices. It would also mean the students might be able to ask the employees some questions.
Candidate B: <u>Yeah, they wouldn't be able to talk to employees if they were in one large group, you're right.</u> We could also take students to the Research and Development centre. There is a lot of interesting work there and the students can see how we think of new ideas and work in teams to deliver projects. <u>Do you agree?</u>
Candidate A: Yes, sure, that's a good idea. <u>Do you think going to Human Resources is a good idea?</u> They have lots of

information about the company and they can also tell the students what they have to do if they want to work here.
Candidate B: Yes, but the HR office is very small, so I think it will be difficult to get the students in. Maybe we could get the HR team to come down to the canteen and talk to the students there?
Candidate A: Yes, OK, I like that idea. Let's see, we've talked about the canteen, Research and Development and Human Resources. What else might be interesting for students?
Candidate B: I think we should show them the boardroom, where the directors have their meetings. It's big and serious, and I think students would like to see what the bosses do.
Candidate A: Yes, good. It also has lots of space for walking around and computers and WiFi, which is a good thing.
Candidate B: Do you think we should talk about how to get the rest of the company involved?
Candidate A: Yes, I do. We talked about asking Human Resources to come to the canteen, so we could have a meeting with them to explain what we want. Should we do the same for the other departments?
Candidate B: It will take a long time to talk to people from all the other departments individually. Personally, I think we should send an email to the heads of the departments and ask for ideas, things each department would like to do.
Candidate A: Yes, but it is very easy to ignore an email. What about organising a meeting for one person from each department? If we get one of the directors to send the email, then it will be difficult to ignore it!

Training Exercise 4

22 *Examiner:* Do you think open days like this are useful for students?
Candidate A: That's a good question. I think they are because it lets students understand what work is really like, so they can be more prepared when they leave school or college. I never did anything like this, but I think it would help.
Examiner: What other things could companies do to help students prepare for the world of work?
Candidate B: I have never thought of that. In my country, lots of students go to college at night and work during the day, so this helps us to be prepared for work because we are doing both at the same time. Students get very tired and maybe they don't learn as much at college, but they do learn a lot of practical things.
Examiner: How important do you think it is for companies to have a good image with the public?
Candidate A: Well, I would say that for some companies it is vital. If a company is selling to the public, then they need a good public image as part of their marketing. However, if the company is more involved in selling to other businesses, then maybe their public image is not so important.

 Test 3

LISTENING PART 1

23 Conversation 1

Woman: Hi, George, how's our presentation coming along for tomorrow's meeting with the tyre company? We really need this client; you know that.
Man: I know, Amy, don't worry. I'm planning to use cue cards to help me remember what we want to say. I'll be starting with a brief overview of our company, then talk about what we could offer them.
Woman: Perfect. Just make sure you don't use more than six words on any of the slides this time, please. And perhaps make slides that reinforce your words, not just repeat them?
Man: So they are really visual, you mean?
Woman: Yes, very colourful. Use professional stock images for this, please.
Man: No problem. Anything else you recommend I do or avoid?
Woman: Well, I have a thing against annoying transitions between slides. They really don't create a professional impression. Oh, and sound effects – they can be really distracting. Please keep it all silent this time.
Man: Will do. Thanks for the tips, Amy.

Conversation 2

Man: So, Miley; can you tell me a bit about what this whole 'Athleisure' movement is in clothing?
Woman: Sure. 'Athleisure' simply means casual clothing meant to be worn both for exercising and for general use.
Man: And should my firm pay attention to this trend, really?
Woman: I think you really should, because it seems that it is here to stay.
Man: But what's the big deal? I mean we've had fashionable sports clothes before!
Woman: That's true. However, this time it's more than just a trend, because it is a complete lifestyle shift, on a large scale. People seem to be embracing healthier lifestyles and demanding more functionality from their wardrobes to go with these.
Man: So we should participate as well, you say. And who are these 'fitfluencers' you mentioned earlier?
Woman: Athleisure products' marketing is often boosted by what we call 'micro influencers' – amateur athletes pursuing different sports, typically running, rock climbing or yoga.
Man: OK, this is definitely food for thought. Thanks, Miley!

Conversation 3

Good morning, and thanks for coming. Today, I'll talk about what a press kit is and why every company needs one. When a journalist asks you for yours, you should first provide them with a fact sheet of your enterprise; the key component of your kit. In it you should include some basic information about you, your partners, the company and the market. Ideally, you should try to include enough material in it that they do not have to ask follow-up questions. Also, you need to be objective, otherwise they might feel they need to research you more. Some other details companies often find useful to mention are the year the company was founded, who the founders are, where it was founded, where it currently operates and how many employees it has. You might also decide to add some pictures and videos to your kit. These should be well-shot and high resolution, of about 1MB per file tops, and could be headshots or short clips of the founders.

LISTENING PART 2

Section 1

13

I know there are many features to look for in a potential new colleague for our company, beyond solid knowledge of our software as well. What I tend to prioritise in an applicant above all is that they come from a background of leadership during their studies already. Applicants who were actively involved in any activity where they took on a managerial role could be identified as prospective staff with us, even if they didn't study something clearly business-related.

14

Leaders should think long term and always act on behalf of the entire company, beyond just their own teams. And they never say 'that's not my job', or worse, 'that's not my fault'. We seek employees for our managerial level positions who are curious enough to learn and, even more so, to tackle any issues that come their way. And when something goes wrong, even despite all that, they don't try to blame it on anybody else either.

15

Despite the cut-throat competition in the market today, I deeply believe that the only companies that survive are those that focus on the customer first instead of the competition. Our leaders also start with the end-user in mind and work backwards when making any decisions. All our employees work vigorously to earn and keep customer trust, and are expected to actively share this passion with each other as well.

16

We expect our leaders to require innovation from their teams and always find ways to streamline our processes. The colleagues we want working for us will all be very aware of the existing problems in our field and will be keen on working on improving the services we are offering our clients – no excuses. Our motto is 'the less complex the better', and if somebody proves they have this ability, they may be the right fit for our team.

17

I've said this before, but it bears repeating: speed matters in business. Many decisions are reversible and, therefore, do not need extensive study or approval from higher levels of management. I really value calculated risk-taking, because having independent enough leaders means that we get to save on important resources, mostly time, and these can be allocated for use elsewhere in the company. While you're not closely supervising an employee, you more easily innovate or focus on the bigger picture.

Section 2

18

I've noticed that many companies make the mistake of thinking that a professional-looking website will do all the work of convincing customers of their company's legitimacy. A serious web presence is a must, of course, but only if it still contains your address and call centre's phone number. I regularly talk to older customers especially, who mention that they feel more comfortable if they see an actual geographical address as well on a site.

19

People feel bombarded by all sorts of scams and fake websites today. This results in customers becoming increasingly wary when coming across a new brand for the first time. Small businesses that, in an effort to save time and money, use generic stock images, risk appearing like they are hiding something. Such a lack of personality and transparency, signals to customers that your site could be a scam. Upload pictures of the people who work with you to avoid this.

20

Online customer reviews are crucial to staying alive as a business today, but it's as if smaller companies didn't know this, or, at least, didn't care. I'm very surprised to see how many brands let third-party review sites and apps speak for them. It should be obvious that a website without, at least, a few accounts of satisfied customers or colourful case stories will seem less credible to the public.

21

You should demonstrate your expertise, yes. After all, a key part of building credibility is showing to your followers and prospective clients that you know what you're talking about. However, when a brand releases blog entries and other types of online content, increasingly on their apps too, including too many 'big words' to seem more authoritative in the field, they often achieve the opposite. Unnecessarily fancy vocabulary that confuses your audience will only alienate the very people you're targeting.

22

Look, we all want to position ourselves as the best in the business, don't we? But, rather than showcase their best work in an online portfolio, many businesses instead choose to use non-specific adjectives such as 'top-quality', 'best of the best' or 'experienced staff'. Such vague expressions destroy a brand's credibility more than, I don't know, a website that regularly crashes, by inadvertently communicating that you don't actually know what it is that your business has to offer.

 LISTENING PART 3

26 *Woman:* Hello everybody, and thanks for tuning in. With me today is Dan Powell, the CEO of AviaTra, to discuss how he changed the company's meetings culture when he took over last year. Dan, welcome.
Man: Thanks, Holly. Great to be with you.
Woman: Most people dread meetings, but you decided to actually do something about them at AviaTra. Can you tell us why?
Man: Principally because inefficiently run meetings are a drain on precious resources. To avoid this, meetings need to be better defined. Before I introduced our checklist, people would call their conversations or presentations 'meetings', for example.
Woman: So how's a meeting different from these?
Man: In many key ways. One, there's one person responsible for calling it. Two, the time allocated matches what's realistically needed. Three, there's no better way forward than to have this meeting; and four, the desired outcome is clearly stated.
Woman: You mean the meeting has an agenda.
Man: Yes, with maximum five items on it, with the time allotted for each. Another trick that saves time is to make all the relevant information available to everybody in plenty of time to be reviewed in advance.
Woman: I know some executives like to open meetings with 30 minutes of silence too, which participants use to read a summary of any important reports, then think and make notes.
Man: Exactly. This also helps avoid organisations spending the most time on trivial issues and the least time on the most important ones, which is very common.
Woman: Why is that?

Man: Because the more complicated, and often important, a matter is, the fewer people really understand it to meaningfully contribute to discussing it.
Woman: And does everybody have to agree on one thing before moving on to the next point?
Man: I actually don't think they do. If an individual has clear decision-making responsibility, they are the one in charge on that topic. But abandoning the concept of consensus takes some getting used to. However, I noticed that often the wrong people might be present in a meeting. We also changed this by doing away with the old default of 'when in doubt, invite them'. Now it's 'when in doubt, leave them out'. There's also the 'two-pizza rule', which prohibits meetings where two pizzas couldn't feed the entire group. Now, only those who need to understand, buy into or act on the topics being discussed are invited.
Woman: Interesting!
Man: Having said that, it's crucial too that no key party be missing.
Woman: And when do you hold your meetings at AviaTra?
Man: Meetings used to be scheduled at the wrong time, and interrupted the day in other illogical ways by interfering with people's work flows or peak concentration times. So we asked around to find out when people are most productive, then blocked off certain times and days as 'meeting-free', based on their replies.
Woman: Major changes all right!
Man: Yes, but they were necessary. I have a theory that whatever you see in meetings is what happens at the company outside of the meetings as well.
Woman: What do you mean?
Man: For example, if you see people tuning out in meetings, getting anxious, looking to the authority figure in the room for the final say on a matter, when they aren't curious about each other's point of view ... all this is probably present in the company in general.
Woman: Now I especially see why you wanted the reforms! Dan, thank you for coming in today.

Test 4

 LISTENING PART 1

27 **Conversation 1**

Man: Hi Erin! Do you remember when I said I needed a better way to be in touch with our growing team?
Woman: You mean when we were talking about how meetings, video conferencing and the old weekly employee newsletter are just not the way to go any more, with 600+ employees?

Man: That's right.
Woman: So what's the plan now?
Man: I'll be shooting weekly 'CEO videos', to address everybody across all departments, including our colleagues abroad.
Woman: That's an awesome idea, Nick! So what are the details?
Man: Well, the idea is not to spend too much time preparing the videos. I do want to be able to share any important company news, however, and ask for or provide feedback. And this all has to be done from wherever, obviously, because of my travels.
Woman: And how well produced are the videos going to be?
Man: Not at all. I wouldn't have the time to deal with sound, lighting, writing scripts, etc. Instead I'll just shoot them selfie-style on my phone.
Woman: Great plan!

Conversation 2

Woman: Hi Josh, I'm free now to talk about the new virtual reality application I developed to showcase our furniture.
Man: Wonderful. We should really release it early next year. It might even boost our first quarter's figures.
Woman: Let's hope so.
Man: So what have we got here?
Woman: Well, I wanted it to allow our customers to imagine how our products would fit into their offices. Besides marketing, I believe it could actually really help them because currently about 22% of them take away furniture that is the wrong size for its intended spot.
Man: That is unfortunate. So the app would help with measurements?
Woman: And, you know, show our products in the most impressive and modern way possible; give them ideas about interior design.
Man: Sure, sure. I think it would also be useful in helping them see whether the colours of their existing furniture might match those of the new pieces, don't you think?
Woman: Exactly! I'll have the prototype ready by November, as agreed.

Conversation 3

The problem with asking customers for their opinions on your product or service is that either they don't know, they think they know but they're wrong, or they do know, but they won't tell you what they really think. Therefore, it is always recommended that you use implicit data, that is to say information about observed customer behaviour, as opposed to explicit data, such as any customer-provided information. The problem with surveys is that they require a lot of time, money and energy, but only an unrepresentative group typically responds, namely the clients who already like what you have to offer. Also, you don't get enough responses to achieve real statistical significance and results often prove that customer intent doesn't actually match future behaviour. To get more reliable and unfiltered customer feedback, customer support calls and emails are excellent. From these, you can acquire a more refined idea about them and can predict their future choices too. Another effective feedback source is paying for a user-testing service.

LISTENING PART 2

 Section 1

13

If you put your high performers on your hardest projects over and over again, it is only fair that you should provide them with some help to avoid them burning out along the way too. It's logical to put your best people on the company's key projects, but when they are under non-stop pressure while *also* being asked to help out with smaller tasks, these extra demands can lead to their becoming completely exhausted. Be careful not to overburden them.

14

A lack of advancement options is one of the main factors influencing turnover among key employees. To prevent their careers from arriving at a plateau within your organisation, have yearly one-on-one meetings with your high performers to discuss their long-term learning goals. Pay attention to what they say in these and, depending on what you hear, seek out or create these challenges for them. They can range from participating in a mentorship programme to taking online courses.

15

In my experience, a sure-fire sign that an important employee might be considering leaving, is that they start taking on fewer responsibilities and become less of a team player than usual. While you won't necessarily detect a significant decrease in their performance, you will most likely perceive a decline in their engagement, both for their own work and the company's mission. Watch out for such disengagement and sit down with them to see how you could get them motivated again.

16

When high performers commit to something, you can count on them to do it right, even if you can't pay them the same your rivals would. However, when they lose interest, these same employees are likely to stop volunteering for new responsibilities. Try tempting them with more creative or bigger scale projects to win them back for the company and you will both win: they'll stay and you get to launch the new project more confidently with them on board!

17

No one likes to feel like their work is being taken for granted. For top performers who are frequently asked to step up to compensate for weaker employees, it's even more important that they know that their work is valued. Besides, or in some cases even *instead of*, handing out generous bonuses or offering the option to work from home, maybe also consider that sometimes merely by acknowledging your staff's contributions you can drive employee engagement quite successfully.

 Section 2

18

The same rules will not apply for every industry. I work in travel, where we have noticed that the most successful response rates seem to come from subject lines under about 18 characters, written in capital letters. I have friends in other sectors though, including finance and publishing, where the numbers are 33 and 45 respectively, according to them. So you see, it's worth looking into what's expected or considered standard in your field, before wording your subject.

19

It has been found that subject lines that included the recipient's name or recently purchased or browsed items had 67 per cent higher open rates than emails that were not so tailor-made. I just wish more people were this forward when sending an email and writing their subject! Somehow, we all seem to have been trained to send out our bulk emails with our bulk subject lines, but it doesn't seem to be working so well, according to research.

20

Another common sales strategy brands often resort to these days is to send their users emails about their abandoned carts with unpurchased items in their online shops. The results don't appear to be spectacular, however. Approximately 85 per cent of these messages get a below-average open rate, which is a very small number indeed. The issue may be that companies are too upfront about their agenda, but recipients appear to be more easily enticed by subjects that read 'you forgot something'.

21

In my field, what we discovered works wonders is when we generate interest by including a number of specific key words relevant to the recipient. These can typically be related to the topic of the newsletter they signed up for, such as 'Foundations of data science: A beginner's course'. The reader would most likely want to know the subject of our course, in this case 'data science'; and the level of the course, before clicking on to read more.

22

Don't you find it fascinating that we go to all this trouble to make sure we don't send out anything that is factually incorrect, and then write subject lines in a hurry? I recently embarrassed our company with a subject line to an email I sent out that read 'Get 25% of any of our products', instead of 'off', with double f. I also got the extent of the discount slightly wrong, but that was the least of it.

LISTENING PART 3

Man: Hello everyone and welcome to another episode of *Ask the Expert*. With me today is Ashley Quinn, who is here to tell you how to secure some much needed media coverage. Hi Ashley!
Woman: Hey Logan! Thanks for the invite!
Man: So how can an entrepreneur make sure they are well informed regarding the target media they want to approach?
Woman: I'd say by reading the publications and watching or listening to the shows they want to be on. This will help them figure out what they like to cover. Also, you need to know who to talk to, to avoid funny mistakes and misunderstandings.
Man: Any secret tips on how to do this?
Woman: Well, it can really help if you look for things you and the journalist you are approaching have in common. Doing so might help you grab their attention more easily.
Man: Like hobbies, interests – things you've noticed about them on social media?
Woman: Exactly. Be subtle about this though. More importantly, a successful pitch will always answer the query 'Why should I care?'. I always open emails from entrepreneurs asking myself this and if I don't find a convincing answer to it after a brief read through, I move on.
Man: Ruthless.
Woman: I know, right? Having said that, I often read amazing pitches from people who help me imagine how the story would run. Providing journalists with any background information or ideas on how to present it may more easily convince them to pick it up.
Man: And when should you reach out?
Woman: That's important too! Too many entrepreneurs make the mistake of assuming that just because their product or service is useful throughout the year, it's automatically interesting as a story at any time. It isn't. The media are obsessed with remaining relevant to their audiences. You need to 'hook' your message on to whatever's currently happening.

Is your story based on an emerging trend? Does it speak to a breaking news story? etc.
Man: Does that mean negative news too?
Woman: It does. In fact, I recommend creating a crisis plan so that when a major negative event occurs, your company is prepared to handle things appropriately. No matter what line of business you're in, you probably already have material about industry issues you could use as a guide, such as blog posts.
Man: I've heard the term 'hijacking the news' though …
Woman: That should be avoided. It may seem like good practice to tie your company's news to some major national news story, but no matter how hard you try, there's probably no realistic connection between your new dry-cleaning service and, say, the general election. This move will come off as unnatural and forced, and most journalists will probably ignore the pitch.
Man: Fair enough. What else *can* help instead?
Woman: Being prepared to provide expert insight when needed. Every start-up founder should sign up with 'Help a Reporter Out', or HARO, as it is typically referred to. This free platform connects journalists to industry experts, sending out three requests daily to its members. There are several categories you can subscribe to, providing you with plenty of opportunities to get featured by major media outlets.
Man: Excellent. And your last tip?
Woman: … is to use infographics as outreach bait. Visual content such as infographics is very appealing to websites. It tends to receive a lot of attention and social sharing, and this translates into more page views for the media outlet.
Man: Ashley, thank you for your time.
Woman: My pleasure.

Test 5

LISTENING PART 1

Conversation 1

Woman: Generation Z, the name given to people born in 1995 or after, currently makes up a quarter of the American population and contributes $44 billion to the US economy. One of the main differences between earlier generations and Gen Z is that members of the latter are better multi-taskers. They can more effortlessly shift between work and play, with multiple distractions going on around them. This generation is also full of what we would call 'early starters', which means that between the ages of 16 and 18 they already go into the workforce, often opting out of traditional higher education. At work they are more entrepreneurial too. They prefer more independent work environments and while they are not the first truly global generation, members of Generation Z are fast becoming even more global in their thinking, interactions and use of their digital devices than their predecessors. In addition, some of their skills, such as reading comprehension, are being radically transformed as a result of their constant use of digital devices, platforms and online materials.

Conversation 2

Woman: I can't believe it's already Thursday!
Man: I know – the week's gone really fast.
Woman: It really has, and I still haven't told them about management's decision of the layoffs. I hate to break any bad news to my team, Tim!
Man: Who doesn't? Can I give you some advice? What I find crucial, is to always start by giving them a good reason. In my experience, you can usually talk to adults, even if they are disappointed at first. Last year, we had to dismiss most of our sales team. It was an incredibly hard decision, but it was necessary and they accepted it.
Woman: Did they all find new jobs?
Man: Interestingly, two years later we could hire most of them back! I actually made this promise to the leaving colleagues, that we would welcome them back as soon as we could.
Woman: What a story!
Man: We also made sure we handed out some really impressive severance packages.
Woman: Nice! Not too bad!
Man: Lastly, we also provided the dismissed employees with useful referrals in the industry.

Conversation 3

Man: Rachel, I think we should talk a bit about starting to delegate some of our tasks, don't you?
Woman: I agree. I just read a blog entry about this topic, actually, that made me think the same. In it the author was saying that leaders are often slow to delegate, principally because they don't trust their staff.
Man: That's kind of true, I think!
Woman: … and that when leaders overextend themselves as a result, the company's development slows down unnecessarily.
Man: So true! So, what tips do they mention, how should you start?
Woman: They say you need to start small and that it's totally normal to feel terrified when you decide to give up some of your set routines at first.
Man: I know that feeling. But maybe if we set out by delegating a few administrative tasks, we could survive.
Woman: I hope so! We do need to focus more and more on the things that only we can do. You know, like strategising.

LISTENING PART 2

Section 1

13

I was quite happy at my previous workplace, actually. Doing that job, even if only on a series of short-term contracts, made me realise just how much I care for my profession! I really love this area of HR – benefits is such an interesting part of it. I just came to a point where I wanted something more stable, you know? I felt that I was ready for a bigger commitment and I needed a workplace that wanted the same.

14

It broke my heart, having to quit. Trust me, it wasn't something I would have wanted, especially not right after having been given the department chair position, but I had no choice, given the circumstances. I mean, it's one thing to work from home once or twice a month, but when I started having to attend treatment sessions in other cities, it all got too complicated. It wouldn't have been fair on the company if I hadn't quit, to be honest.

15

We had set up a very efficient routine by then. Mornings are particularly complicated in a family with two working parents, you know, but we were managing it well. I would wake up first, at 5.40, make breakfast and get everybody ready, then Nicholas would drop the kids off at school on his way to the office. When his company moved, it all became impossible, however, as he now has a longer commute to his new office. Something had to give, as they say …

16

I always knew that I'd only want to be in management for a while. It was never my idea to stay in it, as is often the case with others. I just needed some first-hand experience of what it is like having my own team, before eventually signing up for my course. Having said that, I never would have thought that the requirements would be this demanding! I was quite surprised at first, but it was clear what I had to do.

17

Thirty years as a corporate lawyer! Can you imagine that? So many companies, so many cases … so much adrenaline too! And I have to say, I liked it! The environment, the challenges, even the difficult colleagues, and I had quite a few over the years! But when my children left home, I decided I wanted to dedicate myself to something less intellectually demanding and more creative. I always loved baking as a hobby, so opening a small bakery seemed like a fun idea.

Section 2

18

I think last year we got a bit overwhelmed by our other day-to-day tasks and ended up only publishing content related to job openings on our various sites. I plan to change this as of next year because top-quality candidates typically want more than this. We will pay more attention to sharing valuable posts as well, beyond the ads. I hope this way they will engage with us more and realise we might be a good fit for them.

19

I had to tell my recruiters that simply using a prospective candidate's name at the beginning of their messages does not count as a personalised offer. In my experience, high-quality candidates know a template when they see one. Unfortunately, even if they were originally interested in our company, an impersonal outreach will have them hitting the delete button immediately. It may be a little time-consuming, but being patient enough to spend some time researching each candidate is a must.

20

The worst mistake I made was when we urgently needed a senior analyst before this huge project, and although I knew we had found the right candidate for the job, I didn't quite consider just how much it would cost to lose them. Finding and replacing our second choice, and the lost opportunity from hiring someone performing much worse, ended up being way more expensive overall than making a better offer would have been to the first candidate.

21

It took me some time to learn that during the hiring process we're not the only ones choosing, so we must learn to listen better. Now I make sure I help the candidate think through whether or not we'd be a good fit for them too, by paying attention to and addressing at least some of the details that come up along the way. This can be anything that prompts them to see themselves working for us.

22

As a candidate, I hated this too. After all, it should be quite obvious to anybody that every workplace will have its unique opportunities and challenges. Yet there are companies and recruiting strategies that focus only on talking about the positives while glossing over the issues. This is an approach that tends to backfire, so I now explicitly ask my HR team to own up to the difficulties we are facing. The ideal candidate will choose us anyway.

LISTENING PART 3

Woman: Hello and welcome back to *Business Talk*. I'm Sharon Bailey and with me today in the studio is Ryan Page, entrepreneur and amateur martial artist. Ryan, thank you for accepting our invitation.
Man: My pleasure.
Woman: Can you tell us why you spend so much of your time doing martial arts?
Man: Well, I'm very dedicated to my company, which is actually why I decided to take up Mixed Martial Arts nine years ago.
Woman: So what's the connection? How does this serve your enterprise?
Man: In multiple ways. There are several parallels between martial arts and starting a company that I feel have made me a better entrepreneur.
Woman: Can you tell us a few?
Man: I think the main lesson I've learnt from all these years of fighting is that to succeed, you must learn to control your emotions and get used to discomfort.
Woman: What emotions, for example?
Man: Well, running a company, like being in a fight, will push you beyond your comfort zone. Whether you're firing, negotiating, handling customer complaints or maintaining quality control, you will most likely be handling uncomfortable situations in unfamiliar territory.
Woman: That's so true.
Man: Connected to this is the skill of learning to embrace failure. Getting used to entering training sessions knowing that you will fail builds a certain toughness of character. I really used to fear defeat. Now I accept it as just a necessary component of the road to success.
Woman: So, being happy with failure is important.
Man: Having said that, to beat your competition or qualify to compete in a championship you need to be 'complete'. This means that during your preparation you leave no 'holes' in your game. You practise your moves standing up or on the ground, and create contingency plans in advance. You need to be well-rounded as a leader too.
Woman: And what do martial arts teach you about patience? When should you persevere, when should you swiftly change tactics? It's not always easy to decide these things and in business they are crucial, right?
Man: Indeed. Fighting shows you that mastery takes time and practice. You shouldn't move past the beginner level until you have first got good at the basics. It's easy to get excited about trying cool new techniques, but you need a good strong foundation to build on.
Woman: So you should be persistent?
Man: Right. Fighting also teaches you how to avoid the 'shiny-object syndrome'. Entrepreneurs often easily get distracted by new strategies or approaches. They move from one new thing to the next, before they've implemented something well enough to get results from it. Often less is more, if you're consistent.
Woman: Tell us a bit about who's helping you.
Man: Great question. Although when you are fighting, you're facing the opponent by yourself, a team of highly specialised professionals, from massage therapists to trainers, are behind you. Ask any manager and they'll tell you that in business too, teamwork is very important. You need a team of people who can see things you can't and make you strong where you are weak.
Woman: So another lesson is that you must be stronger than your enemy.
Man: Not necessarily. Instead I'd say that the really successful entrepreneur learns to use their opponent's force against them. In other words, it is not enough to just push back when something comes at you, you should always take it a step further and ask yourself 'How can I leverage this? Where is the opportunity in this?'. Challenges are there to be used, not just survived.
Woman: Ryan Page, thank you.

Test 6

LISTENING PART 1

Conversation 1

Woman: Hi, Nicolas! Welcome on board!
Man: Hi, Christina! Thank you. I'm so excited to get started!
Woman: Me too, you'll love working here. Our customers are amazing. Just make sure you always teach them something new about each one of our essential oils. A feature, or another use they haven't considered.
Man: Great point, noted!
Woman: You'll also have to become an expert on their use in the home, not just personal hygiene and health. We need to come across as a credible authority in our industry, after all.
Man: I know! That's why I like to attend any beauty conferences and trade shows my customers attend.
Woman: Perfect! Do you also read journals and research reports?
Man: To be honest, so far only blogs. Could you share some of the most relevant ones with me, do you think?
Woman: Of course! They will help you nurture our relationship with customers. If we keep on educating them about the multiple uses of our oils, they will consider us a valued resource they can count on ... that's always the hope anyway!

Conversation 2

Man: Hello, Catherine. Why did you want to see me?
Woman: Hi, Timothy! I'm trying to get promoted and I wanted your advice. Talking to you about work proved to be really useful last time, so I thought I'd ask again.
Man: Sure. I think what usually tends to impress the decision makers about promotions is when an employee proactively starts acting like a leader. This demonstrates that you can inspire your co-workers and are quite capable of independently coming up with and completing projects.
Woman: Without abandoning my current responsibilities, you mean.
Man: Obviously. Make sure you set goals that you can use to measure your success. Check that you and your supervisor both understand how success looks in your context.
Woman: What a great point!
Man: You should also be very conscious not to engage in office politics. Instead, try to become a calming office presence, I'd say. At most organisations the people who typically get promoted are the ones who keep their cool under stress.
Woman: Thanks, Timothy! I knew I should talk to you! These are very useful ideas.

Conversation 3

Before a company decides to choose a new name, symbol or design, there are a few things worth considering. Not getting rebranding right can potentially ruin years of accumulated brand equity. To prevent this, you should inform any stakeholders such as key clients, partners and vendors in advance. Before picking a new name you should also always consider any important naming guidelines, including checking the availability of any URL domains and making sure they fit your price range. It is also very important to be careful not to make the common mistake of choosing a trademark that is already taken. Purchase your new domain name and switch your social media profiles to it but keep the old name too, in order to redirect traffic to your new accounts. If this is done, you can go ahead and create the new email addresses that you will use. After all this is done, all that is left is updating your website and promotional materials, and, there you are, a new brand is born!

LISTENING PART 2

 Section 1

13

I got the feedback from many of our clients that when they first searched for us online, they were surprised by the lack of information available on our site. A recurring comment was that they would have liked to know much more about how long we've been in business, the size of our company, the experts working for us, and so on. So I hired this web developer and now you can read all about our history at www …

14

The coach we hired criticised this aspect of our website. He said that the information we provided in this section of the site should be based on our clients' everyday queries that come in through all the channels: emails, chat, our social media or the call centre and preferably be much more recent. According to him, ours was full of generic issues that don't really address the doubts our customers currently have while shopping with us.

15

I wanted the new site to feature this section more prominently for our prospective customers to read and told my colleagues this too. I figured that anybody interested in buying from us will surely be curious to find out what previous buyers thought of our services in the past, so it really shouldn't be hidden. I'm quite happy with the new layout overall, and glad our visitors get to read all our satisfied past users' accounts first thing.

16

We were told to include an entire page describing each, and now I see how right the IT consultant was about this! I can't believe how many websites I still come across, including our competitors', where there is only a joint page for all the items! Customers need more information than this. They want to see photos too, preferably with zoom and rotation, if possible. I also learnt that you should include not just the names but model numbers too.

17

Our main rival had a section called *Methodology*, and it sounded so professional I thought we needed something like this too. Or rather, that we needed to boost the info that we already had about all the national and international quality control processes and certifications that we had acquired over the years. Besides good marketing, this helped shorten our *About Us* section greatly, as we could eliminate the need to describe some of our key procedures and permissions too.

 Section 2

18

To me, it seems that in the UK it's more challenging for a company to get its employees to put in the same number of hours, even skipping lunch, as people will automatically do in the States. In the UK, you have to capture the hearts and minds of your employees first.

If they are committed to your firm's mission, they'll complete any task that needs to be done, but only when they are truly invested in the company.

19

I accepted the offer anyway, because working for this company was like a dream come true for me at the time. I had read the contract carefully too, but to be honest, at first it didn't quite register just how few ten days was going to be. That's a mere two weeks off, after all, and this is even supposed to include sick days! It's a good thing the job turned out to be life-changing, so I didn't mind.

20

It was embarrassing at first, but I tried hard to follow what was going on around me in the office. I mean, I had been told in advance that a curriculum vitae is a resume in America of course, but besides this, I wasn't really prepared for all the variations in phrasing and terminology. This lead to quite some misunderstandings at the beginning. If you're planning to work in the US, don't leave without exposing yourself to the culture at home first.

21

First off, I'm not keen on sports. At all. And we don't even have the same ones back home. So, although I really appreciated my colleagues' attempts at welcoming me to their team, I often struggled with these 'water-cooler' conversations. I wanted to connect, but I just couldn't keep up with this. Instead, I kept changing the topic to other neutral ones, such as films and travelling. Now I have the reputation of being the 'movie guy' in the office.

22

The same behaviour that you'd be judged for back home is not only tolerated here but sort of expected. I took my time getting used to it, because back in the UK you're not taught to proactively keep telling people about your achievements like this – it's considered inappropriate. In the States, however, this is apparently actually actively encouraged, especially while networking after work. It is considered a sign of competence and self-confidence! So I'm practising.

🎧 LISTENING PART 3

38 *Woman:* Hello, and welcome to *Business Today*! We've invited business coach Adam Scott to the studio today, to discuss a topic you've all long been interested in: what really makes an entrepreneur? Who should and who shouldn't be one? Adam, welcome.
Man: Hi, Shannon. Great to be on the show!

Woman: So. Business owner? Entrepreneur? Are they the same?
Man: On business cards, sometimes, but, in my opinion, in real life 'business owner' is more of a job title, while being an entrepreneur is a mindset, a lifestyle.
Woman: How so?
Man: Well, a 'business owner' might take over or, occasionally, even start a more predictable, more traditional kind of business because 'it's a great opportunity', 'it's the only thing I enjoy doing or know how to do', or 'I couldn't let this business die'. They've usually been in their industry for a long time and don't innovate so vigorously when they take over. An 'entrepreneur', on the other hand, will often say things like, 'I saw a better way of doing things', or 'I saw a need in the market for X'.
Woman: Sometimes these two categories surely overlap though, right? Can you tell us your opinion on this, please?
Man: Oh, yes. When I'm coaching a new client, one of the first questions I consider is, which approach do they seem to be following: that of an owner or a more visionary entrepreneur?
Woman: In their day-to-day lives, what're the differences between their activities?
Man: Business owners are more concerned with the smooth running of their company. They focus on solving problems. They envision a world where employees do their jobs well, customers pay on time, and software or equipment always functions as it was designed. Whenever there is a glitch in these, they step up to solve the issue. In this sense it's a more reactive approach, I think.
Woman: As opposed to that of an entrepreneur, which is …
Man: Proactive. True entrepreneurs go beyond maintaining things; they learn to question them and sometimes even create new industries if they are really bold.
Woman: And what about their views of their future? How does a business owner think about it as opposed to an entrepreneur?
Man: Excellent question! Very differently, in fact. Business owners tend to name their business after themselves, or build their company on their own skills. They then sometimes struggle to train their employees to standard, and to delegate to them, but this is another topic. We could say that they 'trade in their time for money' as their business model, that is to say they typically don't seek ways to scale their business, just maintain it stable, without delegating or outsourcing much. And they're often not conscious about tomorrow.
Woman: Entrepreneurs on the other hand …
Man: Well, they often have what we call an 'exit strategy', so are not likely to merge their own persona so completely with their firm's. One way to do this is by choosing a more neutral or operational name that anyone could call their

own, and hiring more skilled employees for certain aspects of the work, to be able to delegate more. Their approach tends to be much more consciously hands off. They want to escape getting too involved in the operational aspects of the company to be able to work on expanding their vision instead.

Woman: So what this means is that entrepreneurs like to work 'on' the business, not 'in' the business?

Man: That would be a great summary, yes.

Woman: Adam, thank you for coming in to raise some awareness of this interesting question.

Man: Thanks for inviting me.

Keys

Test 1

Reading

PART 1
Training

1 a
2 **1** endorsement, falling **2** negative feedback, improve **3** persuaded, make a difference to their lives **4** interest, well ahead of **5** traditional way, not effective **6** Be clear, group of people **7** necessary, draw attention to
All the words above give you very important and specific information. They will all be paraphrased in the four sections. Because the idea of cause and effect runs throughout the text, the linking words *lead to* and *in order to* are paraphrased frequently. For this reason, they are not particularly helpful for locating the information needed for statements 1 and 4. The words *product* and *launch* occur throughout the text, as does the idea of *buying*. For this reason, there is little point trying to match any of the statements with parts of the text containing the same words.
3 **1** C: A good review from an influencer (= an endorsement) can mean thousands of fans taking notice and spreading the word about your product. Having said that, choose your influencer carefully. If they somehow damage their reputation, (= this suggests the wrong person) you will quickly see your profit margins decline (= product sales will fall).
2 B: Don't be defensive if they find flaws (= they find problems and give you negative feedback); their comments will allow you to strengthen your product (= improve your product) before it goes to market.
3 D: Another idea is to publish an infographic convincing people of the need for (= people need to be persuaded) your product; explain what problem your product was created to solve or how it will help them do something better (= how the product will make a difference to their lives).
4 C: When you are confident you have the best possible version of your product, start making announcements (= begin to promote) at least eight weeks before it goes on sale (= well ahead of). A pre-launch video campaign, for example, will awaken customers' curiosity (= it will make customers interested).
5 A: Long-established companies may recall a time when launching a new product simply involved arranging interviews with reporters. Reviews would then be published (= the traditional way) around the launch date, guaranteeing publicity. However, unless companies are willing to recognise that this approach no longer holds consumer attention, the product is likely to fail (= companies must accept that the traditional way is not effective because the product won't attract attention and sell).
6 B: Before considering a possible launch date, ensure you know (= be clear about) your target market (= group of people), so you can avoid wasting time making announcements to the wrong audience.
7 D: If sales take off after the official launch date, you can congratulate yourself on a job well done. However, you must now (= it is necessary) intensify your efforts to keep your product in the spotlight (= draw attention to your product).
4 1, 5, 6

Exam Practice

1 B: Text B contains the key *a long history of innovation* and the ability to *look at our back catalogue*. Text D refers to *returning to well-tried concepts*, but this is not described as positive.
2 D: Text D has an example of the experience in the statement, with the employees staying with families to see their car use for themselves. Text C refers to *thinking outside our comfort zone*, but not with reference to experiencing a product.
3 A: Text A explains how a strategy could be changed – *repackaging the existing product or service*. Text C mentions reviews, but not with regard to a changing of company strategy.
4 B: Text B contains the warning that *most innovation will require a period of time to pass before its impact can be felt*. Text A mentions *the first few weeks after launch* but is focusing on the dangers of not being flexible about the decisions you make at this time, rather than the time it takes for benefits to show.
5 D: Text D mentions the need for a willingness to *quickly kill an idea*. Text A also talks about reactions to problems, but with an opposite idea – to try different approaches.
6 A: Text A mentions the dangers of over-testing an idea *to the point where you lose sight of your original concept*. Text B mentions the importance of research and development, but without the negative aspect.

7 C: The idea of surprise comes in Text C with the phrase *unexpected areas of the value chain*. The idea of being 'unexpected' comes through in text A with *goes against logic* but this is with regard to testing, not areas of the business where innovation is important.

PART 2
Training

1 a 3 b 4 c 1 d 2 e 5

2 1 f 2 c 3 g 4 d 5 a 6 b 7 e

3 1 B: For example, <u>it is often stated</u> (= this repeats the idea in the text before the gap of *claims made in the numerous online articles*) that health products or services are <u>best promoted in green, while fast food outlets should stick to red</u> (= these are the suggestions mentioned at the start of the next sentence after the gap).

2 A: In this way, <u>the same, oversimplified messages</u> (= this refers back to the idea of repeating information) about the way customers respond to colour continue to spread. (In the text after the gap, *many of them* refers back to these messages.)

3 E: It's more the case that <u>this group of consumers</u> (= refers back to *women*) may be forced to buy an item in <u>this colour</u> (= *pink*), since there is no alternative. (This sentence shows the real reason why women buy pink products, in contrast with the misconception in the text before the gap.)

4 C: There has recently been <u>a shift in thinking</u> (= companies no longer think that all kitchen appliances must be white), however, and now <u>they</u> (= the appliances) are also available in blue and yellow.

5 F: Similarly, buttons such as 'Buy Now' or 'Get Started' will <u>contrast sharply</u> (= repeats the idea that they can *easily distinguish themselves*) with the other text or images on a webpage. (*Contrast sharply* is also paraphrased in the text after the gap – *stands out*.)

4 In this way = therefore, Indeed = in fact, however = but, In contrast with = unlike, It's more the case = In truth/In fact, Similarly = likewise, For example = for instance

Exam Practice

8 E: The sentence contains *also* which links to the previous sentence start of *One way ...* . The topic also follows on with an example of places to find advice.

9 F: The phrase *the organisation's process* links appropriately with the pronoun *it* in *Find out how it works*. The use of *Additionally* suggests that a new, but related, piece of information is coming.

10 A: This sentence gives an example of the things to include in your business case. The sentence following the gap also refers more specifically to *records of specific achievements and events*.

11 C: The use of *these options* in the sentence following the gap tells us that the sentence must contain more than one idea, as well as following the topic. Sentence C has *elements ... that could be expanded* and a reference to *challenges* and *more responsibility*.

12 D: This sentence contains the phrase *Doing so* (where *so* means *this*, referring back to the sentence before the gap). It is also referenced after the gap with the idea of considering an offer carefully, which further links to *making a decision* in the gapped sentence.

PART 3
Training

1 *Make meetings count* can be paraphrased as *how to make meetings useful and important*. The subheading suggests that it is not necessary to have *a lot* of meetings. Instead, we can achieve more and fulfil aims if we have fewer, but more effective meetings.

3 1 C: The writer explains that 'Every minute spent at a meeting is time *they* (= the employees) could otherwise have spent on getting through *tasks actually assigned to them* (= they can't do the work they are supposed to do, so they have low personal productivity)'.

2 A: The writer suggests that 'the employee can *enquire* (=seek information) what their colleague specifically *hopes to achieve* (= the purpose) by having the meeting and how they can help their colleague achieve it'.

4 1 A: Candidates might be distracted by 'Respondents report having to spend up to 25% of their working day sitting around tables with colleagues, <u>often listening in</u> to discussions about projects that do not directly concern them.' However, all we know from this part of the text is that employees frequently listen to other people talking; we don't know whether they want to give their point of view or not.

B: The sentence 'the responses to recent workplace surveys may surprise some CEOs' might be distracting because the option refers to 'senior management'. However, the writer doesn't mention anything about the CEOs criticising staff.

D: The writer begins the first paragraph with 'It goes without saying that <u>collaboration</u> (= teamwork) is vital to the success of any business'. However, there is no suggestion that employees fail to realise this. The point is simply that many meetings are a waste of time, and don't lead to success.

2 B: The writer concludes the second paragraph by saying 'In some cases, the sender may decide a sit-down meeting is unnecessary after all'. However, this decision to cancel a meeting is the invitation sender's decision. There is no suggestion that employees should demand a reduction in the number of meetings.

C: Some candidates might be distracted by 'how they can help their colleague achieve it'. However, this is referring to the purpose of a meeting, not to general organisation.

D: The line 'a respectful "The project sounds interesting" might be distracting. This could certainly be a tactful way to initially respond to an invitation. However, the writer does not refer to people who might be *over-sensitive* (= easily upset) if their invitations are refused.

Exam Practice

13 C: This option mentions *increasing ... storage capabilities* which appears in the text as *measures to maximise capacity in ... the warehouses*.

14 A: This option explains that Atmos's success made FrontRow attractive – this is implied in the text by the phrase *in the run up to flotation, this parallel proved useful ...* .

15 B: This option is paraphrased in the text by the phrase *being able to set its own charging structure ...* .

16 D: This option is reflected in the text with the idea that products need to be *new and exciting*, so limited amounts of stock are bought, which ensures rapid turnover.

17 A: The phrase *popular celebrity bloggers and social media influencers* shows they have driven the company success with the target market, giving the answer A.

18 B: The phrase *trading updates are unlikely to disappoint ... remains encouraging* gives the answer B.

PART 4
Training

1 **a** The CEO, Graham Stapleton, plans to reduce the range of goods that Halfords sells, and focus on cycling and motoring. The plans include selling electric bikes, and increasing the number of bike shops, garages and repair services. It's not yet clear whether the plans include making a bid for Evans Cycles.
   b Investors are worried because the cost of the changes and improvements will be about £60m a year. This means that the company won't make a profit for two years, and share prices have already fallen as a result.

2 1 g 2 f 5 b 6 e 8 d 9 a

3 1 a–i, b–ii 2 a–i, b–ii 3 a–ii, b–i 4 a–ii, b–i 5 a–i, b–ii

4 1 D 2 A 3 B 4 C 5 D 6 B 7 A 8 C 9 A 10 B 11 D

Exam Practice

19 D: the collocation of *adopting a technique* leads us to option D. While we can also 'value a technique' the idea of 'choosing to value something' doesn't work here.

20 B: *Perks* best fits the idea of an extra benefit here. *Bonuses* tends to be used when talking about salaries; *additions* is very general and, like *promises*, doesn't fit the context.

21 A: *Award* is the only one of the set that reflects the idea of giving something of value to customers. The other verbs all express the general idea of giving or receiving, without the idea of value.

22 C: *Redeem* is the only one with the meaning of 'exchanging'; the others do describe managing the awarded points but don't have the idea of getting something in return.

23 B: *Specifically* fits with the idea of targeting a plan or policy at a customer; the other adverbs do not have this precise meaning.

24 D: *Build* is the only option that collocates with *trust* and has the idea of describing an action that businesses need to do.

25 A: *Advantage* collocates with *take* and gives the meaning of 'allow customers to access something worthwhile'. Although *note* and *control* also collocate with *take*, the meaning does not fit here.

26 A: *Incentive* expresses the idea of providing a reason. The other options do not include this (*resolution* and *determination*) or work with the following word (we could say a *purpose for* but not *purpose enough*)

27 D: *Awareness* fits the context; *notification* and *enjoyment* do not express the idea of customers recognising your product. The option *response* is not followed by *of* in this context.

28 B: *Stand out* has the meaning of 'being different', and also collocates with *from*. Although the others are common phrasal verbs, they express different ideas, e.g. *bounce back* means to recover from a problem.

29 A: *Recognition* best gives the idea of what a customer should experience when seeing your brand. The remaining options do not express this, e.g. an *obligation* is a requirement for someone to do something and *appreciation* has the meaning of 'liking', but that is not the same as customers remembering your logo, which is the context.

30 C: *Differentiate* is the only one that fits the context of understanding the importance of being different to other brands. The other options include words meaning 'change', which does not fit the context; they also would not be followed by *from* here.

31 A: *Connect* has the idea of communicating on an emotional level. Although *join* fits grammatically, this word has a more physical meaning so isn't appropriate for the context. The remaining two options would not be followed by *with* here.

32 C: *Attention* completes a common phrase, especially with the preposition *on* that follows. Other options do not collocate accurately – you would be more likely to say '*give*' time/consideration (to something) and '*raise*' concern is more natural.

33 D: *Highlight* means showing something to others, which fits the context. The options *advertise* and *feature* would

be something a business would do, not a customer, and *support* does not express the idea of telling others.

PART 5
Training
1 **1** H **2** G **3** B **4** E **5** F **6** A **7** D **8** C
2 Sentence 4 is correct.

Exam Practice
34 CORRECT
35 WHICH: *which* would be followed here by *result from*, not *resulting from*
36 MANY: *much* would fit here, but *many* doesn't fit with a singular idea of 'benefitting'
37 UP: not used in the phrasal verb *come together*
38 THE: the definite article (*the*) would only be needed if there were a previous reference in the text to *expertise*
39 AS: there is no comparison made between benefits to companies and consumers
40 CORRECT
41 THOSE: *those* would need to be a reference to a previous mention of *financial resources*
42 OF: this would fit with *the development of* but not with *developing*
43 MOST: *very* would fit the sentence, but there is no superlative meaning in this sentence
44 EACH: does not fit with plural *manufacturers*
45 CORRECT

Writing

PART 1 (EMAIL)
Training
2 **1** True **2** True **3** False. You should write between 40 and 50 words
3 Text **A** is too short and too direct, for example the reader might not know the name of the writer. Using *I want a meeting* instead of *I'd like a meeting* might be too rude for the reader. The student has also used some of the same words from the question instead of using their own words, e.g. *Some of our clients have recently complained about problems accessing the building our company works in* is almost exactly the same as the words in the question. It would be better to say something like *Some of our customers have mentioned they are having difficulties accessing the building.*
Text **B** is a better text, but it is too long and perhaps too informal with words like *Hi John* and *reckoned*.
Text **C** is the best answer. It covers all the points, is neutral to formal in style and is the right length. The writer of the email has used their own words, e.g. *complaints* instead of *complained* and *enter* instead of *access*.

Exam Practice
1 **1** All the staff in the company.
2 In this question, *saying what* and *explaining* have a similar meaning, so for each point you need to give some extra details or say why something is happening. *Telling* means giving an instruction to the reader. In this case, you will often use language like *you should …* or *I would like you to …*
3 You could be quite formal: *Dear staff / Best regards*. Or you could be more informal: *Good morning everyone / Thanks*. But remember that you are writing to staff, not friends, so you can't be too informal. Whichever register you choose, be consistent all through the email.

2 **Model answer**
Good morning everyone
I am writing to invite you to a special meeting next week about our new marketing campaign. The meeting will be on Thursday at 13.30 in meeting room 4. If you are unable to come to the meeting, please let me know by 17.00 on Wednesday.
Thanks
[your name]

Notes
- *A good answer which fully addresses the question*
- *All three content points are clearly covered and expanded in an appropriate way*
- *Uses a good range of language even in such a short price of writing, including present continuous, modal verbs (will) and a conditional structure (If you are unable …)*
- *No grammar mistakes*
- *Successfully re-phrases language from the question e.g. to ask → to invite*
- *Slightly mixed register: 'Good morning everybody' is more informal than 'I am writing to invite you'*

PART 2 (REPORT)
Training
1 **1** False. You have one compulsory task. **2** True **3** True **4** False. You must use all of the handwritten notes.
5 True. You can spend more than 30 minutes, but this will mean you do not have enough time to complete the other part of the writing paper.
2 **1** business correspondence **2** proposal **3** report
3 You have to include everything in the handwritten notes.
4 All of the information is included. This is a good answer with a clear structure.
5 **1** While **2** and **3** as **4** As a result
6 **1** Although **2** as well as **3** because **4** Due to this

Exam Practice

1 **1** The purchasing manager (NOT the manager of the supplier, MCP Ltd)
2 To review the work of the supplier over the past year and, using this information, recommend whether or not to give them a new contract when the current contract ends.
3 With a clear recommendation **of whether to renew** the contract with the supplier.

2 **Model answer**

Report on MCP Ltd

The aim of this report is to review the current contract with our supplier, MCP Ltd.
MCP have been supplying our company for nearly one year now and we need to decide whether to renew their contract. The contract finishes on 21st May.
This report will look at MCP's deliveries, quality and price.

Deliveries
Although a number of MCP's deliveries were late, this was not the fault of MCP as they were caused by bad weather in the winter.

Quality
MCP's product quality was consistently very high and we never had to return anything they supplied us with.

Price
MCP's prices were very competitive at the start of their contract, but some new competitors such as Wilsons are now offering similar products at a lower price.

Recommendation
It is recommended that we sign another contract with MCP, because of their high quality and reliable deliveries, but that we should try to negotiate lower prices.
[your name]

Notes
Positive
- A clear answer with all five of the content points covered
- Content points are expanded on and reasons are given for answers where needed
- Effective use of headings to help organise the report
- Appropriate register all through the report
- A good range of language with past, present and future forms used accurately

Negative
- Slightly over the word limit
- Includes information which was copied from the question and which the Purchasing Manager already knows: 'MCP have been supplying our company for nearly one year now and we need to decide ...'

Listening

PART 1
Training

1 **1** a surname **2** a number **3** an address or the name of a town
2 **1** Lipton **2** 700 **3** TS17 5PJ
3 a 3 b 1 c 2 d 2 e 3 f 1
4 **1** 9(th) **2** quarterly report **3** sandals and shorts **4** delays **5** recruiter **6** social media **7** environment **8** shoes **9** decision-making **10** judges **11** eat **12** morning routine

Exam Practice

1 April: Amanda wants to join the course that is *starting soon*, and although she first thinks it is in May, the man tells her that its *first workshop will be on 30th April*.
2 keyword optimisation: The man asks what Amanda *might find most useful to learn about*, then adds *Besides keyword optimisation, obviously* and *The course will deal with that a lot!*
3 bloggers: The man tells Amanda that *other popular issues include if you should have one or multiple* (= many) *bloggers*.
4 field experts: He says the course will also deal with *if you should seek out experts in their fields* (= field experts) *rather than just online content writing ...*
5 old mill: The woman says that the building complex is going to be *right next to* (= near) *the Cathedral*, but this is given in the notes already. She also says it will be *behind the old mill*, which also means *near*.
6 €900: The woman states that *apartments will typically cost about €900 per month*. Later on she mentions another number (€1,500), but this is what *renting a studio apartment in the area* costs.
7 WiFi: The woman says that the apartments will *come with utilities and WiFi, and even housekeeping*, of which *utilities* and *housekeeping* are already in the notes, so the answer is *WiFi*.
8 three months: The woman says that another competitive advantage is that tenants will be able to rent for *as little as three months*.
9 55 billion: *projected number of* is introduced as *there will be ...* .
10 9 billion: The man states that *this* (= the number of IoT devices by 2025) *is way higher than the 9 billion in 2017*.
11 wearables: The man says that *we also expect* (= (is) projected to) *the wearables market to grow*, then when the woman asks what that means, he gives the examples of *smart watches, fitness trackers, etc.*, of which *smart watches* is included as a clue in the notes.
12 healthcare industry: *is going to seriously impact* is the same as *likely to influence*

PART 2
Training

1 Possible answers
A manage, uncertainty **B** pay attention **C** work, alone **D** modest **E** understand, complex, problems **F** not waste time **G** cautious **H** handle money

2 A unsure / not sure, unclear / not clear, (no) guarantee, questionable, (to) doubt
B good at listening, distracted
C on their own, isolated / in isolation, without, (a) team
D arrogant, conceited, to boast, humble, humility

3 Possible answers
E (to) grasp, complicated, difficult, harder, issue, question, matter
F spend, be aware of, be conscious of, time management, to manage one's time
G (to) (take) risks, safe, responsible / responsibility
H financial(ly), good / better at, manag(ing), spend (carefully)

4 1 G 2 B 3 C 4 A 5 D

5 Speaker 2: good at listening
Speaker 3: on their own, isolated
Speaker 4: unclear
Speaker 5: humble

Exam Practice

Section One

13 D: *Nothing is worse than trying to give a presentation on a topic* (= subject) *you are not fully confident about* (= an expert of). The man also says that it helps him when he remembers why he is an *authority on* (= expert of) *the subject*.

14 F: Being *familiar* with a presentation means that you have rehearsed it and know it well. Also, *prepared (enough)* is the same as *rehearse (a lot) in advance*.

15 A: *check the … technology* is the equivalent of *considering your tools*. *Equipment failure* or *no internet connection* are also examples of the latter.

16 B: First the woman mentions presentations that were *just not right for the participants* (= audience). She then goes on to say that from this she learnt to *always be sensitive* and *identify* (= tailor it to) *the participants' concerns*, etc.

17 H: The phrase *upcoming material further along* implies a connection among the parts of a presentation, while the expression *move from one part onto the next more smoothly* gives the idea of the material being *linked*.

Section Two

18 F: The man says he likes to *approach* (introducing any major change) by *talking together about a problem we've been struggling with* and then referring back to the change as a *necessary response* (= reason).

19 H: Being *completely aware* (of) or *acknowledging* something equals *admitting* it. *Annoying, confusing* and *tough* are negative adjectives and are the same as *difficult*.

20 B: *Getting* (somebody) *on board* is the same as *convince* them, and *senior team members* can be considered as *key employees* in this context. When the man says *I often tell them why I believe …* , he also describes the process of convincing somebody, while *sell it to the rest of the team* implies that not all the workers are involved at first.

21 A: The woman says it is important to keep *checking for signs* (= monitoring) that everybody is *on board and cooperating*, although workers might *disagree with* or even *sabotage* things (= resistance.)

22 D: *Schedule to meet up with* somebody means the same as *follow up* with them. The man also says *a few days after*, which is the same as *later*.

PART 3
Training

1 Possible answers
1 believes **2** first key thing **3** second (question)
4 freedom **5** after a networking event **6** better at sales
7 family **8** charging money

2 Students' own answers
Some possible answers:
– the lifestyle of being an entrepreneur might mean more freedom; some thoughts on what this might mean in practice
– how to become better at sales (i.e. some practical tips mentioned / discussed)
– being an entrepreneur and having a family; time management, etc.

3 Students' own answers

4 1 B 2 A 3 C 4 C 5 A 6 A 7 C 8 B

Exam Practice

23 C: Vanessa says that a podcast is produced by people *coming from any sector* (= various industries).
Distraction A: The host invites Vanessa to clarify what *podcasts* and *monetising* are *for the sake of our less tech-savvy listeners*. He is talking about the show's audience, not that of podcasts.
Distraction B: Vanessa is not saying that podcasts can be *produced* by anybody with a mobile device, but *downloaded* (= consumed).

24 A: Vanessa says that *podcasts often come in a series* (= bulk).
Distraction B: She says that content is produced *by* people *coming from any sector* (= different fields), not audiences *in* them.
Distraction C: Although Vanessa says that *monetising is finding ways to make it* (= your podcast) *earn you some money*, she does not explicitly state that this necessarily comes before deciding *to start producing (…) content*.

25 B: The man says that it is hard for the average listener to understand monetisation *while accessing content (...) without having to pay* (= do not cost money).
Distraction A: Although Vanessa is talking about how *podcasters frequently (...) show that they're an expert on their topic*, she does not say that they find this surprising.
Distraction C: Although the man is talking about the listeners accessing content that is *sometimes of top quality*, he does not claim that listeners find this surprising; only that they do not have to *pay for an episode or a subscription*.

26 B: When she introduces the term, Vanessa also says *or as it is also sometimes called* (= has another common name), *performance marketing*.
Distraction A: Vanessa says that *You will earn money only when someone makes an actual purchase*, which is the opposite of *yields a reliable income*.
Distraction C: Although *online courses* (= educational content) are mentioned earlier, Vanessa does not say that affiliate marketing should only be used by retailers specialising in this.

27 C: In Vanessa's opinion affiliate marketing works best when you promote products or services that *you also happily use* (= like).
Distraction A: Vanessa only says that the *small start-up owners* she coaches ask her if recommending products can *ever be authentic*. She does not say that affiliate marketing is *ideal* (only) for them.
Distraction B: She uses the phrase *familiar with*, not to talk about the audience but the podcaster.

28 B: Vanessa explains that *sponsorship* (= traditional advertising) is *calculated based on 'Cost Per Mile'*, then describes that this means that you receive a fee for every thousand downloads. The man also says that *for sponsorship to be effective you need a large, engaged audience*, which Vanessa confirms by saying *Indeed*.
Distraction A: When asked *who seeks out whom* (i.e. podcaster the sponsor or the other way around), Vanessa says that it *varies*.
Distraction C: The words *calculate* and *purchase* are used, but it is not highlighted that podcasters should *calculate the number of purchases accurately* as such.

29 A: Vanessa says that affiliate marketing is preferred by beginner podcasters because *they don't need to have a minimum number of listeners* (= a large audience).
Distraction B: The word *engaged* is used by the host, but differently, to talk about the sponsorship model, not affiliate marketing. He says that *for sponsorship to be effective you need a large, engaged audience*.
Distraction C: According to Vanessa it is in the sponsorship model where the podcaster receives *a fee for every thousand downloads*.

30 C: Vanessa describes the purchasing process and says that the listener of a podcast will often be able to claim their discount (*voucher*) by using a *promo code* (= a key word).
Distraction A: The words *voucher* and *download* are used, but nothing is said of how the vouchers actually have to be *downloaded* for the discount to become available.
Distraction B: A given name (*Tom*) is used, but only as an example of a possible promo code of a podcast whose host (not listener) may be called Tom.

Speaking

PART 1
Training

1 **1** paper **2** marksheet **3** examiners **4** morning **5** three **6** anything

2

Home	Studies	Job
a, e, i	b, c, g	b, c, d, e, f, g, h, i

3 Phase 1 – a, b, c, d, f, g; Phase 2 – e, h, i

4 For all of the questions, the **first** answers are the worst because they are too short and do not show the examiner how much you know. The **second** answers are better, but they still do not provide a lot of information for the examiner to give you marks. The **third** answers are excellent as they give extra information but are not too long.

5 **1** report to **2** in charge of **3** responsible for **4** deal with **5** producing **6** oversee **7** involves **8** intern

PART 2
Training

1 **1** three **2** make **3** stop **4** brief **5** pay
3 1, 2, 4, 7, 8

PART 3
Training

1 Sentence 2 is false – You should keep talking for the full three minutes (or four minutes if you are in a group of three candidates).

2

Starting the discussion	Giving an opinion	Making a suggestion
• Are you ready to start? • Would you like me to start? • Let's start. • Shall we start by talking about ...?	• In my opinion ... • Personally, I believe ... • From my experience, I've found ... • I'd say ...	• What do you think about ...? • How about if we ...? • Would it be possible to ...? • Do you think it would be a good idea to ...?
Agreeing	Disagreeing	
• Yes, absolutely. • I couldn't agree more. • That sounds good to me. • That's right.	• I understand what you're saying, but ... • I agree to a point, but ... • I'm not sure I agree. • OK, but what about ...?	

3 1 would 2 actually 3 seems 4 view 5 believe
4 1 b 2 c 3 e 4 d 5 a

Test 2

Reading

PART 1
Training

Review 1 7 **2** different **3** specific information and detail **4** No, they will be paraphrased.
1 1 d 2 h 3 c 4 f 5 e 6 a 7 g 8 b

Exam Practice

1 C: Section C refers to *poor weather* to give the key. Section A is talking about difficult situations, but not in *one region*.
2 B: Section B compares viewpoints on customer needs, with Kingfisher disagreeing with a previous comment. Section D focuses on a different section of the market, rather than having a different view about them.
3 A: Section A says that the *changes go deeper*, accounting for the benefits taking longer. Section B talks about doing business in a range of countries, but without the idea of taking longer to see benefits.
4 D: Section D states Kingfisher has *rejected attempts to impose a more central management structure*.
5 D: Section D mentions that Kingfisher is coming under *increasing calls to split it* (= Screwfix) *off, which they will resist*. Section C refers to another US company fighting off a takeover.
6 B: Section B talks about problems of a rival (Homebase), but of another cheaper company (B&M) moving into the business.
7 C: Section C mentions the property owned by Kingfisher. Section D mentions out-of-town retail parks and industrial estates, but not as assets to attract investors.

PART 2
Training

Review 1 five (out of six remaining sentences) **2** b, c, d
1 1 AM 2 AM 3 N 4 AM 5 AM 6 AM 7 AM 8 AM 9 AM 10 N
2 a 2 b 5, 7 c 1, 3, 4, 6, 8, 9, 10 d 1, 8, 9

Exam Practice

8 E: The words *The outstanding balance* refer back to *split into two parts, with the first ...* and the sentence after again mentions the candidate starting, which is also in the gapped sentence.
9 A: The use of *It* here goes back to the rebate, and the pronoun *this* in the sentence before the gap. The idea of the sliding scale is continued with the mention of *negotiate the structure* (of the scale) in the next sentence.
10 D: The use of *Even better* suggests that one idea has already been given previously, and the sentence after the gap refers to *Reading these* which links back to *customer testimonials*.
11 F: The sentence refers to *this crucial initial* stage, and again continues the theme with the reference to speaking to candidates in the sentence following the gap, and the use of *they* refers back to the *agency*.
12 C: *References* are in the plural, linking to the pronoun *these* in the gapped sentence. There's also a link between *on your behalf* and *give you more confidence* in the following sentence.

PART 3
Training

Review 1 6 **2** Names and dates, and business-related phrases which would occur in one paragraph only, rather than throughout the text. There may also be a line or paragraph reference, e.g. *The writer uses the expression 'back to the drawing board' in line 62 to show that ...*, or *What is the writer's main point in the third paragraph?* **3** a, d

1 **1** f **2** g **3** d **4** b **5** h **6** c **7** e **8** a

2 **1** set **2** turn **3** ended **4** called **5** pay **6** drawn **7** put **8** spell

Exam Practice

13 D: The answer comes from Andy's observations about the drinks market while he was working.

14 A: The answer comes from the phrase *this proved a great starting point to pitch to a company.*

15 B: The answer comes from the reference to getting a minimum viable product to market, then making changes as needed.

16 A: The answer is supported by the idea that the general design was good, and therefore only needed small changes on each product run.

17 C: The answer comes from the line *the opportunities are there for start-ups to disrupt markets ... .*

18 D: The answer comes from the beginning of the last paragraph *... public sentiment will lump Natural Power in with its competitors.* Andy's opinion comes later, when we learn he's not sure whether this will be a problem – so therefore must be of concern.

PART 4
Training

Review 1 15 **2** vocabulary, e.g. collocation, fixed expressions, phrasal verbs **3** similar **4** a, c (b: Part 4 only tests your understanding of the meaning of verbs, not the way they are formed; d: Three options will definitely be wrong, not 'less correct' than the right option.)

1 **1** d **2** c **3** a **4** b **5** c **6** b

2 **1** strategy **2** investment **3** drawback **4** application **5** appointment **6** impression

3 **1** c **2** b **3** a **4** a

Exam Practice

19 B: *Response* is the accurate collocation in the set. Option C, *answer*, could work with *as an answer to ...* but not with the sentence as it stands.

20 D: *Picking up* is the phrasal verb with the meaning that fits with the *happen to meet* idea in the text. Options A and C refer to creating a new business, and option B has the meaning of finding information.

21 B: *Financial* has the meaning of buying / providing a service which fits the context. The other adjectives do not have the meaning of 'a business transaction'.

22 B: *Commitment* has the idea of giving time to a plan, and also collocates with *make*. While options A and D also collocate with *make*, A does not fit the business tone and D does not work with the idea of the timescale.

23 B: *Caution* collocates with *advise*, and also supports the idea later in the following sentence, where strategists suggest a more sensible networking idea, which is missing from the others in the set.

24 A: *Agreement* is the only one in the set which has the idea of a promise to do business.

25 B: *Highly* is the only adverb in the set that has a strong collocation with *likely*.

26 D: *Recommend* works with the overall context, and is the only one in the set which fits logically with the preposition *to* which follows.

27 B: *Resulting* has the idea of linking the networking event with future work possibilities. The other options do not explain this connection.

28 A: *Deal* collocates with *struck* further in the sentence, unlike the others in the set.

29 B: *Efficiency* brings in the idea of saving time, and explains why you might see a *positive effect* and also be *more productive*. Both these phrases link to *efficiency* in a way that the other options, although positive in meaning, do not.

30 C: *Leads* refers to information about who might be interested in doing business with you in future, which fits with the phrase *could become sales* in a way that the others do not.

31 A: *Opportunity* collocates accurately with *miss out*. The other options do not have the idea of 'having a good chance for something', which is the context here.

32 B: *Beneficial* expresses the idea of the overall advantage of a situation, which is lacking in the other options.

33 D: *Recognition* explains best how a networker should see a networking situation, which the others do not. Option A, *evaluation*, for example, refers to judging success or failure, which does not fit the context here.

PART 5
Training

Review 1 12 **2** Lines may contain one error, but not two. Sentences which spread across two or more lines may contain two or more errors – but only one per line. **3** No **4** You should write CORRECT.

1 **1a** incorrect **b** correct **2a** incorrect **b** correct **3a** correct **b** incorrect **4a** correct **b** incorrect **5a** correct **b** incorrect **6a** incorrect **b** correct **7a** correct **b** incorrect **8a** incorrect **b** correct

Exam Practice

34 CORRECT

35 AN: the plural *lines* mean that *an* is incorrect here

36 BEEN: the tense used here is present simple passive; *been* would be used for present perfect passive

37 THOSE: *those* would generally refer to something outside of, or further back in, the text

38 CORRECT

39 AS: reading the previous and the following lines shows us that *as* is incorrect here – there's no comparison given

40 SUCH: this would refer back to a previous reference to *clear communication lines* – there is none here

41 OF: *suppliers* is part of a list following on from *communication lines with* and is unnecessary

42 WHO: there is no clause in this sentence that provides the 'extra information' that this pronoun would require (i.e. a relative clause)

43 CORRECT

44 SO: this word would be used to refer back to and expand on a previous idea – this link is not present

45 HAD: the tense here is present simple, expressing general advice; the present perfect is therefore incorrect here

Writing

PART 1
Training

1 1 explaining 2 apologising 3 complaining 4 requesting
5 offering 6 apologising 7 explaining 8 informing
9 requesting 10 informing 11 complaining 12 offering

2 1 to 2 for 3 for 4 to 5 for

3 1 I would like to apologise for not being able to go to the meeting.
2 I was very dissatisfied with the information I received.
3 Unfortunately, there was a problem with scheduling.
4 I can let you know my answer by the end of the week.
5 I would like to know when you can make the payment.
6 Please return your comments as soon as possible.

Exam Practice

1 1 Staff in the writer's department (which means that a more informal register could be appropriate).
2 In some cultures, the relationship between managers and staff is quite formal; in other cultures, it is less formal. Also, if you are writing to people above you in the company hierarchy, it is usually best to use a more formal register. In this task, most people will use a neutral register – not too formal or informal. The most important thing is to be consistent: don't use a mixture of formal and informal language.
3 The reason why the meeting room will be closed, how long it will be closed and what staff can do if they need to have meetings while it is closed.
4 You could explain what staff should do if they need to have meetings while the room is closed. Also, it is a good idea to say exactly which room is closed, e.g. room 2.

2 **Model answer**
Dear staff
Just to let you know that meeting room 2 will be closed on Monday and Tuesday next week, because we are going to install some new IT equipment for giving presentations. In the meantime, please use meeting rooms 1 and 3. Apologies in advance for any inconvenience.
Best regards
[your name]

Notes
- *A successful answer which addresses all three content points clearly in an appropriate and consistent register*
- *Well organised, although it would be better if the points were in the same order as the points in the question*
- *Content points 1 and 2 linked effectively*
- *Uses appropriate register*
- *Correct length*
- *Good range of language, with present and future forms and some more advanced vocabulary: 'to install'; 'in the meantime'*
- *No language errors*

PART 2
Training

1 1 a, report 2 a, business correspondence 3 b, report
4 b, proposal 5 b, business correspondence 6 a, proposal

2 1 It is recommended that …
2 In conclusion, we can see …
3 I look forward to hearing from you.
4 If there is anything you need, please do not hesitate to contact me.
5 There are the following recommendations:
6 It can be concluded that …

Exam Practice

1 1 To customers of the company you work for.
2 Probably not. For some points, you need to give the customers detailed information, but for others, such as the second note, you just need to say clearly which phone has the problem.
3 It is written to customers, so it should be more formal. An informal letter might not sound serious enough to a customer who has spent a lot of money on a product which doesn't work properly.
4 As the letter is to all the customers who have had a problem, the letter should begin *Dear customers*. The most appropriate ending to letters where the person is not addressed by name is *Yours faithfully*.

2 **Model answer**
Dear customers
I am sorry to have to tell you that some customers who have bought the Alphafone 5 might experience a minor technical issue.
When trying to access the internet using WiFi, there may be problems staying connected. This is because

of a problem we discovered during the manufacturing process.

I am pleased to inform you that the Alphafone 5 is still completely safe to use and, if you do not experience this problem, there is no need to return or replace your phone. If you would like a refund of your money, please return the phone to the retailer where you purchased your phone and we will be pleased to give you a full refund.

I apologise for any inconvenience caused. I hope you will continue to use Alphafone in future.

Yours faithfully

[your name]

Notes

- A clear answer with some advanced vocabulary used well: 'experience a minor technical issue'; 'manufacturing process'; 'purchased'
- All five content points are clearly covered and appropriately expanded. The real apology is at the end of the letter, which is fine.
- Correct length
- The register is appropriately formal and uses language typical of this type of letter
- The organisation is good, with the information effectively organised into paragraphs
- Key vocabulary has been rephrased, e.g. 'can continue using' → 'is still completely safe to use' 'money back' → 'refund'
- There is a range of language used including modal verbs: 'might', 'may', 'would', relative clauses: 'customers who ...' and conditional structures: 'If you do not ...'
- The overall effect on customers will be reassuring
- No language errors
- There is some repetition: 'problem', 'phone', 'refund'

Listening

PART 1
Training

1 **1** g, h: A noun is missing from this gap. Logically *a request* and *a complaint* would make sense in this context.
   2 c, f: A noun is missing from this gap. The answer has to be something that can be sold.
   3 b, e: A noun is missing from this gap. Companies either sell products or services. The question says *Maggie's company does* (and not, e.g. *produces*), so it probably provides *a service / some services*.
   4 a, d: A noun is missing from this gap. The answer is something that typically appears on a company's website or social media profile.

2 **1** g **2** c **3** e **4** a

3 **1** advice: The gap requires a noun. *Advice* is an (uncountable) noun. *Advise* is a verb, and *advises* is its form in the third person singular: *She advises me to ...* .
   2 see through: Although in the conversation you hear *But you saw right through it*, *saw* has to be changed to *see* to grammatically fit the gap, which includes the auxiliary *didn't*.
   3 contact request: The correct form of this compound noun is *contact request*. While compound nouns can often take the *-ing* form of a verb, this one does not.
   4 unlimited access: *excess* means 'too much of something' and it is pronounced with an /e/. *Access* means 'a means of approaching or entering a place' and it is pronounced with an /æ/.

4 Student's own answers

Exam Practice

1 trend: The woman says that *this is clearly* a *growing* (= increasing) *trend that is worth paying attention to* (= following).
2 work: *more control* is the same here as *more authority* (over your work)
3 vendors: Among the advantages in the notes it says that *you pick the people you do business with* (= choose business partners), *your customers* (= clients), which cue in the answer *vendors*.
4 creative occupations: *most typical* is expressed as *constitute the largest part of*, while *until now* is *so far*
5 business name: *must go with* is *(that it) matches* in the conversation
6 branding: When the woman asks why it is important, the man says that this *keep(s) your branding cohesive* (= unified).
7 visual: *memorable* is already expressed as *catchy* in the recording
8 relevant: The man suggests that a domain also needs to be relevant *to your business* (= your company) and *reflect* (= show) what it is about.
9 emails: The woman uses various phrases to signal that she is going to talk about the *reason* for the change (e.g. *as our team grew ...*, *I realised that ...*, *we would need a* and *To combat this ...*). After this she says that the *quantity of emails especially got overwhelming* (= too many).
10 project management: When she starts describing the new system, Sylvia first mentions that it is an *online (...) programme* (= software).
11 goals: She says that everyone *inputs* (= posts) four significant points from the previous week under the categories of *achievements* (= accomplishments), *disappointments* (= setbacks), *worries* (= fears) and goals.
12 senior team: Sylvia says that she *introduced it to* (= applied (it) with) the *senior team* first.

PART 2
Training

1. **1** c **2** d **3** e **4** a **5** b
2. *not a bad way to* = a good way to
   isn't uncommon = common
3. **C** (*Refrain* from using *un*balanced language = Use balanced language) and **H** (*Don't* assume *bad* motives = Assume good motives)
4. **1** C **2** A **3** E **4** H **5** G

Exam Practice

13. **D**: The man says that *there's so much more to be learnt at any workplace than just technological tricks* (= computer skills). He also seems to disapprove of *fancy mentoring programmes* that focus on *the latest apps*, which is another technological example.
14. **G**: The woman recommends *match(ing) employees to one another in an intentional manner* (= pairing the right people up), and also talks about dysfunctional programmes where people were assigned to one another *based on some random factor*.
15. **B**: The man mentions their failed mentoring system, which was a *disaster* because they forgot to *provide* (= give) some *key guidelines* (= clear instructions) from the outset (= beginning).
16. **A**: The woman talks about how if the *atmosphere* (= work environment) is not *supportive* (= positive), no mentoring programme will succeed at a company either.
17. **F**: After describing some current trends in mentoring programmes, the man says that these should not influence what *purpose* (= goal) is given to the programme at your company, as these should be *defined more by your company's* (= own) *needs*.
18. **H**: The woman talks about content that offers their customers *practical value* (= functional benefits), then goes on to give an example (their *'How-to' videos*).
19. **A**: The man says that writing *longer* (= lengthy) *blog entries* (= content) is a *winning strategy*, and that he no longer thinks that *the shorter the better*.
20. **C**: The woman talks about how there's *nothing more original than telling and listening to stories* (= (using) narratives).
21. **F**: To *engage* with something is the same as *interact* with it, so that it will be *discussed* and *shared*. The man also says that they like to create material that *invites our customers to do something in response to our ads*.
22. **D**: The words *brave* and *polarising* and the phrases *evokes* (= provokes) *some kind of strong* (= intense) *reaction* (= emotions) and *doesn't create indifference* are all cues for option D.

PART 3
Training

1. **1** B **2** A **3** C **4** B **5** B **6** C **7** A **8** C
2. **1** Option A is incorrect because the word *young* is used differently by Rebecca. She is not talking about some young *board members* but *young companies*. Option C is incorrect because although both words (*feasible* and *expanded*) are used, she is saying the opposite, namely that *If your company has expanded, it's time to* leave this *Me, Myself and I* mentality behind and assemble a board of directors.
   2 Option B is incorrect because although a *formal board of directors is only required (...) upon the interest of venture capital investors*, Rebecca is not saying that *entrepreneurs* think this. Option C is incorrect because although the word *argue* is used, it is not stated that *entrepreneurs* think that *boards* argue too much.
   3 Option A is incorrect because Rebecca recommends hiring an *advisory board*, as a *test drive* for when a *formal board of directors* is required. Option B is incorrect because the word *responsibilities* is used to talk about *advisory board* members' (legal and financial) responsibilities.
   4 Option A is incorrect because the interviewer is asking Rebecca for some rules or *recommendations*. Rebecca is not stating that the first board of directors should be chosen *through* recommendations. Option C is incorrect because the distraction *even if only advisory* refers to the first board of directors a founder / entrepreneur chooses. Rebecca does not say that the first board of directors should serve only as advisors.
3. **5** Answer: they tend to become 'yes people'
   Distractions: *they're going to give you* ~~advice~~ *whether you want it or not*; *These advisory boards are voluntary and have no legal and* ~~financial responsibilities~~.
   6 Answer: *you already pay those people* (= your accountant, attorney or marketing consultant) *to advise you*
   Distractions: *Why not? They might actually* ~~know~~ *a lot about your company!*; *You should be looking for people external to your company instead who are going to* ~~challenge~~ *you*.
   7 Answer: *a board too easily influenced by investors and their desire for short-term profit can be in conflict with the CEO's mission*
   Distractions: *You should be looking for people* ~~external~~ *to your company*; ~~legal or marketing~~ *consultant*.
   8 Answer: *You need to choose members who counterbalance your weaknesses. Many founders are tempted to choose board members who possess the same skills set as their own, but the best boards are those that bring strengths that are important to the company but aren't possessed by the founders.*
   Distractions: *If you're an* ~~IT expert~~, *bring on* ~~advisors that are good at sales~~.

Exam Practice

23 B: The cue introducing the woman's answer is *I think success in sales* (= selling anything) *today* (= nowadays) *all comes down to …*, after which she says companies need to be more *genuine* (= honest).
Distraction A: Although the concept of *traditional marketing* is mentioned, she actually says the opposite about them, namely that their time (era) is *over*.
Distraction C: Although the interviewer introduces the subject of the interview as *successful product launches*, Heather expands it to talk about selling in general and how it needs to be based on genuineness today.

24 A: To the interviewer's prompt: *I thought all advertising (…) was built on* (manipulation = controlling the client's mind), Heather replies with *Yes, 'was' being the operative word here*, which means she thinks advertisers are no longer doing this.
Distraction B: Heather believes live launches *should be avoided*, but she does not say that advertisers do this.
Distraction C: Again, it is Heather herself who disapproves of live launches, not advertisers.

25 C: A lot of examples of *engagement* are mentioned, e.g. *attention, instant exposure, traffic, many exciting leads*.
Distraction A: Heather talks about *expenses on* (= spending on) *ads*, not any revenue coming in from them.
Distraction B: Only *opportunities for partnerships* are mentioned, no details of actual partnerships caused by live launches.

26 B: She talks about how *new leads* (= subscribers) *have since unsubscribed* (= opted out of) *your mailing list*.
Distraction A: The word *afterwards* is not used here to talk about *subsequent* launches, and while the phrase *not that profitable after all* is used, it refers to live launches in general, not only future ones.
Distraction C: Heather only talks about how, if you take into account your *expenses on ads* after a live launch, you realise that they are not that profitable.

27 C: According to Heather it is not ideal to be *at the mercy of* (= dependent on) product launches, if these are *your only sources of income* (= single revenue).
Distraction A: Heather says about live launches (not evergreen campaigns) that these are a lot of work and leave you *totally exhausted*, but this is not why she says evergreen launches are *safer*.
Distraction B: While it is implied earlier that live launches require advertising (i.e by the mention of *expenses on ads*), this is not why evergreen launches are safer either.

28 C: Heather talks about the problems connected to not knowing how effective your *conversion funnel* is, and mentions a few examples of what might go wrong (e.g. *you might not know whether your video works, unsure if your emails and social media ads are on point*).
Distraction A: She is talking about optimising *targeting* customers (e.g with *emails and social media ads*), not about them struggling to *find you*.
Distraction B: Although she mentions that *you might not know whether your video works*, nothing is said of improving your *videos*, plural.

29 A: After she introduces the idea of companies respecting their clients (*it's time companies really started to respect their customers more*), she also talks about customers *buy(ing) your product* (= shop) *at a time relevant to them* (= when best for them).
Distraction B: While the idea of *highlighting their problems* is mentioned, the importance of *timing* anything is not.
Distraction C: Heather talks about how you might (erroneously) base your strategy on *assumptions*, not that companies have assumptions about their clients' problems (nor of this being respectful).

30 B: Heather believes that live launches will *entirely go out of fashion* (= disappear completely).
Distraction A: She says live launches do not *create a robust business model*, but does not say that she thinks this might change in the future.
Distraction C: Similarly, of live launches she says that these *do not help build trust with your clients* but does not imply that this will change.

Speaking

PART 1
Training

1 1 I'm sorry, could you repeat the question?
2 I didn't quite catch that. Could you say it again, please?
3 Would you mind repeating that, please?
4 What do you mean by …?
5 Could you be more specific, please?
6 Would you elaborate on that, please?
7 Do you mean …?
8 Could you give me an example, please?

2

Linking ideas	Giving an example	Giving a reason
as well, so, and, then, also	such as, like, for example	as, because

3 a I'm sorry, could you repeat the question? so b I didn't quite catch that. Could you say it again, please? also, because, and c Would you mind repeating that, please? because, and, like

4 1 I <u>have been studying</u> publicity at university for the last two years.

2 I am responsible for <u>creating</u> advertising campaigns.
3 After my studies, I would <u>like to be working / like to work</u> in a management position.
4 I <u>studied</u> Business Administration when I was at university.
5 In my sort of work, patience and communication <u>are</u> the two most important soft skills.
6 The thing I like about my job ~~it~~ is developing other people in my team.
7 The <u>biggest</u> challenge I face is balancing my working life with my family life.
8 I first <u>became</u> interested in logistics when I was working as an intern.
9 You have to be able to understand a lot of <u>information</u> very quickly in my job.
10 I <u>really</u> like the fact that every day is different at my company.
5 Student's own answers

PART 2
Training

1 **6** This is not a good thing to do in the exam. When you have spoken for a minute, the examiner will tell you to stop. Try to keep speaking until then.
2 **1** b **2** a **3** c **4** f **5** d **6** e
3 **a** I would choose **b** would prefer **c** you could say **d** I'm not really sure **e** I suppose **f** it depends
4 **1** b **2** a **3** c **4** d **5** e **6** f

PART 3
Training

2 **1** T **2** T **3** T **4** F (They ask questions to encourage their partner to talk.) **5** T
This is a good example of how to do Part 3 of the speaking test.
4 **1** Do you think open days like this are useful for students?
2 What other things could companies do to help students prepare for the world of work?
3 How important do you think it is for companies to have a good image with the public?
5 **1** That's **2** never **3** Well

Test 3

Reading

PART 1

1 C: *When workers know what they're doing and why, and have empathy for the company's objectives, this creates loyalty ...*
2 B: *Some managers may assume that keeping workers happy means trying to make the workplace fun. However, people come to work in order to work, and do not necessarily wish to be distracted from the task at hand ...*
3 D: *Companies have to be aware not only of what makes their company attractive to their customers but to potential employees, too ...*
4 C: *People are expensive to replace, so looking after your workforce is of major importance.*
5 A: *In order for employees to really enjoy their work, they must not only feel that their jobs are secure, but that their managers care about their well-being.*
6 D: *... if certain needs are not fulfilled, they may well look elsewhere. A supportive atmosphere, clear goals, reasonable working hours and a decent pay packet are necessities.*
7 B: *Managers should, instead, focus their attention on providing supportive and timely feedback, ensuring employees have a sense of purpose about their work.*

PART 2

8 E: *It* refers to *change* in the main text. E continues the list of what change can entail.
9 A: *This is because they are happy with the way things are* provides the reason for *Any big change can make employees feel uneasy. ... fear change* links to *While this may be the case, their worry is not without grounds.*
10 D: *interested parties* refers back to the workers, managers, shareholders and stakeholders in the main text; *support and direction* links to *Such leaders must embrace the new approaches, and be able to motivate those around them.*
11 F: *This is so that* introduces an explanation for how change must be managed and why plans are required.
12 C: *These leaders* refers back to *the right people to lead the company* and *individuals* links forward to *each and every person* in the next sentence of the main text.

PART 3

13 C: *Psychometric tests are often used by HR departments to build up a picture of their employees, and may be used as part of the recruitment process, to ascertain whether a candidate is suitable for the role they have applied for.*
14 B: *The results indicate how an individual's attributes can be useful to and have an impact on a team.*
15 A: *Experts discovered that how successful a team was ...*; *Different behaviour types were categorised, and distinct 'roles' identified*; *Most people are not confined to one particular role, but instead display different elements to a greater or lesser extent.*
16 B: *... logical thinkers ... are able to weigh up* (= consider) *what the team's options are without getting emotionally involved*
17 D: *... teams can become so absorbed in the task at hand that they forget to look beyond the team and at whether what they are doing will work ...*

18 C: *For a team to work effectively, it is crucial to have a balance of each of these roles, which may be no easy feat.*

PART 4

19 C: This forms part of the compound noun, *cash flow*.
20 A: *Determine* means 'discover the facts about something' which fits the context and links back to *know* in the second sentence.
21 B: *Covers* collocates with *costs* in this context.
22 D: *Expenses* relates to *costs*.
23 B: *Sustainable* means 'able to continue over a period of time' which relate to *over time*.
24 C: This relates to measuring *performance* which is the best collocation.
25 D: This forms part of the phrase *take a hit* meaning 'be negatively affected by'.
26 A: *High* collocates with *quality*. *Top* also collocates with *quality* but cannot be followed by *enough*.
27 D: This is part of the phrase *within budget*.
28 C: *Fully* is the only adverb which fits with the verb (*integrated*) in this context.
29 B: *Expand* is the only correct verb, which means 'grow' in this context.
30 A: *Ensure* is the only verb which means 'make sure'.
31 C: This forms part of the phrase *take into account*, meaning 'consider when judging a situation'.
32 D: This forms part of the phrase *base on*, meaning 'using those facts and ideas' (in this case, *providing value*).
33 B: *Respond to* means 'react to' in this context.

PART 5

34 ITS: does not refer to anything in the text and is not required
35 TO: *in to* or *into* suggest movement, but the text only refers to what is in the budget; no movement is suggested
36 CORRECT
37 IF: We already have *whether* in the text and this covers both *services* and *products* as it comes before them. *Whether* is the more accurate word to use in the context.
38 EVEN: *even* is used for emphasis, but there is none implied in the sentence
39 CORRECT
40 NOT: the negative does not fit with the meaning of the whole sentence, and it does not make sense here
41 CORRECT
42 AN: *one such* is not followed by *an* but the noun only
43 IT: *as is the case* is the complete phrase, without *it*
44 ARE: the tense is present tense as indicated by the main verb, so this word is not required as it would be for the passive tense
45 UP: the collocation is *make calculations* not *make up*

Writing

PART 1

Model answer

Dear staff
I need to tell you that one of our products, the Gen 10 mobile phone, is losing sales. This is our main phone product and makes 25% of our profits. We're going to start a new TV advertising campaign next month to boost sales.
Best regards
[your name]

Notes

- *A good answer which fully addresses the question*
- *All three content points are clearly covered and expanded in an appropriate way*
- *Uses an appropriate range of tenses including present and future forms*
- *No language errors*
- *Successfully re-phrases language from the question, e.g. falling → losing; improve → boost*
- *Suitable register*

PART 2

Model answer

Report on Target IT Ltd

The purpose of this report is to review the installation of the department's new IT system by Target IT Ltd and recommend whether this system should now be used by the rest of the company.
The new IT system was needed because the old system was out of date and no longer supported by the manufacturer. It was also unable to run the latest software.
We chose Target IT for the work because they were highly recommended by several suppliers and customers.
The installation was successful, although there some minor problems at first with accessing data. Also, some of the old hardware needed to be upgraded to run the new system.
It is recommended that the system is used by the rest of the company as it has increased efficiency in this department already and is more user-friendly than the old system. Target IT should do the work as they were on time and on budget with the first installation.

Notes

- *A clear answer with all five of the content points covered, including the recommendation as required*
- *Content points are expanded on and reasons are given for answers where needed*
- *No headings used, but still well organised*

- *Appropriate register all through the report*
- *Good use of passive forms which are appropriate to a more formal register*
- *A good range of language with past, present and future forms used accurately, as well as appropriate business language e.g. 'on time and on budget'*
- *No unnecessary or irrelevant information*
- *Some language is repeated from the question instead of being rephrased, e.g. 'out of date'; 'minor'*

Listening

PART 1

1 overview: George says he'll be *starting* (= begin) with a *brief* (= short) overview of the *company* (= firm).

2 slides: Amy asks George to make sure he doesn't use *more than six words on* (= overcrowd) the slides.

3 stock images: Amy also tells George to use *colourful* (= vivid) stock images to reinforce his presentation with.

4 (annoying) transitions: After he asks *Anything else you recommend I do or avoid?* she replies that she has *a thing against* annoying transitions between slides, which means she is asking him to *avoid* using them *when changing slides*.

5 movement: The man starts the conversation by asking Miley to tell him about *this whole Athleisure movement* in clothing.

6 lifestyle shift: Miley says Athleisure is *more than just a trend*; it's a complete lifestyle shift, *on a large scale* (= in society).

7 functionality: According to Miley, people are *demanding* (= want) *more functionality (…) to go with these* (= their clothes).

8 influencers: Miley says that its products are *often boosted* (= frequently advertised) by *micro influencers*, that is *amateur athletes* (= people doing certain sports as a hobby).

9 fact sheet: The man says that you should *provide (journalists) with* (= include) a *fact sheet* of *your enterprise* (= your firm).

10 objective: After he listed the basic components of a typical fact sheet, he says that you *need to be* (= should be) *objective*, otherwise *they* (= journalists) might feel they need to *research you more* (= further enquiry).

11 employees: He also lists *some other details* (= possible extra info) that might be mentioned in a fact sheet, then lists these and ends with *and how many* (= number of) *employees it has*.

12 headshots: He says that you might also decide to add *some pictures and videos* (= visuals) to your kit, then mentions some examples for these *headshots or short clips of the founders*.

PART 2

13 H: The woman says that what she looks for in an applicant *above all* (= more than anything else) is that they *come from a background of leadership* (= management experience) *during their studies* (= at university).

14 C: The man says that leaders should act *on behalf of the entire company*, which suggests *taking responsibility*; as does the phrase *they never say 'that's not my job' / 'that's not my fault'*. Employees who *tackle any issues* (= problems) are also *taking responsibility* for them. The last sentence *And when something goes wrong (…), they don't try to blame it on anybody else either* is also a description of the latter.

15 D: The idea that *only those companies that focus on the customer first (…) survive, start with the end-user in mind and work backwards* and *work vigorously to earn and keep customer trust* are all examples of a *client-focused perspective*.

16 G: *innovation* and *find ways to streamline our processes* are the same as being *inventive*

17 E: *calculated risk taking* is the same as *being brave enough to try things*.

18 D: The man says that besides a *professional-looking website*, companies also need to provide their clients with an *address* and *geographical address* (= physical location) as well.

19 A: The woman explains that if you *upload pictures of the people who work with you*, it will *humanise your brand*, while if you *use generic stock images*, it does the opposite as it suggests a *lack of personality and transparency*.

20 G: *A few accounts of satisfied customers or colourful case stories* is a description of the concept of a *testimonials page*.

21 B: The phrases *too many 'big words'* and *unnecessarily fancy vocabulary that confuses your audience* are the opposite of *simple language*.

22 F: The phrase *showcase their best work in an online portfolio* is the same as displaying *concrete achievements*. The speaker also advises against using *non-specific adjectives*, which is the opposite of using more *concrete* language to talk about your *achievements*.

PART 3

23 B: Dan says that to avoid meetings becoming a drain on precious resources they need to be *better defined* (= more precisely described).
Distraction A: Dan introduced a *checklist* to improve the meetings culture at his firm. He also mentions *presentations* (sometimes being confused with meetings) but he does not talk about *presenters* or presenters *using checklists*.
Distraction C: Although the word *conversation* (= dialogue) is used, Dan is not proposing more discussions *about* meetings.

24 B: Dan says an agenda should have maximum five items, with the *time allocated* for each (= how long every item will be discussed).
Distraction A: He says there needs to be one person *responsible for calling* the meeting, but it is not stated that this should be included on the agenda.
Distraction C: Similarly, while he says that a meeting should only be held if *there's no better way forward* than to have it, it is not stated that this should be included on the agenda.

25 C: Participants who *read a summary of important reports*, *think and make notes* are *doing research*.
Distraction A: Dan talks about making all the *relevant information* available in advance, but employees collecting their *questions* is not explicitly mentioned.
Distraction B: He says participants use this silence to *read a summary of important reports*, not each other's *summaries*.

26 A: Dan says that *the more complicated (...) a matter is, the fewer people really understand it*, i.e. more employees can probably say something about *trivial* ones.
Distraction B: Dan uses the words *organisation* and *important* but not to mean that trivial matters are discussed *when* these are *most important at an organisation*.
Distraction C: *if not enough people understand 'the more complicated'* ones would be correct to say about Dan's opinion. *If not enough people really understand them* (= the trivial ones) is not what he is saying.

27 B: The interviewer asks Dan if it is always necessary that everybody *agree on one thing before moving on to the next point*, to which he says he doesn't think they do, as long as it is clear who is *in charge* on that topic.
Distraction A: 'deciding' who is in charge is not talked about.
Distraction C: Dan says that *abandoning* consensus *takes some getting used to* (= hard for some people to adapt to), not consensus itself.

28 C: After describing why they implemented the 'two-pizza rule', Dan introduces a contrast by using the linking expression *Having said that* (= despite), then says that *it's crucial too that no key party be missing* (= the principal participants be present).
Distraction A: Dan talks about *doing away with* (= discarding) the *old default* of automatically inviting more people than absolutely necessary, *not* old default *topics*.
Distraction B: It is true that in Dan's opinion it is essential all participants *understand the topics*, but this is not so *despite* the two-pizza rule.

29 A: Dan says meetings used to *interrupt the day*, people's *work flows*, *peak concentration times* (= employee focus).
Distraction B: Meetings used to be scheduled at Dan's company without checking when people were *most productive*. The word *free* is only used to talk about the times / days that were then *blocked off* as *meeting-free*.
Distraction C: According to Dan, meetings used to interfere *with people's work flows*, not with *other meetings*.

30 C: Dan believes that *whatever you see in meetings is what happens at the company outside of the meetings as well*. He also lists some example behaviours, e.g. *people tuning out*, etc. of which he says these are *probably present in the company in general* (= are representative of its culture).
Distraction A: *getting anxious* is only one of the behaviours he lists as an example, not his entire theory about meetings.
Distraction B: *Authority figures* and employees (not) being *curious* are mentioned, but it could not be said that Dan's theory about meetings is that they *raise people's curiosity about authority figures*.

Test 4

Reading

PART 1

1 B: *This is where making different products at the same time can result in reduced costs. Companies which merge, say, different health and beauty products, will be able to lower their marketing and product development costs per product.*

2 A: *However, it is important to get it right.*

3 C: *Merging with a similar company which is located in a different market, such as another country, helps to avoid having to start from nothing there to build up a distribution network.*

4 D: *The main reason that companies merge horizontally is to reduce opposition, which may be in the form of new companies entering the market, substitutes or established rivals.*

5 A: *Reasons given for doing so are numerous and may include a desire to increase in size, widening the range of products and services on offer, achieving economies of scale, and accessing new customers or markets.*

6 D: *But, as with anything, there are, of course, disadvantages. ... This can happen when companies become too big to manage well.*

7 B: *And, in addition to economies of scale, where costs are saved when production is increased, there may*

be economies of scope. This is where making different products at the same time can result in reduced costs.

PART 2

8 D: *These* refers back to *industry trends and changes* and *keeping up* corresponds with keeping knowledge current. *It* in the next sentence of the text refers back to *foolish*.

9 F: *This is because* refers back to *it is vital to gain ...*; *acquire new approaches* relates to *doing things the way you've always done them*.

10 E: *This* in the main text after the gap refers back to *know as much as possible about*.

11 A: *Professions such as this* refers back to the *field of medicine*, and also to *high-risk fields* following the gap; *advances and safety procedures* links to *codes of conduct or ethics*.

12 B: *But* is the contrast with the previous sentence in the main text (*hard work*); *employees* links to *those* in the following sentence in the main text.

PART 3

13 D: *... highly successful entrepreneurs seem to be particularly good at working out what went wrong; they also look at their successes and analyse what went right.*

14 B: *They will tell you that they probably already had an idea that things weren't right at the time, but they went ahead anyway without listening to their instinct.*

15 C: *The steps depend on the nature of the business and may need to be adapted to the situation at hand.*

16 B: *What this means is being able to quantify the gaps between your expectations for a venture and what has actually occurred.*

17 D: This refers back to the action that should be taken: *Look at the cause of inconsistencies. This will enable you to see where you misjudged things and provide you with a wider perspective.*

18 A: *... use the knowledge you've gained to learn lessons and develop better judgement.*

PART 4

19 D: *stand still* is a strong collocation
20 A: *business climate* is a strong collocation
21 D: *adopt* is the only verb which fits the context
22 C: *Keeping* means *staying* which fits the meaning required of the context.
23 B: *maintain* means *keep* or *retain* which is the only verb which fits the context
24 A: a *clear vision* is a strong collocation
25 B: This forms part of the phrase *return on investment*.
26 C: This forms part of the phrase *be the case* + *for* + noun.
27 D: This is the correct verb for the phrase *make (an) investment(s)*.

28 C: *ability* refers to companies 'being able to' get new products on the market quickly
29 A: *outdated* means *old-fashioned*, which is the meaning required of the context
30 C: This forms part of the phrase *result of*.
31 B: *traditional* refers to former versions of products which have been modernised
32 D: This forms part of the verb phrase *to move on*, meaning keep going forward.
33 A: This is the only verb which fits grammatically and semantically into the sentence.

PART 5

34 THE: no article is required for things in general (*health*, *noise*, etc.)
35 CORRECT
36 TO: the second *to* is not required as part of the phrase *impact on*
37 AND: this is redundant, as there is only one thing being talked about (*psychological well-being*)
38 SO: no emphasis is needed in this sentence
39 THEIR: *their time off* would refer to planned time off, but this is not what is being talked about
40 SUCH: the phrase needed is *things like* to give an example
41 CORRECT
42 OUT: The correct phrasal verb required by the context is *look after*. *Look out for* has a similar meaning, but this does not fit here.
43 THAT: this does not fit grammatically in the verb phrase
44 AT: this is not part of the phrase *be a must*
45 CORRECT

Writing

PART 1

Model answer

I am writing to let you know that there is a vacancy for a sales executive in our marketing department. If you are interested in applying for this job, please contact the manager of the HR department directly by phone or by email.

Notes

- All content is relevant to the question and is given in a straightforward, efficient manner
- All three content points are clearly covered although there could be a little more detail on the job and what it involves
- Effectively links the first two points in one sentence
- Uses quite a good range of language including a conditional structure ('If you are interested in ...')

- *No grammar mistakes*
- *There is no greeting, e.g. 'Dear staff', or closing remark, e.g. 'Best regards', or name of the manager*

PART 2
Model answer
Proposal on new retail store
The aim of this proposal is to consider whether or not to open a new store in Wigston.
It is definitely a good idea to open another store in this town as it is growing in size every year and doesn't have another department store offering our range of products.
After considering a number of sites it is suggested that the best location for the new store would be in the town centre in Oxford Street. This is already a well-established shopping area with good public parking.
We need a store of at least 8,000m². A smaller store would not be as profitable.
To find a suitable building for the new store it is suggested that an estate agency would be the best option. Novostate is an agency with a good reputation.
The new building should be on a lease because it will give us more flexibility in the long term.

Notes
- *A successful answer with all five of the content points covered*
- *Content points are expanded on and reasons are given for answers where needed*
- *The writer's opinion is clear throughout the answer*
- *A reasonable range of language with passive forms used correctly, e.g. 'it is suggested ...'*
- *Paragraphs, although short, are appropriate for a business context*
- *The second paragraph is one long sentence. This could be broken up into shorter sentences or separated by commas*
- *Slightly over the word limit at 154 words. This is not a serious problem, but could be reduced by keeping the answer as relevant as possible to the question (e.g. the reference to 'well-established shopping area with good public parking' is not required).*
- *Some copying from the question, e.g. 'definitely a good idea'; 'the best location ...'. These could be rephrased: 'certainly makes sense'; 'the ideal place'*

Listening

PART 1

1 **employee newsletter**: The woman says that *meetings, video conferencing* and the old *weekly employee newsletter* are *just not the way to go any more*, which is the cue for *will replace* in the notes.

2 **(colleagues) abroad**: The man says that he'll be shooting the videos to address everybody *across* (= *from*) *all departments, including our colleagues abroad*.

3 **feedback**: The man says that in the videos he wants to be able to *share any important company news (...), and ask for or provide* (= exchange) *feedback*.

4 **sound**: When the assistant asks him how *well produced* the videos are going to be, the man says that he wouldn't have the time to deal with *sound, lighting, writing scripts* – of which the first two are *aspects* and of these the first one (*sound*) is missing in the notes.

5 **first quarter**: The man says releasing the app *might even boost* (= may improve) (our) *first quarter's figures* (= numbers).

6 **offices**: The woman says that she wanted the customers to *imagine* (= visualise) how the *products* (= items) would *fit into their offices*.

7 **interior design**: She states that it will also *give* (= provide) *them* (= the customers) *ideas about* (= inspiration) *interior design*.

8 **prototype**: She ends by saying that she will have the *prototype ready by November*.

9 **implicit data**: The woman first defines implicit data as *information about observed customer behaviour*, then compares it to explicit data, which is *customer-provided information* (= info provided by customer). The phrase *is better than* in the question shows that you need to catch a comparison.

10 **surveys**: You hear the cue *The problem with surveys is that they ...*, which introduces the section in the notes beginning with *... are problematic*.

11 **statistical significance**: Another problem listed by the woman after the fact that only an *unrepresentative group ... responds* (= results not representative) is that *you don't get enough responses to achieve* (= ensure) *real statistical significance*.

12 **user-testing**: *Another effective feedback source ...* introduces the section of better *sources of feedback*, of which the first is already given (customer support calls), so the answer is *user-testing* service.

PART 2

13 **F**: The woman is talking about how important it is to *provide them* (= your high performers) *with some help* to avoid them *burning out* and suggests being *careful* not to *overburden them* (= reduce their workload).

14 **H**: The man says that key employees often leave because of a *lack of advancement* (= growth) *options*, to which he suggests discussing the employee's *learning goals* and setting *challenges* for them, which will help them grow, as these will *prevent their careers from arriving at a plateau*. *Mentorship* programme and *online courses* are further examples of *opportunities for growth*.

15 C: The woman talks about *sure-fire sign(s)* of disengaged employees. She mentions that they *start taking on fewer responsibilities* and *become less of a team player* (= lack of cooperation) and their *engagement* starts to *decline* and they will need to be *motivated again* somehow.

16 G: The man talks about when high performers *stop volunteering for new responsibilities*, which can be reversed by *tempting* (= involving) them with *more creative or bigger scale projects* (= exciting upcoming tasks), *to win them back*.

17 D: *Being taken for granted* is the opposite of being *recognised* and the woman says that *No one likes to feel* this. Therefore, it is important that they *know that their work is valued*. The speaker also mentions that sometimes it is enough if you are just *acknowledging* your staff's contributions to *drive employee engagement*.

18 D: The man starts by saying that the same *rules* (= characteristics) will not apply for every *industry* (= trade). He then mentions other *sectors* (e.g. *finance* and *publishing*) and ends by saying that you should *look into* (investigate) what is *considered standard* (= characteristic of) in your *field* (= trade).

19 G: The woman says that including *the recipients' name* or their *recently purchased or browsed items* (= personalising) is a good strategy because these emails had *higher open rates* than others that are *not so tailor-made*. She also talks about how we have been trained to send out *bulk emails* with *bulk subject lines*, which are the opposite of *personalising your message* and don't seem to be *working so well*.

20 A: The man says that sending *users emails about their abandoned carts* (or being *too upfront about their agenda*) is not a successful strategy. However, *recipients appear to be more easily enticed by subjects that read 'you forgot something'*, which are examples of subject lines worded as *reminders*.

21 F: The woman recommends generating interest in the recipient by including a number of *specific key words* (= leading vocabulary). She also gives an example in which she describes what details she thinks should be mentioned (i.e. *data science*).

22 B: The man talks about how while we make sure *we don't send out anything that is factually incorrect*, we tend to write subject lines *in a hurry*. He then describes an example of his own *proofreading* error (*25% of* rather than *25% off*).

PART 3

23 B: Ashley says that *reading, watching, listening to* one's target media will help *figure out* (= become familiar with) what they *like to cover* (= their topics), then adds that you also need to know *who to talk to* (= staff).

Distraction A: Although Ashley talks about approaching journalists, she only says you should use the information that can be found out about them, to which the interviewer introduces the idea of social media.
Distraction C: Nothing is said about what an entrepreneur should or should not share about themselves on social media; only what you should check about a journalist (e.g. hobbies, interests). (The word *secret* is used, but by the interviewer and differently – to elicit further tips from Ashley.)

24 B: Ashley says that a successful pitch will always *answer the query 'Why should I care?'* (= raises the journalist's interest), to which she adds that if she doesn't find a *convincing answer to it after a brief read through* (= immediately), she moves on.
Distraction A: *I always open emails from entrepreneurs* does not necessarily mean that a successful pitch is *always sent via email*.
Distraction C: Ashley recommends being *subtle about* using the personal information you can find on social media to approach a journalist, but she doesn't say a successful pitch is subtle.

25 C: She says that some *amazing pitches* help her imagine *how the story would run* and provide *ideas* (= tips) *on how to present* (= feature) it.
Distraction A: When talking about approaching journalists she says you should know who to talk to, *to avoid funny mistakes and misunderstandings*.
Distraction B: *Mistakes* are only mentioned in the same context of approaching journalists. Nothing is said about a *company's* past mistakes.

26 A: She says that because *the media are obsessed with remaining relevant to their audiences*, you should *hook your message on to whatever's currently happening*, then mentions two examples for this (*emerging trend* and *breaking news stories* (= the news)).
Distraction B: She says that entrepreneurs make the mistake of assuming that just because their product or service is *useful throughout the year*, it is automatically interesting at any time. She actually says the opposite, namely that you should pay attention to offering something *relevant* to the media in a pitch.
Distraction C: She uses the phrase *just because their product or service is useful throughout the year* and talks about *news* stories but does not imply that the timing of a pitch should be *about a new product or service* but current affairs.

27 C: When talking about putting together a crisis plan, Ashley mentions *material about industry issues* and *blog posts* (= old publications).
Distraction A: She recommends doing this before any crisis occurs (*I recommend creating a crisis plan so that*

when a major negative event occurs, your company is prepared).
Distraction B: She says that *No matter what line of business* (= industry) *you're in*, you should have a crisis plan, which does not mean it will *depend on* the industry.

28 B: Ashley talks about how although it may seem like good practice to *tie* (= connect) your company's news to some major national *news story* (= big news), it should be *avoided*.
Distraction A: She says that this move will come off as unnatural and *forced*, and most *journalists* will probably ignore the pitch. She does not talk about forcing journalists to run a story.
Distraction C: She mentions journalists ignoring the pitch, not because of the news, but rather an entrepreneur's attempt to tie their story to the news when it is clearly not relevant.

29 C: HARO is a *platform* (= tool) that *connects journalists to industry experts*. Ashley says it provides *plenty of opportunities to get featured by major media outlets* (= gain media exposure).
Distraction A: Ashley says entrepreneurs should be *prepared to provide expert insight when needed* (not gain it from HARO).
Distraction B: The platform *connects journalists to industry experts*, so it is not true that it is *only* for *start-up experts*.

30 A: *It tends to receive a lot of attention and social sharing* is the same as *tends to be shared (more)*.
Distraction B: All this *social sharing* then *translates into* more page views for the media outlet. Nothing is said about translating the infographics themselves.
Distraction C: Ashley says about infographics that these are good *outreach bait* to raise the journalists' attention, not that media outlets use them as such to reach their customers.

Test 5

Reading

PART 1

1 C: *Instead of having to walk the length of the office or go up a flight of stairs to talk to a colleague, it is possible to message them instantly. Instead of having to get on a plane to visit counterparts in other countries, it is possible to set up video calls.*

2 B: *... it enables companies to promote themselves via an online presence, target customers and sell to a wide audience. And of course, there is the added advantage of being able to keep an eye on competitors.*

3 C: *Thoughtful, timely communication can even build reputation and attract new business.*

4 D: *It is crucial that a company, regardless of what it does, invests in advanced technologies to enable it to produce cutting edge goods and, therefore, stay relevant.*

5 A: *... making these more efficient, and making the business an effective player in the marketplace.*

6 B: *One of the greatest advantages of technology is its ability to ensure accuracy* and *What once took hours can now be achieved in a matter of minutes.*

7 D: *Whatever the industry or profession, there is technology to make its activities easier.*

PART 2

8 A: *Doing so* refers back to doing research, and *be able to assess ...* links to *If they can*.

9 E: *Attributes like these* refers back to *be curious* and *able to cope with uncertainty*, and *things change quickly and constantly* links to *generation of solutions* in the sentence after the gap.

10 B: *This data* refers back to *vast amounts of information* and *determine trends* links with *be able to spot what is likely to happen* in the next sentence.

11 C: This sentence contrasts with the ideas in the previous sentence. *Understands their weaknesses* links to *knowing how to deal with limitations* in the second sentence after the gap.

12 D: *Enthusiastic and likeable* links to *positive people* in the sentence after the gap.

PART 3

13 B: *While most managers have their own distinct style, the most successful are flexible, shifting the way they do things as the need arises, depending on the situation.*

14 A: *... things continue to be done in the same way, not always with the best results.*

15 C: *Feeling valued and heard, employees with consultative managers are more likely to stick around and remain loyal to the company, knowing that they can approach their managers to discuss issues or concerns in the workplace.*

16 C: consultative: *Employees are encouraged to give their opinions, but decisions are ultimately made at the top.* Persuasive: *... managers are still in charge of the decision-making process.*

17 B: *Together, they can create a strong vision for the company ...*

18 A: chaotic: *Managers who employ the chaotic style allow employees to make decisions.* Laissez-faire: *Here, the manager plays the role of mentor rather than leader, not getting too involved in what workers are doing. Employees make their own decisions and consult the manager only when necessary.*

PART 4

19 A: *go ahead* means to move forward, which fits the context
20 D: This is part of the phrasal verb *weigh up*.
21 B: *potential* means *possibility* here, which fits the context
22 C: *grow your brand* is a strong collocation
23 A: *Interacting with* is the only verb which fits the context. Options C (*discussing*) and D (*exchanging*) cannot be used with *with*.
24 B: This means *dedicated* and is the only verb which fits both grammatically and semantically in the context.
25 D: *Direct mail* is a kind of *marketing campaign* which is a commonly used compound noun with a specific meaning.
26 C: This forms part of the phrase *last but not least*.
27 D: *highly* is the adverb which collocates best with *cost-effective*
28 B: *time consuming* is the adjectival phrase which means *taking up a lot of time*
29 C: *published* is the correct verb to use when referring to written material in this way
30 A: This forms part of the phrase *on a regular basis*.
31 B: *relevant to* means *of interest to* which is the word which fits the context
32 C: *respond* means *react*, which is the meaning required of the context
33 A: meaning *immediately*

PART 5

34 SO: *so* indicates emphasis but this is not required here and the word does not fit grammatically
35 THE: this is a general reference to *heavy traffic* so it does not need the article
36 CORRECT
37 OF: the phrase is *not too* + adjective + *a* + noun and therefore does not require the *of*
38 ITS: *it* is redundant as a pronoun here and does not refer to anything in the sentence
39 IF: the sentence is in the present simple and does not require the conditional *if*
40 CORRECT
41 AT: this line is a continuation of a list and *operations* also follows *in*
42 TOO: *many and varied* is a phrase which does not include the word *too*
43 THEIR: *knowledge* is mentioned generally and does not need a pronoun
44 AND: only the last two items in a list are separated by *and* so the second *and* is not required at this point in the sentence
45 CORRECT

Writing

PART 1

Model answer

Dear staff
I have some exciting news. A new manager, Mr Paul Keays, will be starting with us next Monday. He will be responsible for developing a new marketing strategy. You'll be able to meet him on Tuesday at 10.00 in room 4.
Best regards
[your name]

Notes

- *A good answer which fully addresses the question*
- *All three content points are clearly covered with plenty of appropriate extra detail*
- *Friendly, quite informal style, appropriate for an internal email*
- *A reasonable range of tenses and no grammar mistakes, but with some repetition of 'will be'*
- *A positive feature is the use of a mixture of short and long sentences*

PART 2

Model answer

Dear Mr Fellowes,
I am writing in response to your advertisement for Quadrant Equipment Supplies.
The company I work for, Wyford Construction, specialises in building houses and apartments. We are based in the south of England.
I was very interested in your offer of fast delivery times. We often need equipment to be supplied at very short notice, usually within 24 hours.
Regarding price, we usually expect our suppliers to offer us a minimum 10% discount on orders, but I was wondering if you could improve on that.
I was very pleased to see that your advert states that there is no minimum order. This is good for us because it would give us more flexibility.
If you are available, I would like to suggest a meeting to discuss everything in more detail. Please let me know a suitable time.
I look forward to hearing from you.
Yours sincerely,
[your name]

Notes

- *A very successful answer with all five of the content points covered*
- *All the content points are expanded on and reasons are given for answers where needed*
- *The text is well organised into clear paragraphs, each covering one content point.*
- *The register is appropriately formal all through the letter*
- *There is a clear early reference to the reason for writing: 'I am writing in response to ...'*
- *Appropriate opening and closing remarks: 'Dear Mr Fellowes', 'I look forward to hearing from you', 'Yours sincerely'*
- *There is a good range of language with present, future and conditional forms used accurately*
- *The length is appropriate. (The answer is slightly over length but this is not a problem.)*

Listening

PART 1

1. **multi-taskers**: The woman says that one of the main differences between *earlier generations* (= previous age groups) *and Gen Z is that the latter are better* (= more efficient) *multi-taskers*.
2. **early starters**: About Generation Z the woman says that it is *full of (...) early starters*, then explains that this means that *between the ages of 16 and 18* (= as teenagers) *they already go into the workforce* (= begin working as).
3. **higher education**: The cues on the recording are *often* (= might), *opting out of* (= choose not to take part in) and *traditional* (= conventional) *higher education*.
4. **reading comprehension**: The key words in the question are *dramatically changing*, which is expressed as *are being radically transformed* in the recording.
5. **reason**: The man says to *start by* (= 1st step) *giving (...) a* (= sharing) *reason*.
6. **promise**: The man tells the story of how at his company they had to *dismiss most of (the) sales team*. Then he adds that he had *made (the) promise to the leaving colleagues that we would welcome them back* (= they would be 'hired back later').
7. **severance packages**: The cue on the recording is *handed out* (= give) *some really impressive* (= generous), after which the man mentions *severance packages*.
8. **referrals**: The man says that they also *provided the dismissed employees with*, which introduces the answer *referrals* because it is the same as *help leaving staff with*.
9. **trust**: The woman says that leaders often *don't* (= can't) *trust their staff* (= employees).
10. **development**: The cue introducing the answer is the woman saying that *as a result* (of leaders overextending themselves) because this is the same as *This affects the ...* in the notes.
11. **routines**: *It is OK to be scared* is expressed as *it's totally normal to feel terrified*.
12. **(administrative) tasks**: The man says that *if we set out* (= begin) *by delegating a few administrative tasks, we could survive*.

PART 2

13. **E**: The woman says she was doing her previous job *only for 20 hours a week* and wanted something *more stable*, a *bigger commitment*. (Although she mentions *benefits*, it is clear from the context that this is her work area, not the reason why she changed companies, so option H is incorrect.)
14. **F**: The fact that he says he *had no choice* about quitting his job implies a negative reason and you usually *attend treatment sessions* if you are ill.
15. **C**: The woman describes her family's morning routine, then talks about how Nicholas's (presumably her husband's) company moved and this upset their old schedule, so she had to quit (*Something had to give*). (While the word *moved* is used, it is her husband's company that moved, not them, so option A is incorrect.)
16. **G**: The man says that he always knew he'd only be in management *for a while*, then talks about signing up for a *course* and it being *demanding*.
17. **B**: The woman starts by saying that she was a corporate lawyer for 30 years, then describes what her old life was like. (She also mentions that she had *difficult colleagues*, but does not say this was the reason for her leaving the field.) She mentions that she wanted to dedicate herself to something *less intellectually demanding and more creative*, then says that *opening a small bakery* seemed like a fun idea.
18. **G**: The man talks about *sharing valuable information* on their *various sites* (= social media) to *engage* top-quality candidates, as opposed to what they used to do, i.e. only publishing content related to job openings.
19. **C**: The woman complains that her colleagues used to only use a *prospective candidate's name at the beginning of their messages* (= emails) and that this is not *personalised* (= the opposite of *generic*). Other words she uses such as *template* and *impersonal* are also synonyms of *generic*, while the *outreach* she refers to is the *emails*. (Although she also adds that a recruiter should be *patient enough* to research each candidate, this is not her main focus, so option A is incorrect.)

20 E: The man tells the story of hiring the wrong person because he hadn't considered how much having to replace them would *cost* (*way more expensive*). He says that from this he learnt that he needs to make a *better offer*, i.e. not be *thrifty*. (While option F also includes the word *performance*, and the man mentions *someone performing worse*, he doesn't describe *tracking* their performance, so this is not the answer.)

21 H: The woman says that it took her some time to learn *to listen better*, which means that she is admitting that she wasn't attentive enough in the past (i.e. used to be *inattentive*). She also suggests *paying attention* to the details of each candidate.

22 D: The man talks about companies having *challenges*, *issues* and *difficulties* and *only talking about the positives* (= hiding the 'issues'). (He also uses the phrase *ideal candidate*, but nothing is said of *defining* their profile, so the answer is not option B.)

PART 3

23 C: The linking expression Ryan uses to introduce the answer is *I think the main lesson I've learnt*. Also, *unpleasant circumstances* is the same as *uncomfortable situations*, as well as (being pushed) *beyond your comfort zone*.
Distraction A: handling *customer complaints* is mentioned only as an example of 'unpleasant circumstances' among others, but it is not the most important lesson.
Distraction B: Similarly, (maintaining) *quality control* is just one example of the bigger category of *discomfort*.

24 A: Ryan says that he now sees *defeat* (= failure) as a *necessary component* (of success).
Distraction B: He talks about his training but doesn't say anything about failure being a *necessary* part of good training.
Distraction C: According to Ryan, failure builds *toughness of character*, which is a quality, but option C uses the word *character* in the meaning of 'person' or 'personality'.

25 C: (Leaving) *no 'holes' in your game* and (creating) *contingency plans in advance* are synonyms of *being prepared* (for many different situations).
Distraction A: Ryan talks about practising your moves *standing up*, not about the action of standing up, nor does he say it equals being *complete*.
Distraction B: He says that to *beat your competition* or *qualify to compete in a championship* you must be *well-rounded*, but he doesn't say that these are the same.

26 B: Ryan says that *mastery takes time and practice*, which means it *requires perseverance*.
Distraction A: Although the word *time* is used, *saving time* is not talked about.
Distraction C: The interviewer uses the phrase *(swiftly) change tactics*; Ryan doesn't define mastery like this.

27 A: Not moving *past the beginner level* until you have *first got good at the basics* equals not *hurrying it*.
Distraction B: Ryan says that *It's easy to get excited about (...) new techniques*. He does not say that *being a beginner* is exciting, however.
Distraction C: The idea that *many people never master the basics* is not stated, only that you *shouldn't move past* being a beginner before getting *good at the basics* first.

28 B: Ryan expresses the idea that entrepreneurs shouldn't *change tactics* so much in various ways. First he says that *Entrepreneurs often easily get distracted by new strategies or approaches* (= tactics), and that they *move from one new thing to the next before they (...) get results from it*. These are negative things, as is the adverb *unnecessarily*. He also says that *less is more* if you're *consistent*, i.e. don't unnecessarily change tactics.
Distraction A: The words *new* and *approach* are used, but *a new approach to entrepreneurship* suggests a positive new trend, while Ryan is criticising the phenomenon.
Distraction C: Similarly, words of the same root (*implementation* / *implemented*, *strategy* / *strategies*) appear in option C and the recording, but not as a compound noun (*implementation strategy*).

29 C: Ryan says a team can *make you strong* (= add to your strength).
Distraction A: He talks about massage therapists and trainers, being *behind you* but not to mean that they want to *betray* you; on the contrary, to support you.
Distraction B: The words *manager* and *highly specialised* are used differently, as (separate) examples. Ryan is not explicitly saying that teams *always need a highly trained manager*.

30 B: He says challenges *are (...) to be used* (= exploited), *not just survived*.
Distraction A: He asks the rhetorical question *How can I leverage this?*, which includes the false cue *leverage*. He also uses the word *opponent*, but his focus is again different. He's discussing what *successful entrepreneurs* do, not what their *opponents* might do.
Distraction C: He asks another rhetorical question, *Where is the opportunity in this?*, and he uses the word *survived* but doesn't talk about *opportunities for survival*.

Test 6

Reading

PART 1

1 C: *Remember that naming conventions change. For example, until recently, names which used 'u' for 'you' and '4' for 'for' were on trend.*
2 B: *Replace this with the name of the area in which it operates – 'London Cakes' – and some headway is made.*
3 D: *… it's also important to check out whether a name is already in use before adopting it.*
4 A: *People who hear the name should have an immediate understanding of what the business does.*
5 B: *While 'Johnson's' may carry meaning within the family, it conveys nothing to customers about the goods or services on offer.*
6 D: *Depending how big a brand will be, it may be worth considering trademarking its name. This not only helps customers with the identification of the source of goods and services, but it also prevents others from operating under the same name.*
7 C: *Numbers can have some purpose if they help to describe what a business does: 'Ten-min Thai Takeaway' tells you not only that its meals will be ready in ten minutes, but what kind of food it is and where it will be consumed.*

PART 2

8 C: *Presentation* links thematically as it is described as a visual process in option C, which fits the context of the paragraph.
9 E: *Diagrams and charts* links to the references to *those in the creative arts*; rather than *listening* links to *prefer a quiet learning environment*.
10 D: *Background noise* links to the following sentence in the text, *In fact, they benefit from (…) having music on.*
11 A: *Only around 5 per cent* links to *a minority*.
12 F: *The learning process* in the main text links to *training programmes*. *It is not necessary* links to *Instead* in the sentence after the gap.

PART 3

13 C: *… it can be worthwhile investing time and energy in finding out whether there's a good fit between you and the company in question. Understanding a company's culture will help you determine whether your personality and that of the company's match.*
14 B: *For example, if you prefer to work quietly away on your own, but the company has large, open-plan offices and encourages discussion, you may find it difficult to be as efficient as you would like to be.*
15 D: *… with few opportunities to try something new unless you progress formally through the ranks.*
16 A: *It is therefore crucial to find out as much as you can about potential employers if (…) you intend to find a job where you will stay for a long period.*
17 A: *The 'About us' page will fill you in on what the company is about: what their mission is and what their core values are. Employee testimonials can give you a flavour of what it's like to work there.*
18 C: *It may be that you already know someone who works for the company – or you have connections on business social media. If so, talk to them and learn about the company.*

PART 4

19 B: *require* is the closest in meaning to *need*, which is the meaning required by the context
20 A: *Virtually* means *almost* and can be followed by *nothing* rather than *anything* as options B and C require. Option D does not fit the context.
21 D: This is part of the phrasal verb *work out* which means *understand*.
22 B: *initial* means *first* and is the best fit for the context
23 A: This forms part of the phrase *find ways round* meaning *deal with or avoid a problem*.
24 D: This forms part of the phrasal verb *set up*, meaning *establish*.
25 C: *supplies* means *an amount of something available to use*, which is the best fit for the context
26 B: *fees* is the correct term for the amount of money you pay for a service
27 A: This forms part of the phrase *single-handed*.
28 C: *limited* is the adjective which collocates best with *funds*
29 D: This forms part of the phrasal verb *cut out* meaning *stop doing* or *remove* in this context.
30 B: This forms part of the phrasal verb *take out* and collocates with *a loan*.
31 A: This means *deal with* or *speak to* and fits both grammatically and semantically, unlike the other options.
32 C: This forms part of the noun phrase *marketing strategy*.
33 D: This fits the metaphor of building using bricks.

PART 5

34 SO: *so* for emphasis is not required in the context
35 MUST: only *must* or *have to* is required, and *must* cannot be followed by *to*
36 CORRECT
37 A: *time* is uncountable in this context and does not need the indefinite article
38 TO: the second *to* is not required; *in to* or *into* suggest movement, which is not the case here
39 THE: the phrase is *in return* which does not need the article
40 CORRECT

41 OF: *of* is not required in the phrase *the result is ...*
42 CORRECT
43 CORRECT
44 WHICH: if *which* were needed in this context, it would be preceded by *in*
45 WHAT: *an understanding of* + noun phrase without pronoun

Writing

PART 1

Model answer

Hi

I'm going to be out of the office from Monday next week as I have to go to a sales conference in Berlin. If there are no problems, I'll be back on Wednesday morning.

If you need to get in touch while I'm in Berlin, please let my secretary know and he'll pass on any messages. I'm going to be too busy to take calls or deal with emails.

See you next week

[your name]

Notes

- A good answer which fully addresses the question but is about 20 words over the word limit (rectify this by omitting: 'I'm going to be too busy to take calls or deal with emails.')
- All three content points are clearly covered and expanded in an appropriate way so the message is clear and the target readers would understand the situation
- Uses a good range of future forms: 'I'm going to be ...', 'I'll be ...' and conditionals: *If there are ...*
- No grammar mistakes
- Successfully rephrases language from the question, e.g. 'away from the office' → 'out of the office', 'need to' → 'have to go to', 'contact' → 'get in touch'
- The register is consistently informal, which is appropriate for an internal email

PART 2

Model answer

Report on customer complaints

The aim of this report is to examine the recent rise in customer complaints and to suggest ways of responding to and improving the situation.

Background

Over the last month, customer complaints to this company have risen by over 50%. The main reason for this dramatic rise in complaints may be because of the success of the new online customer feedback system that we have just set up. This makes it much easier for customers to complain than in the past.

Reason for complaints

The majority of complaints have been about poor delivery service, including late deliveries and goods arriving in damaged condition.

Recommendations

It is recommended that all people or companies recently making complaints should be offered a full refund of the cost and/or a replacement product where necessary.

In the long-term, we must review and improve our delivery service. If we do not, we risk losing more customers.

Notes

- A very well organised and clear answer with all five of the content points covered
- Clear recommendations for action are given as required in the task
- Effective use of headings which helps with the organisation of the report
- Appropriate formal register throughout the report
- Uses a range of language including some good business vocabulary: 'customer feedback system', 'poor delivery service', 'replacement product'
- Effective use of cohesive devices/referencing, rather than just linking words: 'may be because of ...', 'This makes it much easier', 'If we do not, we risk ...'
- Only slightly over the word limit

Listening

PART 1

1 teach: The woman recommends *always teach(ing) [the customer] something new* about the products, such as *a feature*, or *another* (= a different) *use they haven't considered*. The cue to this question is *Just make sure you always ...*, because it means *try to*.

2 trade shows: After the cues of *expert* and *home*, (...) *hygiene and health* we hear the man saying that he likes to *attend* (= go to) beauty conferences, which is the cue for the missing word *trade shows*.

3 journals: The woman asks him if he also *reads* (= subscribes to) *journals and research reports*, of which the second is given as a cue. Another cue is when the man says *so far only blogs* afterwards.

4 valued resource: ... *they will consider us a* is the same as *become ... in their eyes*.

5 leader: The man says that what impresses decision makers is when an employee starts *acting* (= behaving) *like a leader*.

6 projects: The man tells the woman that people seeking a promotion should be capable of *independently* (= on your own) *coming up with* (= proposing) *projects*.

7 **set goals:** After the cue of *without abandoning my current responsibilities*, referring to the fourth bullet point in the notes (*don't abandon your current tasks*) we hear the man recommend *set(ting) goals that you can use to measure* (= track) *your success* (= achievements).

8 **office politics:** The last tip is not to *engage in* (= participate in) *office politics* but *become a calming office presence*.

9 **stakeholders:** *Inform* is the same as the cue *notify*, and *in advance* appears as *before starting* in the question. *Key clients, partners and vendors* are listed as examples of *stakeholders* as well.

10 **price range:** The cue to this question is when the woman starts talking about URLs. First she mentions *checking the availability of any URL domains*, then talks about making sure these *fit* (= meet) *your price range*.

11 **trademark:** ... *not to make the common mistake of choosing a trademark that is already taken* is the same as *check if it is available*.

12 **email addresses:** After talking about *switching your social media profiles*, which is given as a cue in the notes, the next item in the rebranding process is to *create* (= set up) *the new email addresses*, introduced by the cue *If this is done, you can go ahead and* and followed by the cue of *After all this is done, all that is left is updating* (= changing) *your website and promotional materials*.

PART 2

13 **C:** *How long we've been in business, the size of our company, the experts working for us* are examples of the type of information typically included in the About Us section of a website, as is *our history*. The fact that the woman says her clients *were surprised by the lack of information* shows that this section was *not detailed enough* before the change. (Although *experts* are mentioned, a *blog* is not, so the correct answer is not option A.)

14 **B:** The cue is *clients' everyday queries* as this is what a typical website's FAQ section usually includes. The man also says he had got the advice from the coach that these should be *much more recent*, i.e. that theirs was not *up to date*. (The man mentions the phrase *our social media* but only as a *channel* through which the messages also come in. There are no other clues indicating that a Contact page is being described, so the correct answer is not option F.)

15 **D:** The phrases *what previous buyers thought of our services* and *satisfied past users' accounts* (= stories) shows that it is their Testimonials and Case Studies section she is talking about. She also says that all this shouldn't be *hidden* (= concealed). (While we hear the phrase *users' accounts*, this refers to previous customers' stories, not any kind of access (= login) so option G is not the correct answer.)

16 **H:** There are various cues implying *products* (e.g. *an entire page describing each, items, names* and *model numbers*). The sections *only a (...) page* and *Customers need more information than this* indicates that this section was originally *too short*.

17 **E:** The woman says that they *needed something like this* after describing their competitor's Methodology section. Methodology is how somebody works. Further cues include *national and international quality control processes and certifications, (some of our) key procedures and permissions*. (Although she mentions their About Us section, she says that *shortening it* was an added benefit, so the answer is not option C).

18 **F:** The woman talks about the number of hours employees *put in* (= work) in the two countries. She also describes a key difference she perceived between people's dedication and how it affects their work habits (i.e. that in the States employees are committed to their companies almost by default, while in the UK this has to be 'earned' by the company first). (Although *lunch* is mentioned, *eating lunch at your desk* is not, and neither is this the main point here, so the answer is not option B.)

19 **C:** The man says that he had *read the contract*, which, among other things, tends to include the amount of time off an employee is going to have in a job. He also says that he didn't really realise *just how few ten days was going to be*. Other expressions relating to holidays include *a mere two weeks off* and *sick days*.

20 **D:** The woman mentions that she *tried hard to follow* what was going on around her. The example of a *curriculum vitae* being *resume* in America, and the expressions she uses to talk about *variations in phrasing and terminology* and *misunderstandings* also indicate that she is talking about the language problems she encountered. (The word *leave* is used but as a verb, not as a noun, as in option H (*paid parental leave*.)

21 **A:** *Sports* is typically a topic of *small talk* in many cultures, and the phrase *water-cooler conversations* implies casual / informal discussions. The man also mentions the notion of *neutral* topics (such as films and travelling), which is a characteristic of small talk as well.

22 **G:** The woman starts by referring to a certain *behaviour* that is frowned upon in the UK and considered normal in the US (or even a sign of *competence and self-confidence*), then uses the phrase *telling your environment about your achievements*, which is a synonym of *self-promotion* as well. (While the phrase *networking after work* is used and there is an option about this (E, socialising after work), this is not the main point of what the woman is saying overall.)

PART 3

23 A: Adam says that being an entrepreneur is a *mindset*, a *lifestyle*; both of which are synonyms of *way of life*.
Distraction B: According to Adam, being a business owner, on the other hand, is more of just a *job title*.
Distraction C: While both entrepreneurs and business owners are mentioned and Adam also uses the word *mindset*, it is not true that both are a *way of life* in their own right if you have the *right mindset*.

24 A: Adam mentions a few ways that business owners get started, including how they might *take over* (= inherit) a business.
Distraction B: Although the phrase *take over* is used, nothing is said of how before they do this business owners are entrepreneurs first.
Distraction C: The words *innovate* and *industry* are used, but not to mean that business owners start in *innovative industries*.

25 C: Adam says that when he is *coaching* (= works with) a new client, one of the first questions to *consider* (= tries to understand) is, *which approach do they seem to be following* (= how they lead), i.e. as an owner or an entrepreneur.
Distraction A: Although he considers the differences (*between entrepreneurs and owners*), it is not stated that he *tells* his clients about them too.
Distraction B: The word *follow* is used differently in the recording: Adam does not ask his clients who their role model is (= which entrepreneurs they are following), he only considers which approach (i.e. owner versus entrepreneur) they are following.

26 B: He says owners are *concerned with* (= concentrate on) the *smooth running of their company / solving problems* (= resolving operational issues), as well as *whenever there is a glitch (...) they step up to solve the issue*.
Distraction A: Adam says owners *envision* (= imagine) *a world where employees do their jobs well, customers pay on time*, etc., but it is not clear that he *expects* these things to happen.
Distraction C: Adam talks about both *customers* and *equipment* but more as two (equal) examples of sources of problems. He does not say that owners would *prioritise* one over the other.

27 C: He says that *if they* (= entrepreneurs) *are really bold* (= bravest), they *sometimes even create new industries* (= fields).
Distraction A: Although the words *software* and *question* are used, they are not used together in this sense. Adam talks about entrepreneurs questioning things, but he doesn't mention questioning the design of software.
Distraction B: Although the words *reactive* and *customers* are used, Adam does not talk about entrepreneurs *handling* (reactive) customers.

28 A: Adam says that business owners are often *not conscious about tomorrow* (= not well-defined view of the future).
Distraction B: While Adam talks about business owners *train(ing) their employees*, he does not say that this is their *view of the future*.
Distraction C: Adam says the opposite, namely that business owners generally don't *delegate or outsource* much, nor does he mention that they plan to do so in the future.

29 B: According to Adam, entrepreneurs often have an *exit strategy*, which is to say they consciously plan to *leave their business behind* at some point in the future.
Distraction A: Adam says the opposite, i.e. that entrepreneurs *are not likely to merge their own persona* (= identity) *with their firm's*.
Distraction C: Entrepreneurs don't *change* their company's name, because they tend to choose *a more neutral or operational name* for them in the first place.

30 B: According to Adam, entrepreneurs tend to be more *hands off*. They want to *escape* (= avoid) *getting too involved in the operational aspects* (= running) *of the company*.
Distraction A: Adam talks about *employees* (*hiring more skilled employees*) and uses the word *involved* to talk about the entrepreneurs themselves. He does not mention anything about employees becoming too involved.
Distraction C: Adam states the opposite when he says that entrepreneurs hire more skilled employees precisely to be able to *delegate more*.

Sample answer sheets for Reading

OFFICE USE ONLY - DO NOT WRITE OR MAKE ANY MARK ABOVE THIS LINE

Cambridge Assessment English

Candidate Name:
Candidate Number:
Centre Name:
Centre Number:
Examination Title:
Examination Details:
Candidate Signature:
Assessment Date:

Supervisor: If the candidate is ABSENT or has WITHDRAWN shade here ○

Business Vantage Reading Candidate Answer Sheet

Instructions
Use a PENCIL (B or HB).
Rub out any answer you want to change with an eraser.

For **Parts 1 to 4**:
Mark one box for each answer.

For example:
If you think **A** is the right answer to the question, mark your answer sheet like this: | 0 | ● B C |

For **Part 5**:
Write your answer clearly in CAPITAL LETTERS.
Write one letter in each box.

For example: | 0 | E | X | A | M | P | L | E |

Part 1
1. A B C D
2. A B C D
3. A B C D
4. A B C D
5. A B C D
6. A B C D
7. A B C D

Part 2
8. A B C D E F G
9. A B C D E F G
10. A B C D E F G
11. A B C D E F G
12. A B C D E F G

Turn over for Parts 3 - 5 →

OFFICE USE ONLY - DO NOT WRITE OR MAKE ANY MARK BELOW THIS LINE

REPRODUCED WITH PERMISSION © CAMBRIDGE ASSESSMENT 2020

Photocopiable

Sample answer sheets for Reading

Sample answer sheets for Listening

OFFICE USE ONLY - DO NOT WRITE OR MAKE ANY MARK ABOVE THIS LINE   Page 1 of 2

Cambridge Assessment English

Candidate Name:
Centre Name:
Examination Title:
Candidate Signature:

Candidate Number:
Centre Number:
Examination Details:
Assessment Date:

Supervisor: If the candidate is ABSENT or has WITHDRAWN shade here ○

Business Vantage Listening Candidate Answer Sheet

Instructions
Use a PENCIL (B or HB).
Rub out any answer you want to change with an eraser.

For Part 1:
Write your answer clearly in CAPITAL LETTERS.
Write one letter or number in each box.

For example: | 0 | E | X | A | M | P | L | E |

For Parts 2 and 3:
Mark one box for each answer.

For example:
If you think A is the right answer to the question, mark your answer sheet like this: 0 ● ○ ○

Part 1 - Recording One

		Do not write below here
1		1 1 0 ○ ○
2		2 1 0 ○ ○
3		3 1 0 ○ ○
4		4 1 0 ○ ○

Continue on the other side of this sheet ➡

OFFICE USE ONLY - DO NOT WRITE OR MAKE ANY MARK BELOW THIS LINE   Page 1 of 2

REPRODUCED WITH PERMISSION © CAMBRIDGE ASSESSMENT 2020   Photocopiable

Sample answer sheets for Listening

Acknowledgements

Our highly experienced team of Trainer writers, in collaboration with Cambridge Assessment English reviewers, have worked together to bring you *B2 Business Vantage Trainer*.

We would like to thank Helen Chilton (writer), David Clark (writer), Amanda French (writer), Stephen Greene (writer), Fatime Losonci (writer), Melissa Thompson (writer), Carole Bartlett (reviewer), Michael Black (reviewer), Sarah Dymond (reviewer) and Fiona McGarry (reviewer) for their work on the material.

The authors and publishers acknowledge the following sources of copyright material and are grateful for the permissions granted. While every effort has been made, it has not always been possible to identify the sources of all the material used, or to trace all copyright holders. If any omissions are brought to our notice, we will be happy to include the appropriate acknowledgements on reprinting and in the next update to the digital edition, as applicable.

Text Acknowledgements:
Key: T = Test

T1: Text adapted from 'How to negotiate a pay rise' by Sarah Shearman, *The Guardian*, 05.04.2017. Copyright © 2018 Guardian News & Media Ltd. Reproduced with permission; Text adapted from 'Halfords plan back-to-basics turnaround plan' by Safiya Bashir, *The Guardian*, 27.09.2018. Copyright © 2018 Guardian News & Media Ltd. Reproduced with permission; Text adapted from 'Service with a smile: how to keep customers coming back' by Emma Featherstone, *The Guardian*, 02.06.2017. Copyright © 2018 Guardian News & Media Ltd. Reproduced with permission; Text adapted from 'Smart companies see the importance of collaboration' by Jason Clay, *The Guardian*, 31.03.2011. Copyright © 2018 Guardian News & Media Ltd. Reproduced with permission; **T2**: Text adapted from 'Essential questions to ask a recruitment agency' by Andy Setterfield, *The Guardian*, 09.09.2012. Copyright © 2018 Guardian News & Media Ltd. Reproduced with permission; Text adapted from 'Kingfisher shrugs off doubts about success of turnround' by Jonathan Eley, *Financial Times*, 18/09/2018. Used under licence from the Financial Times. All Rights Reserved; **T5**: Text adapted from 'The 4 different types of workplace Learning Styles', Copyright © 2018 Cornerstone on Demand. Reproduced with kind permission.

Photo Acknowledgements:

Front cover photography by Shomos Uddin/Moment.

Audio recordings by DN and AE Strauss Ltd. Engineer: Neil Rogers; Editor: James Miller; Producer; Dan Strauss. Recorded at Cambridge Assessment, Cambridge.